THE NEW MIDDLE AGES

BONNIE WHEELER, *Series Editor*

The New Middle Ages is a series dedicated to pluridisciplinary studies of medieval cultures, with particular emphasis on recuperating women's history and on feminist and gender analyses. This peer-reviewed series includes both scholarly monographs and essay collections.

PUBLISHED BY PALGRAVE:

Women in the Medieval Islamic World: Power, Patronage, and Piety
edited by Gavin R. G. Hambly

The Ethics of Nature in the Middle Ages: On Boccaccio's Poetaphysics
by Gregory B. Stone

Presence and Presentation: Women in the Chinese Literati Tradition
edited by Sherry J. Mou

The Lost Love Letters of Heloise and Abelard: Perceptions of Dialogue in Twelfth-Century France
by Constant J. Mews

Understanding Scholastic Thought with Foucault
by Philipp W. Rosemann

For Her Good Estate: The Life of Elizabeth de Burgh
by Frances A. Underhill

Constructions of Widowhood and Virginity in the Middle Ages
edited by Cindy L. Carlson and Angela Jane Weisl

Motherhood and Mothering in Anglo-Saxon England
by Mary Dockray-Miller

Listening to Heloise: The Voice of a Twelfth-Century Woman
edited by Bonnie Wheeler

The Postcolonial Middle Ages
edited by Jeffrey Jerome Cohen

Chaucer's Pardoner *and Gender Theory: Bodies of Discourse*
by Robert S. Sturges

Crossing the Bridge: Comparative Essays on Medieval European and Heian Japanese Women Writers
edited by Barbara Stevenson and Cynthia Ho

Engaging Words: The Culture of Reading in the Later Middle Ages
by Laurel Amtower

Robes and Honor: The Medieval World of Investiture
edited by Stewart Gordon

Representing Rape in Medieval and Early Modern Literature
edited by Elizabeth Robertson and Christine M. Rose

Same Sex Love and Desire Among Women in the Middle Ages
edited by Francesca Canadé Sautman and Pamela Sheingorn

Sight and Embodiment in the Middle Ages: Ocular Desires
by Suzannah Biernoff

Listen, Daughter: The Speculum Virginum *and the Formation of Religious Women in the Middle Ages*
edited by Constant J. Mews

Science, the Singular, and the Question of Theology
by Richard A. Lee, Jr.

Gender in Debate from the Early Middle Ages to the Renaissance
edited by Thelma S. Fenster and Clare A. Lees

Malory's Morte D'Arthur*: Remaking Arthurian Tradition*
by Catherine Batt

The Vernacular Spirit: Essays on Medieval Religious Literature
edited by Renate Blumenfeld-Kosinski, Duncan Robertson, and Nancy Warren

Popular Piety and Art in the Late Middle Ages: Image Worship and Idolatry in England 1350–1500
by Kathleen Kamerick

Absent Narratives, Manuscript Textuality, and Literary Structure in Late Medieval England
by Elizabeth Scala

Creating Community with Food and Drink in Merovingian Gaul
by Bonnie Effros

Representations of Early Byzantine Empresses: Image and Empire
by Anne McClanan

Encountering Medieval Textiles and Dress: Objects, Texts, Images
edited by Désirée G. Koslin and Janet Snyder

Eleanor of Aquitaine: Lord and Lady
edited by Bonnie Wheeler and John Carmi Parsons

Isabel La Católica, Queen of Castile: Critical Essays
edited by David A. Boruchoff

Homoeroticism and Chivalry: Discourses of Male Same-Sex Desire in the Fourteenth Century
by Richard E. Zeikowitz

Portraits of Medieval Women: Family, Marriage, and Politics in England 1225–1350
by Linda E. Mitchell

Eloquent Virgins: From Thecla to Joan of Arc
by Maud Burnett McInerney

The Persistence of Medievalism: Narrative Adventures in Contemporary Culture
by Angela Jane Weisl

Capetian Women
edited by Kathleen D. Nolan

Joan of Arc and Spirituality
edited by Ann W Astell and Bonnie Wheeler

The Texture of Society: Medieval Women in the Southern Low Countries
edited by Ellen E. Kittell and Mary A. Suydam

Charlemagne's Mustache: And Other Cultural Clusters of a Dark Age
by Paul Edward Dutton

Troubled Vision: Gender, Sexuality, and Sight in Medieval Text and Image
edited by Emma Campbell and Robert Mills

Queering Medieval Genres
by Tison Pugh

Sacred Place in Early Medieval Neoplatonism
by L. Michael Harrington

The Middle Ages at Work
edited by Kellie Robertson and Michael Uebel

Chaucer's Jobs
by David R. Carlson

Medievalism and Orientalism: Three Essays on Literature, Architecture and Cultural Identity
by John M. Ganim

Queer Love in the Middle Ages
by Anna Klosowska

Performing Women in the Middle Ages: Sex, Gender, and the Iberian Lyric
by Denise K. Filios

Necessary Conjunctions: The Social Self in Medieval England
by David Gary Shaw

Visual Culture and the German Middle Ages
edited by Kathryn Starkey and Horst Wenzel

Medieval Paradigms: Essays in Honor of Jeremy duQuesnay Adams, Volumes 1 and 2
edited by Stephanie Hayes-Healy

False Fables and Exemplary Truth in Later Middle English Literature
by Elizabeth Allen

Ecstatic Transformation: On the Uses of Alterity in the Middle Ages
by Michael Uebel

Sacred and Secular in Medieval and Early Modern Cultures: New Essays
edited by Lawrence Besserman

Tolkien's Modern Middle Ages
edited by Jane Chance and Alfred K. Siewers

Representing Righteous Heathens in Late Medieval England
by Frank Grady

Byzantine Dress: Representations of Secular Dress in Eighth- to Twelfth-Century Painting
by Jennifer L. Ball

The Laborer's Two Bodies: Labor and the "Work" of the Text in Medieval Britain, 1350–1500
by Kellie Robertson

The Dogaressa of Venice, 1250–1500: Wife and Icon
by Holly S. Hurlburt

Logic, Theology, and Poetry in Boethius, Abelard, and Alan of Lille: Words in the Absence of Things
by Eileen C. Sweeney

The Theology of Work: Peter Damian and the Medieval Religious Renewal Movement
by Patricia Ranft

On the Purification of Women: Churching in Northern France, 1100–1500
by Paula M. Rieder

Writers of the Reign of Henry II: Twelve Essays
edited by Ruth Kennedy and Simon Meecham-Jones

Lonesome Words: The Vocal Poetics of the Old English Lament and the African-American Blues Song
by M. G. McGeachy

Performing Piety: Musical Culture in Medieval English Nunneries
by Anne Bagnell Yardley

The Flight from Desire: Augustine and Ovid to Chaucer
by Robert R. Edwards

Mindful Spirit in Late Medieval Literature: Essays in Honor of Elizabeth D. Kirk
edited by Bonnie Wheeler

Medieval Fabrications: Dress, Textiles, Clothwork, and Other Cultural Imaginings
edited by E. Jane Burns

Was the Bayeux Tapestry Made in France? The Case for St. Florent of Saumur
by George Beech

Women, Power, and Religious Patronage in the Middle Ages
by Erin L. Jordan

Hybridity, Identity, and Monstrosity in Medieval Britain: On Difficult Middles
by Jeffrey Jerome Cohen

Medieval Go-betweens and Chaucer's Pandarus
by Gretchen Mieszkowski

The Surgeon in Medieval English Literature
by Jeremy J. Citrome

Temporal Circumstances: Form and History in the Canterbury Tales
by Lee Patterson

Erotic Discourse and Early English Religious Writing
by Lara Farina

Odd Bodies and Visible Ends in Medieval Literature
by Sachi Shimomura

On Farting: Language and Laughter in the Middle Ages
by Valerie Allen

Women and Medieval Epic: Gender, Genre, and the Limits of Epic Masculinity
edited by Sara S. Poor and Jana K. Schulman

Race, Class, and Gender in "Medieval" Cinema
edited by Lynn T. Ramey and Tison Pugh

Allegory and Sexual Ethics in the High Middle Ages
by Noah D. Guynn

England and Iberia in the Middle Ages, 12th–15th Century: Cultural, Literary, and Political Exchanges
edited by María Bullón-Fernández

The Medieval Chastity Belt: A Myth-Making Process
by Albrecht Classen

Claustrophilia: The Erotics of Enclosure in Medieval Literature
by Cary Howie

Cannibalism in High Medieval English Literature
by Heather Blurton

The Drama of Masculinity and Medieval English Guild Culture
by Christina M. Fitzgerald

Chaucer's Visions of Manhood
by Holly A. Crocker

The Literary Subversions of Medieval Women
by Jane Chance

Manmade Marvels in Medieval Culture and Literature
by Scott Lightsey

American Chaucers
by Candace Barrington

Representing Others in Medieval Iberian Literature
by Michelle M. Hamilton

Paradigms and Methods in Early Medieval Studies
edited by Celia Chazelle and Felice Lifshitz

The King and the Whore: King Roderick and La Cava
by Elizabeth Drayson

Langland's Early Modern Identities
by Sarah A. Kelen

Cultural Studies of the Modern Middle Ages
edited by Eileen A. Joy, Myra J. Seaman, Kimberly K. Bell, and Mary K. Ramsey

Hildegard of Bingen's Unknown Language: An Edition, Translation, and Discussion
by Sarah L. Higley

Medieval Romance and the Construction of Heterosexuality
by Louise M. Sylvester

Communal Discord, Child Abduction, and Rape in the Later Middle Ages
by Jeremy Goldberg

Lydgate Matters: Poetry and Material Culture in the Fifteenth Century
edited by Lisa H. Cooper and Andrea Denny-Brown

Sexuality and Its Queer Discontents in Middle English Literature
by Tison Pugh

Sex, Scandal, and Sermon in Fourteenth-Century Spain: Juan Ruiz's Libro de Buen Amor
by Louise M. Haywood

The Erotics of Consolation: Desire and Distance in the Late Middle Ages
edited by Catherine E. Léglu and Stephen J. Milner

Battlefronts Real and Imagined: War, Border, and Identity in the Chinese Middle Period
edited by Don J. Wyatt

Wisdom and Her Lovers in Medieval and Early Modern Hispanic Literature
by Emily C. Francomano

Power, Piety, and Patronage in Late Medieval Queenship: Maria de Luna
by Nuria Silleras-Fernandez

In the Light of Medieval Spain: Islam, the West, and the Relevance of the Past
edited by Simon R. Doubleday and David Coleman, foreword by Giles Tremlett

Chaucerian Aesthetics
by Peggy A. Knapp

Memory, Images, and the English Corpus Christi Drama
by Theodore K. Lerud

Cultural Diversity in the British Middle Ages: Archipelago, Island, England
edited by Jeffrey Jerome Cohen

Excrement in the Late Middle Ages: Sacred Filth and Chaucer's Fecopoetics
by Susan Signe Morrison

Authority and Subjugation in Writing of Medieval Wales
edited by Ruth Kennedy and Simon Meecham-Jones

The Medieval Poetics of the Reliquary: Enshrinement, Inscription, Performance
by Seeta Chaganti

The Legend of Charlemagne in the Middle Ages: Power, Faith, and Crusade
edited by Matthew Gabriele and Jace Stuckey

The Poems of Oswald von Wolkenstein: An English Translation of the Complete Works (1376/77–1445)
by Albrecht Classen

Women and Experience in Later Medieval Writing: Reading the Book of Life
edited by Anneke B. Mulder-Bakker and Liz Herbert McAvoy

Ethics and Eventfulness in Middle English Literature: Singular Fortunes
by J. Allan Mitchell

Maintenance, Meed, and Marriage in Medieval English Literature
by Kathleen E. Kennedy

The Post-Historical Middle Ages
edited by Elizabeth Scala and Sylvia Federico

Constructing Chaucer: Author and Autofiction in the Critical Tradition
by Geoffrey W. Gust

Queens in Stone and Silver: The Creation of a Visual Imagery of Queenship in Capetian France
by Kathleen Nolan

Finding Saint Francis in Literature and Art
edited by Cynthia Ho, Beth A. Mulvaney, and John K. Downey

Strange Beauty: Ecocritical Approaches to Early Medieval Landscape
by Alfred K. Siewers

Berenguela of Castile (1180–1246) and Political Women in the High Middle Ages
by Miriam Shadis

Julian of Norwich's Legacy: Medieval Mysticism and Post-Medieval Reception
edited by Sarah Salih and Denise N. Baker

Medievalism, Multilingualism, and Chaucer
by Mary Catherine Davidson

The Letters of Heloise and Abelard: A Translation of Their Complete Correspondence and Related Writings
translated and edited by Mary Martin McLaughlin with Bonnie Wheeler

Women and Wealth in Late Medieval Europe
edited by Theresa Earenfight

Visual Power and Fame in René d'Anjou, Geoffrey Chaucer, and the Black Prince
by Sun Hee Kim Gertz

Geoffrey Chaucer Hath a Blog: Medieval Studies and New Media
by Brantley L. Bryant

Margaret Paston's Piety
by Joel T. Rosenthal

Gender and Power in Medieval Exegesis
by Theresa Tinkle

Antimercantilism in Late Medieval English Literature
by Roger A. Ladd

Magnificence and the Sublime in Medieval Aesthetics: Art, Architecture, Literature, Music
edited by C. Stephen Jaeger

Medieval and Early Modern Devotional Objects in Global Perspective: Translations of the Sacred
edited by Elizabeth Robertson and Jennifer Jahner

Late Medieval Jewish Identities: Iberia and Beyond
edited by Carmen Caballero-Navas and Esperanza Alfonso

Outlawry in Medieval Literature
by Timothy S. Jones

Women and Disability in Medieval Literature
by Tory Vandeventer Pearman

The Lesbian Premodern
edited by Noreen Giffney, Michelle M. Sauer, and Diane Watt

Crafting Jewishness in Medieval England: Legally Absent, Virtually Present
by Miriamne Ara Krummel

Street Scenes: Late Medieval Acting and Performance
by Sharon Aronson-Lehavi

Women and Economic Activities in Late Medieval Ghent
by Shennan Hutton

Palimpsests and the Literary Imagination of Medieval England: Collected Essays
edited by Leo Carruthers, Raeleen Chai-Elsholz, and Tatjana Silec

Divine Ventriloquism in Medieval English Literature: Power, Anxiety, Subversion
by Mary Hayes

Vernacular and Latin Literary Discourses of the Muslim Other in Medieval Germany
by Jerold C. Frakes

Fairies in Medieval Romance
by James Wade

Reason and Imagination in Chaucer, the Perle-*poet, and the* Cloud-*author: Seeing from the Center*
by Linda Tarte Holley

The Inner Life of Women in Medieval Romance Literature: Grief, Guilt, and Hypocrisy
edited by Jeff Rider and Jamie Friedman

Language as the Site of Revolt in Medieval and Early Modern England: Speaking as a Woman
by M. C. Bodden

Ecofeminist Subjectivities: Chaucer's Talking Birds
by Lesley Kordecki

Contextualizing the Muslim Other in Medieval Christian Discourse
edited by Jerold C. Frakes

Ekphrastic Medieval Visions: A New Discussion in Interarts Theory
by Claire Barbetti

The [European] Other in Medieval Arabic Literature and Culture: Ninth–Twelfth Century AD
by Nizar F. Hermes

Reading Memory and Identity in the Texts of Medieval European Holy Women
edited by Margaret Cotter-Lynch and Brad Herzog

Market Power: Lordship, Society, and Economy in Medieval Catalonia (1276–1313)
by Gregory B. Milton

Marriage, Property, and Women's Narratives
by Sally A. Livingston

Heloise and the Paraclete: A Twelfth-Century Quest (forthcoming)
by Mary Martin McLaughlin

MARRIAGE, PROPERTY, AND WOMEN'S NARRATIVES

Sally A. Livingston

palgrave
macmillan

First published in 2012 by
PALGRAVE MACMILLAN®
in the United States—a division of St. Martin's Press LLC,
175 Fifth Avenue, New York, NY 10010.

Where this book is distributed in the UK, Europe and the rest of the world, this is by Palgrave Macmillan, a division of Macmillan Publishers Limited, registered in England, company number 785998, of Houndmills, Basingstoke, Hampshire RG21 6XS.

Palgrave Macmillan is the global academic imprint of the above companies and has companies and representatives throughout the world.

Palgrave® and Macmillan® are registered trademarks in the United States, the United Kingdom, Europe and other countries.

ISBN: 978–0–230–11506–4

Library of Congress Cataloging-in-Publication Data.

Livingston, Sally A.
Marriage, property, and women's narratives / Sally A. Livingston.
p. cm.—(New middle ages)
Includes bibliographical references.
ISBN 978–0–230–11506–4
1. Women—Economic conditions. 2. Married women—Economic conditions. 3. Right of property—History. I. Title.

HQ1143.L58 2012
330.082—dc23 2011041869

A catalogue record of the book is available from the British Library.

Design by Newgen Imaging Systems (P) Ltd., Chennai, India.

First edition: April 2012

I am afraid to own a Body –
I am afraid to own a Soul –
Profound – precarious Property –
Possession, not optional –

Double Estate, entailed at Pleasure
Opon an unsuspecting Heir –
Duke in a moment of Deathlessness
And God, for a Frontier.

– Emily Dickinson

A feminine text cannot fail to be more than subversive. It is volcanic; as it is written it brings about an upheaval of the old property crust, carrier of masculine investments; there's no other way.

– Hélène Cixous, "The Laugh of the Medusa"

CONTENTS

ACKNOWLEDGMENTS

I am grateful to the many people whose support brought this book into reality. Jan M. Ziolkowski championed me from my first class when I returned to academia straight through to the final draft of my doctoral dissertation, on which *Marriage, Property, and Women's Narratives* is based. His rigorous scholarship and intellectual integrity have profoundly shaped my reading of medieval literature. The other members of my dissertation committee, William Mills Todd III and James Engell, both superb teachers, supported the broad comparative nature of my work, offered invaluable reading suggestions, and challenged me to see distinctions as well as similarities in my texts.

The book began as a paper in the Comparative Literature Proseminar my first year as a graduate student at Harvard. I thank its two faculty members, the late Barbara Johnson, who foresaw that it would be a project that would occupy me for many years, and Despina Kakoudakis, who astutely guided me in its earliest stages. I am grateful to my other teachers at Harvard, whose work has deeply influenced my thinking: Lynn Festa, Virginie Greene, Gregory Nagy, Luis Girón-Negrón, and Nicholas Watson. I am especially indebted to Henry Heller of the University of Manitoba, who first introduced me to the world of pre-1600 history many years ago.

In the various stages of this book I have benefited from the suggestions of colleagues who have generously offered sage guidance: Howell D. Chickering, Joanna Hubbs, Ann Jones, Andrew Romig, Suzanne Smith, and the anonymous Palgrave Macmillan readers. Other scholars who have helped in myriad ways as I pursued my path are Kenneth Bartlett, Cynthia Bland Biggar, Anna Bobrov, Christopher Johnson, Ann Jones, Aden Kumler, Valerie Martin, Inna Mattei, Sandra Naddaff, and Phoebe Putnam. My profound gratitude goes to Bonnie Wheeler, the editor of the New Middle Ages series, for guiding the project to completion and her visionary leadership of all things medieval.

I am grateful to the office of the Provost, Ohio Wesleyan University, for its generous financial support in the preparation of the index.

My friends never questioned my ability to finish this work, and I thank them for the many ways in which they supported me: Barbara Akiba,

Lisa Baskin, Ginny Chandler, Deborah Clendaniel, Jean Donovan, Sheila Gewertz, Denise Gilbert, Thom Herman, Sheila Hunter, Margo Jones, Terry Kayne, Susan LaScala, Larry Rossini, Ellen Ryan, Nancy Sokol, Diane Wood, and David F. Woods. I am grateful to the scores of women who were my investment clients for over twenty years and made me realize that the question "Why are women poor" is one worth trying to answer.

Finally, my family has been an inspiration and a blessing, and to them I owe the greatest debt: my mother, Stella Skrzypek, my sister, Mimi Ginsberg, her husband Stuart, and their children, Allison, Sarah, and Adam Ginsberg. Their collective love of reading, belief that all things are possible, and friendship and love have nurtured me and will continue to inspire all that I do.

A NOTE ON TRANSLITERATION

For the Russian texts, I have adopted a modified version of the transliteration system used in the simplified Library of Congress system, omitting hard and soft signs and retaining conventional English spelling whenever possible.

INTRODUCTION: SILENCE AND WOMEN'S AUTHORITY

As the thirteenth-century Old French *Le Roman de Silence* opens, two favorite counts of Evan, king of England, have killed each other.[1] Married to twin sisters, they fought over which sister was the elder and hence the inheritor of the family land. As a result, the king proclaims that no woman will ever again inherit property. When a noble couple gives birth to a daughter, they decide to bring her up as a boy so that their line will not lose its property rights. The girl is named "Silence" and in the text, Nature and Nurture argue over which one has the upper hand in her upbringing. She dresses and fights like a man and has all the rights that accrue to her assumed gender. When, later, she is discovered and marries the king, he announces that he will restore property rights to women. Although this is a triumph for her gender, it is actually a loss for Silence, since for her to empower other women, she must lose the many freedoms, social as well as economic, that she has experienced as a male.

This text raises important issues about how women's legal right to own property impacts their voice in literature.[2] The name "Silence" has many layers of significance: she is silenced by being born female and cannot speak or perform her natural gender for fear of losing not only her ability to inherit, but also her freedom in the world. Once discovered as female, she becomes the wife of the king, but in being the agent of restoration for her gender, she in fact loses all the other rights she has experienced as a man. She is restored to her property, but is "silenced" in other aspects of her life by becoming the property of her husband.

While the story is extraordinary, its subject—the loss of female ownership—is not unique. The *Roman de Silence* combines a remarkable theme that describes a common circumstance with the additional intrigue of possibly being spoken in a woman's voice. The romance explores the intersection of marriage and property rights and investigates how women experience this confluence of social forces and express it through writing.

This book examines how women writers have broken through the silence inflicted by marriage—when, by becoming the property of their husbands, they no longer had property of their own—in order both to criticize the institution and regain their rightful inheritance. Drawing from three disparate time periods and places and representing three distinct legal models of female ownership, I argue that women's ability or inability to own property in their own name directly affects the way they write about marriage. The first case I examine is that of France and England from the twelfth through the early fifteenth centuries, where we see a challenge to women's previous right to own and pass on property. The second is nineteenth- and early twentieth-century England, where the Married Women's Property Act of 1882 restored women legal ownership over their own property. In the third case, mid-nineteenth-century Russia, women had always owned land and serfs. This practice became secure enough to be codified over the course of the century. I have chosen these periods not only because they represent different legal contexts, but also because of the lively debates by both men and women on the property issue in these times.

My research suggests that women writers frame their responses to both owning property and being property within the context of marriage. They use the power of language to tell stories that allow them to access the property they cannot or have not been able to hold materially. Language is bound up with material goods and the right to those goods. Literature thus becomes the site for women to work out their views on marriage; through literature, they *write their rights* through authorship.

Crucial to this book is an analysis of the marriage plot, in which the pursuit of a husband is the core of the narrative. Moving from her father's home to her husband's, the young woman often experiences a shift from idealistic hope to realistic disillusion.[3] Although no such plot device existed in the works of the medieval women writers I discuss, their deep criticism of marriage has a parallel function. What we see in Heloise is an aversion to marriage as the constitutive basis of a relationship; in Marie de France it is the restrictive business arrangement to which the real love interest (which cannot end in marriage) is opposed. In medieval England women such as Margery Kempe used chastity as the commodity to avoid the responsibilities of wedlock. By the eighteenth century, I argue, the gradual change in women's rights places marriage in a prominent position in female-authored narratives.[4] Thus, although Frances Burney, Jane Austen, and George Eliot find ways to subvert the marriage plot, the device drives their narratives. Propertied women must marry for dynastic reasons, unpropertied women for financial ones. Even after women regained their property rights, the memory was too ingrained to dismiss.

Virginia Woolf, for example, portrays an almost exhausted acceptance of marriage in her novels, where the marriage plot is an accepted but worn-out reality. The situation is quite different in the Russian women writers I investigate: the marriage plot is absent. Because women controlled their own fortunes, marriage is not the center of their heroines' lives.

My study reveals one more important characteristic that binds these women together despite their different historical periods and legal situations: they either negotiate their views on marriage in works that are fiercely realistic, or transform their reality through fantasy. In medieval France the first approach can be seen in Heloise's letters to Abelard and the second in three of Marie de France's *lais*, *Guigemar*, *Yonec*, and *Lanval*. Both Heloise and Marie directly criticize marriage as a tyrannical institution in which women are forced to give up their freedom. The brutally realistic Heloise uses economic metaphors to describe her relationship to Abelard, whereas Marie's female characters use fairy tales to escape the fetters of marriage. For medieval English women such as Saint Audrey and Margery Kempe, money is central to their strategies to avoid marriage.

In England, the ability of married women to own property came late. Although women writers of the eighteenth and nineteenth century, such as Frances Burney, Jane Austen, and George Eliot, criticize marriage, they see few alternatives for women, and the marriage plot is the preoccupation of their novels. Using Virginia Woolf, I argue that even with the passage of the Married Women's Property Act, female writers did not immediately assimilate the new legal and economic changes. In her nonfiction works *A Room of One's Own* and *Three Guineas*, she argues vehemently for women's right both to work and own property. However, her fictionalized women are unable to "own" their money fully. In *Mrs. Dalloway*, they allow men to manage their property, and, as a result, are as marginalized as any women in an early nineteenth-century novel. Only in *Orlando*, a fairy tale, does a woman get the property that is rightfully hers.

The Russian women authors I analyze reflect a vastly different situation. Katerina Pavlova, Nadezhda Khvoshchinskaia, and Sofya Soboleva present alternatives for their women characters. They either do not marry and work to support themselves (Khvoshchinskaia), refuse to allow their husbands' control over any part of their lives (Soboleva), or, in the case of Pavlova, use the fantasy of dream sequences to make poetry a parallel existence to marriage. They drew on the sustained right of Russian women to own property as a means to critique marriage and diminish its centrality in their lives.

This project is the first to examine different historical contexts to see how women negotiate their marital status *as* property in relation to their ability to *own* property. Despite a vast body of legal and historical scholarship on women's property rights, no studies attempt to compare different ownership models, nor has marriage as a theme in women's literature been used as a vehicle to analyze the economic issue comparatively in different times and places.

Throughout this book, I refer to women as the property of their husbands. By this I mean that upon marriage, a women's legal and economic existence was submerged in that of her husband—her property in essence became his. Frederick Engels located the source of the problem historically in women themselves who, in tiring of the demands of sexual promiscuity in matriarchal culture, demanded monogamy. As male wealth increased because men owned the implements to procure food, they gained the social status that enabled them to overthrow maternal inheritance. With the need to guarantee the fidelity of the wife when property passes through the male line, women became more and more the property of men.[5] He concludes: "The overthrow of mother right was the *world-historic defeat of the female sex.* The man seized the reins in the house also; the woman was degraded, enthralled, the slave of the man's lust, a mere instrument for breeding children."[6]

Gayle Rubin, in her landmark essay "The Traffic in Women: Notes on the 'Political Economy' of Sex," argues that marriage is the most basic form of gift-exchange and places women in an economically helpless position: "If it is women who are being transacted, then it is the men who give and take them who are linked, the woman being a conduit of a relationship rather than a partner to it... The relations of such a system are such that women are in no position to realize the benefits of their own circulation."[7] Women, she contends, become "encoded" with their status within the system.[8]

Rubin's notion of encoding might explain why legal changes in the property system are not immediately apparent. Gayatri Chakravorty Spivak characterizes this as the "subaltern" mentality, in which "the subaltern has been inserted into the long road to hegemony."[9] Hegemony does not insure equality because in the process the woman has taken on the values of the patriarchy. She remains locked into the old system, even when she has legally been freed. Women remain, paradoxically, "inside" but still "outside" in the margins. In allowing a woman ownership and control of her own property, she is shut outside it by the rest of the social structure she has internalized.[10]

As objects rather than their own subjects, women have been put in the position of the economically marginalized, unable to take full possession of either their property or themselves. This marginalization parallels the way women write. In the Middle Ages, as Caroline Walker Bynum has explained, women's stories are "less processual than men's;

they don't have turning points." Women's narratives, she argues, are more about continuity than sharp change.[11] This tendency holds true in the French and English examples I explore, in which women are responsible for the domestic, internal order and subservient to men's external duties.[12] The Russian women writers, in contrast, see less of a tension between the domestic and the outside worlds. Their heroines interact with the public world, giving them choices that the other women lack. For the Russian writers, therefore, property becomes a signifier of ownership, not only of material goods, but also of one's right to own oneself. Consequently, their heroines find themselves at the center of their own narratives, ones in which they have the power to control their lives.

Nonetheless, given a voice, the marginalized have an important role to play. Michael Camille, writing about physical marginalia in pictorial art, has observed that the "images on the edge" in medieval manuscripts play a crucial societal role; they "add an extra dimension, a supplement, that is able to gloss, parody, modernize and problematize the text's authority while never totally undermining it. The center is . . . dependent upon the margins for its continued existence."[13]

Written texts operate in much the same way. The works that I have chosen in this study act in precisely this crucial, peripheral role as critics of the dominant culture. These women writers, as marginalized individuals within their economic contexts, "unsilence" themselves, on the one hand, by starkly laying out the reality of their positions, and, on the other, by envisioning alternatives. Their literary narratives provide the access by which they can take possession of the property they cannot materially hold.

Before embarking on this study, I spent over twenty years as an investment advisor, counseling women on the management of their money. As I pondered their lack of comfort with, indeed, their fear of financial matters, I understood that the root of this problem goes back centuries. At its very core, therefore, this book tries to answer Virginia Woolf's question, "Why are women poor?" I conclude that owning property not only inflects the way women write about marriage, but also determines whether women in these three distinct moments in history see themselves as property. This conflation, in turn, influences women's financial independence as well as their ability to "own" their own wealth. Even when property rights are restored, I argue, women are unable to free themselves from the historical fact that, for centuries, they were not in control of their own wealth, whatever its size. Money remains a mystery, something to be entrusted to males, whether they be husbands, fathers, or advisors. Love, trust, and money have been intertwined in Western society so that when these connections become fractured, women are marginalized even more.

The book is structured as follows: after discussing how historians have framed the legal rights of women in each period, I explore in detail texts that test my general hypothesis that the way women write about property is influenced not only by legal history but also by prevailing social and intellectual beliefs held by both women and men. I have chosen a relatively small number of authors who exemplify important positions on this issue. Despite putting them in the context of other writing of their time, I do not offer a total survey of women's writing about marriage and property, but rather offer three important snapshots of these issues.

I do not mean to argue that literature reacts immediately to legal and historical changes. Even in a digital age, old ways of thinking take time to modify. At the same time, literary texts can anticipate, can tell us what some people in specific intellectual communities are thinking and feeling long before we see change in tangible ways. Literature also serves as a register of memory, holding in place, as Mary Carruthers has noted, "that which is no longer so in actuality."[14] It gives a kind of power over the past, and consequently, over the present.[15] My aim is this work is to allow the reader to drop in at various points in the broad picture of marriage and women's property rights and, through literature, see similarities as well as changes from the twelfth to the twentieth century. What happened 900 years ago, I suggest, has had a very long and profound impact.

CHAPTER 1

PROPERTY'S HISTORY, PROPERTY'S LITERATURE

If literature both foretells change and then instills it in memory, how can we determine if it portrays an actual historical condition? How does the loss of women's property rights in *Le Roman de Silence* reflect thirteenth-century social concerns, if at all?[1]

Historians disagree on the extent to which women's economic rights diminished in the Middle Ages. In this chapter I present multiple sides of the argument and then look at three romances in which women's right to inherit is a central theme. Although these stories by no means settle the debate, they show, I believe, that literary imagination is a tool by which society asks questions of itself, and, as such, is a valuable key for understanding what might have actually happened with female property rights in certain areas of medieval Europe.

The traditional argument, represented by David Herlihy and Georges Duby, among others, traced a loss of female inheritance in the eleventh and twelfth centuries.[2] Substantial evidence suggests that early medieval women, especially those living in areas that had been under Roman law, had inheritance rights equal to men's. Southern France, which had been an important part of the Roman Empire, continued to follow Roman laws well after the empire collapsed. These laws gave women the right to inherit property and to retain control over that property even after marriage.[3] In the tenth and eleventh centuries, an increasing number of women controlled landed property and with it, the attendant rights of justice and military command. Peasant and urban women as well had increasing responsibilities and opportunities.[4]

David Herlihy suggested that a change occurred in the twelfth century when a bilineal kinship system, in which relationships traced through women were coequal with those through men, became agnatic or patrilineal. Citing Peter Damian's "On Degrees of Kinship," written in 1063, Herlihy's argument points out that women's membership in the kin group allowed them to share in its inheritance of property.[5] He also found that there was a close correlation between the use of matronymics and women landowners: from the ninth to the eleventh centuries, sons showed an increased preference to be identified by their mothers' names. Much of the use of matronymics, he argued, was due to uncanonical clerical marriages, in which the children could not be identified with the father. As the church finally wrested control over this problem in the twelfth century, the use of matronymics diminished.[6] At the same time, the church's long-standing campaign for lay monogamy strengthened patrilineal relationships.[7]

According to the Herlihy-Duby school of thought, as estates were carved into smaller and smaller pieces to satisfy inheritance rights of children, land became scarce, and many landed families became concerned that the family property was becoming eroded. Land was not required to be kept in the family: owners, both male and female, could dispose of it as they wished. Furthermore, husbands and wives controlled their own estates and could sell without consulting one another. The result was the fragmentation of estates, not only into heirs' hands, but also as outright gifts to the church.[8]

Primogeniture, the custom that allowed only the eldest son to inherit, solved this problem of land division, but created other complexities.[9] Younger sons had to find new ways to support themselves, often leaving the family estate to become knights in lords' households or moving to towns in search of new opportunities. The impact of this change was more than merely economic. As Jo Ann McNamara has theorized, it created a masculine identity crisis, the *Herrenfrage*. Because status in the urban environment was "less pinned to urban warrior qualities," men needed to redefine manhood to ensure their superiority over women.[10]

Central to the traditional historical view is the belief that daughters of the landed classes, who previously had been able to inherit, suffered as well. The advantage that women in southern France held in previous centuries was erased.[11] To provide daughters with some kind of settlement since they did not have the same new opportunities as sons, the nature of dowry shifted from the Germanic practice of gifts of land, goods, or money from husband to wife to Roman dowry, a gift to the husband from the bride's family.[12]

The Germanic tradition, as Diane Owen Hughes has delineated, specified three gifts: the bridepiece, the payment made by the groom to his wife's kinsmen in return for relinquishing their guardianship (*mundium*) over her; the *morgengabe*, or morning gift, the groom's payment to the bride on the morning after the consummation of their marriage as a reward for her virginity; and the father's marriage gift to his daughter (dowry).[13] The morning gift, in particular, assured brides of substantial rights to their husbands' patrimonies and took precedence over the inheritance rights of the husbands' kinsmen.[14]

The Germanic practice of dowry as a gift of land, goods, or money from the husband to the wife (thus ensuring her economic independence) was, according to David Herlihy, "the universal rule of marriage throughout the early Middle Ages." For the most part, both sons and daughters had rights to the property of their parents.[15] By the twelfth century, the burden of a dowry had shifted almost exclusively to the bride and her family.[16] As Hughes argues, not only did dowry begin to take precedence over the *morgengabe*, but also its very nature changed between the eleventh and twelfth centuries. While previously the dowry had been given in real property, that is, land, it was replaced by money. This change, Hughes contends, was "a further sign of the daughter's effective disinheritance." Real property was too valuable to be given to daughters, since it could then fall out of family hands. Husbands, as well, preferred cash, which could easily be merged with their own estates.[17] Unlike the eleventh century, wives could no longer sell their dowry without their husbands' authorization, thus limiting a woman's power.

Because primogeniture excluded women (as well as younger sons) from inheriting family land, dowry became the only way that a daughter could share in her parents' property. As Mark Angelos has described it, "No longer simply a wedding gift, a woman's dowry was now considered her entire share of the patrimony...ending her claims to any later division of her father's estate with her brothers."[18] In other words, dowry and inheritance were mutually exclusive.[19] Furthermore, under the system of primogeniture, only a fraction of the marriageable men had a source of income. Families thus paid to have their daughters taken off their hands; grooms welcomed the money and goods that came with their brides. Although some younger sons entered the clergy, there was still a surplus of men, who competed for the attentions of well-dowered women.[20]

Primogeniture, in this construction, thus had a severe impact on both daughters and younger sons, although it appears that women suffered more. In the profound social and economic change that grew out of this practice, female inheritance rights became confined within marriage. Once wed, a woman could no longer own real property. Even her dowry was not hers to control. As Weinburger has described it:

> As dutiful daughters, women helped to stabilize their fathers' estates by accepting a dowry (which in some cases was surprisingly small) in place

> of an inheritance... as wives, they provided a similar service to their husbands by accepting only a lifetime usufruct of the *sponsalitium* while at the same time giving up control of their dowries so that their husband's [*sic*] estates could remain intact.[21]

The notion of usufruct is an important one because having the "use" of property managed by a husband differs greatly from being able to decide how it is used and how it is passed on to others. Women gained control over their dowry only if and when they became widows. Nonetheless, as Penny Schine Gold has shown, even then they often were hindered in their ability to transfer property. Studying property transactions in Anjou in 1000–1249, she found that women were more often consenters to the transfer of property (44.5 percent) than alienors, that is, the donors of property (11.9 percent). Even as widows, they had children as consenters more frequently than men did.[22] Selfish children could restrict the ability of a widow to control her property, as could a second husband.[23]

The practice of usufruct held true in other parts of Europe as well. In tenth-century Saxony, for example, the shortage of males and the longevity of females led to an accumulation of land in women's hands. Rich widows found security in leaving land to the church, which began to own more property than was in secular hands. The balance of land became so distorted that rich widows were forced by the state to remarry.[24] In England, before the thirteenth-century Statue of Westminster, which required land to be passed on to heirs, a woman had full possession of her marriage portion, the *maritagium*. She could pass it on to her younger sons or to daughters, but often in the form of dowry.[25]

While the traditional view of the diminution of property rights that we can trace to Duby and Herlihy remains influential, scholars in the last two decades, such as Theodore Evergates and Kimberly A. LoPrete, have disputed its widespread application. In the introduction to Evergates's collection of essays titled *Aristocratic Women in Medieval France*, they challenge the thesis of Jo Ann McNamara and Suzanne Wemple that women in Western Europe lost property rights in the eleventh and twelfth centuries and were thus excluded from the exercise of powers that were associated with lordship and governance.[26] Adding to the work of a host of historians, LoPrete and Evergates point to "the failure of historians to exploit the vast and varied source materials that do exist" about medieval women who were property owners in the regions of Blois-Chartres, Champagne, Flanders, and Occitania.[27] Several key articles appear in this volume, including Amy Livingstone's analysis of women in the Chartrain. She argues that women could inherit both property and administrative office as well as retain certain rights over their dowries. She admits, however, that it is impossible to know whether or not it was a shared inheritance with brothers.[28] In an earlier article, Livingstone also argues that women were not prevented from inheriting family property under primogeniture in Blois-Chartres.[29] In her most recent work, *Out of Love For My Kin: Aristocratic Family Life in the Lands of the Loire, 1000–1200*, she uses historical documents, such as charters, cartuleries, obituaries, and chronicles, to show that in the Loire region, primogeniture and patrilineage were options, but not the choice of the majority.[30]

Evergates's article in this collection on aristocratic women in Champagne outlines the 1270 High Court of Champagne's "customs" on familial and property rights. Three such customs were important to women: partible inheritance (nonfeudal property shared equally among all children), community property (the equal share of all property acquired during marriage), and dower (the wife's right to a residence and half of her husband's property for her lifetime use).[31] He cautions that, despite the cases of female inheritance he found, the rights of women were diminished:

> This was not a society of equal opportunity. By the twelfth century, daughters were no longer of equal status with their male siblings, if indeed they ever had been. Increasingly, their dowries were explicitly identified as their part of the family inheritance, and they were asked to wait in line behind their brothers for any chance to succeed to the principal portion.[32]

Other historians have provided useful frameworks for understanding the complex relationship between women and property. Martha C. Howell, in her groundbreaking work *The Marriage Exchange: Property, Social Place, and Gender in the Cities of the Low Countries, 1300–1550*, has described the transition from a conjugal system of marital property law in Douai to a patrilineal one. Marriage, she explains, is the way in which property was transferred from generation to generation. It was "the main site for the institutionalization of relations between women and men, a powerful legislator of gender norms."[33] A widow had only usufruct, use of her husband's property, not ownership. During her lifetime, she had the right only to its income and at death it passed to predetermined heirs.[34] This practice developed, she argues, into the marriage contract, which attempted to limit women's ability to control marital property.[35]

According to Howell, women were not deemed competent to manage their own property under the new contract system because it was believed that they did not understand wealth management and needed supervision. Seeing their possessions as "cultural or social capital" rather than "economic capital," women tended to attach themselves to personal property and named clothing and jewels more often in their wills.[36] They gave immovables, however, according to convention, thus serving as "conduits of patrimonial assets."[37]

Shennan Hutton's recent work on Ghent during the period of 1339–1361 finds women acting as principals in 25 percent of the transactions she studies. The marital status of these women did not determine their ability to conduct business.[38] Hutton provides a useful distinction between two constructions of women's economic roles: (1) the patrimonial, which is patrilineal, privileges primogeniture, and results in women losing their legal capability upon marriage; (2) the burgher, which was the legal custom in Ghent. In this construction, all property, with the exception of land held in fief, was equally divisible among all children. Most of her data from the alderman's registers uses the burgher construction; only 3 percent is patriarchal. But, she notes, there were clear limits to women's economic and political authority, which was not seen as a threat to the patriarchal system "as long as the transaction was unimportant."[39] Hutton has found that when women's economic activities became profitable, they were often taken over by men.[40]

What, then, can we determine from the historical evidence about female inheritance and property rights? First of all, it is clear that there was not the widespread acceptance of primogeniture and its relationship to women's property, originally postulated by Duby and Herlihy. Although it was the norm in many regions of Western Europe, there were significant areas in France and the Low Countries in which women could inherit and exercise some control over their assets. Strict primogeniture was rarely the rule. Second, we must distinguish between land held in fief and other forms of property, including business interests. The former was almost certainly passed on to sons before daughters, who could not inherit unless there was not a male line.[41] Other assets were divided according to regional customs and provided an opportunity for women to exercise economic power. Third, a woman's marital status had a great impact on her ability to control her property. Linda Mitchell has categorized three states in thirteenth- and fourteenth-century England: unmarried maidens (under their fathers' control), wives (under their husbands' legal control), and widows (able to control themselves and their property, but did not always control whether or not they remarried).[42] Finally, the sheer volume of surviving evidence that we have from the twelfth century onward might artificially inflate the differences between that period and the earlier Middle Ages. What all of these distinctions show is that while we cannot make a blanket statement that women lost the right to inherit in these centuries, it nevertheless was true in some areas and for some women.

In the rest of this chapter, I broaden the analysis of women's property rights by looking at the literary evidence. Returning to *Le Roman de Silence*, I analyze it and two other romances written in the same century, *La Manekine* and *Havelok*. In all three, the narrative is precipitated by a woman losing her right to inherit. Is this loss simply a device to begin a plot or is it saying something more important, something of substance?[43] Was the practice widespread enough that writers, male authors at that, chose to highlight it and knew that they would have a receptive audience to the issue? If so, the message is subversive, but it is also powerless. Although these women regain the right to inherit, it is within a patriarchal structure: the property rights of all three are restored when they marry. Marriage validates their claims. The woman in each story must, in the end, cede control of the property she never had the chance to own.

I return to my question: Is there a connection between female property rights and the way they are portrayed in literature? If women did not lose the right to inherit, then why does it appear as the action that drives these plots? The three texts I will use all have been studied primarily for other themes: *Le Roman de Silence* for gender identity, *La Manekine* for incest, and *Havelok* for rightful kingship.[44] But they all *begin* and *end* with property, specifically, women's property.

Silence is the most clear-cut of these texts: written most likely in the latter half of the thirteenth century, the romance centers on the story of Silence, whose birth triggers the challenge to King Ebain's decree that women cannot own property.[45] His reason for denying them this right is not economic or political, but purely *emotional*: it is a punishment against all women for the loss of his beloved knights. We see a certain arbitrariness to this decree: the punishment is not because of anything the two sisters have done—in fact, it is really the men who are to blame for their own deaths.[46] The king wants to remove the situation so that it can never happen again. The author creates Silence, who, testing the new law, is so-named because silence, Heldris explains, relieves anxiety (2067–2069). She is brought up as a he so the family can keep their inheritance, thus relieving her parents' worries.

However, her silence does anything but relieve anxiety. The romance is saturated with gender confusion. Silence is neither he nor she, but rather "Malduit" ("very badly brought up")[47] (3177–3178). Furthermore, when she is a child her parents fear that she will be found out. For example, they have to trick a priest into hurriedly baptizing her without removing her cloth, pretending that she is close to death (2084–2124). When she gets older, she cannot partake of sexual pleasure, clearly explaining the problem:

Nel sui, par foi, ains sui honis
Quant as femes voel ester onis.
Gel pensai por moi aäsier.
Trop dure boche ai por baisier,
Et trop rois bras por acoler.
On me poroit tost afoler
Al giu c'on fait desos gordine,
Car vallés sui et nient mescine. (2643–2650)

[No I'm not, upon my word—I'm a disgrace
If I want to be one of the women.
I was trying to make life easy for myself,
but I have a mouth too hard for kisses,
and arms too rough for embraces.
One could easily make a fool of me
in any game played under the covers,
for I'm a young man, not a girl.]

These lines indicate how very confused Silence is. Because she plays the role of a male, she believes herself to be one. With life too difficult at home, she runs away, realizing that to save the family inheritance, she must continue to act as a male. In the process, she becomes a minstrel, not an heir, removing herself from the very class that creates the conflict. She acts as if she is no longer an heir. The anxiety that her name was supposed to calm goes beyond herself and her family. Indeed, it causes an ongoing fight between Nature and Nurture about which one is responsible for her identity. After she is back in the court of Ebain, she is unmasked by Merlin, the *magician*, and marries the king. This outcome suggests that women regain their property by the same arbitrariness by which they lose it.

As a man, Silence exemplifies all that is perfect; she is the quintessential male, all that she cannot be as a woman. She is only restored to her property by losing her freedom in the world. Silence no longer has to be silent because the situation has been magically resolved. There is no more anxiety, no more gender confusion, but only because Silence has gotten married—to a king, no less, the ultimate in patriarchal authority on earth. She becomes a kind of Christlike savior for all women—by her sacrifice, property is restored.

La Manekine, written by Philippe de Remy most likely in the late 1220s,[48] also introduces the idea of women's property rights. At the beginning of the story, the dying queen of Hungary asks her husband, the king, not to remarry except "if the princes and the counts of this country refuse to have my daughter inherit the Kingdom of Hungary" ("se li prince et li contoeur / De ce païs ne voelent mie / Que li Roialmes do Hongrie") (128–134). The narrative is thus driven not only by the dying queen's request to her husband, but also by her premonition that her daughter, Joie, will be prohibited from inheriting. The issue of inheritance is central to the story, as Nancy B. Black has pointed out: the first two illustrations of the only surviving manuscript of *La Manekine* (B.N. fr. 1588) depict the death of the queen and the barons insisting the king remarry in order to produce a male.[49]

As suspected, the barons refuse the queen's deathbed request: although Joie is noble and courteous, they reason, there might be a break in the line of succession if a woman was in power (212–214). What is the king to do? The queen has specified that if he remarries, he must find a woman who resembles her (128–134). One baron suggests that he marry Joie (317). In this conflict between having an heir and committing incest, the inheritance issue is more powerful and overrides the sin and crime of incest. If he doesn't remarry, he will lose his throne to rebellion (362); even the clerics approve of the wedding. Again, the question of property is paramount: the sin can be forgiven if succession is at stake. The problem has been initiated by a woman, the queen, who foresees the problem, and by her demand that her husband marry someone who looks like her. The problem is aggravated by Joie, who refuses. She puts her honor and her soul before thoughts of inheritance and dynasty (571) and retaliates by cutting off her hand. By this action she maims herself to show that she is not worthy to be queen, but also symbolically refuses to give her hand in marriage (712).

Like Silence, Joie loses her right to inherit on the whim of the barons. She too has an arbitrary name ("Manekine" – the girl without a hand); she wants to be silent about her given name because of her father's villany. She also is forced to leave her home and sets out on adventures, which take her in a boat, first to Scotland, where she marries the king of Scotland and is given the dower lands of Ireland and Cornwall (1944–1945). Her disapproving stepmother's machinations force her to leave, now with her newborn son. Back in a boat, Joie blames Fortune for causing her to lose both her husband and her wealth (4707–4710):

Moi a ele fait mo[u]lt dolente;
Car de grant joie et de rikece
M'a mis en [doel] et en tristece.
De la riens que je plus amoie
Et de tous les biens que j'avoie. (4706–4710)

[She has caused me more woe
For from great joy and wealth
She threw me into distress and sorrow.
Separated from the one whom I loved the most
And from all the wealth that I had acquired.]

Twice, therefore, Joie is deprived of her rightful property and leaves her home. Landing in Rome, she is found by fishermen who "sell" her to a senator. She refuses to give the senator her rightful name and exacts a promise that he respect her married state; she becomes his housekeeper and he raises her son as his own. Like Silence, her story has a magical ending: both her husband and her father arrive in Rome at the same time and all confusion is resolved. Joie's hand is found in a nearby fountain and is reattached. She also regains her property, but only because she is married: the barons of Armenia arrive to tell her that she has inherited the entire kingdom "on the side of your good mother" (323) but they give her husband the power to govern them (329). Likewise, her father gives Hungary not to Joie, but to her husband, the king of Scotland. As Carol Harvey has noted, "she will only recover her name and her full identity when she is reunited with her husband and reconciled with her father."[50]

Both of Joie's proposed marriages entail loss. The sanctioned marriage to her father requires that she commit incest in order to retain ownership of her property. The remedy is as severe as the loss: only by replacing her mother can she retain her mother's property. As Margaret Schlauch noted in her now classic book *Chaucer's Constance and Accused Queens*, "The request of a dying queen in fairy tales and romance that her successor should look like her, seems to be due to a distorted reminiscence of the time when she herself had constituted her husband's right and claim to the crown."[51] Even her marriage to the king of Scotland is not without loss: Joie must go to the ends of the earth to regain her hand and her property, which she can enjoy, but not control.

The various versions of the Havelok story provide a variation of the loss of property theme we have seen in *Silence* and *La Manekine*. Both Havelok and his bride are dispossessed of their inheritance by wicked guardians, which seemingly might contradict my point, since it is both sexes who lose this right. However, I believe that the female character in the Havelok stories is emphasized in such a way as to privilege her situation. There are several versions of the story—Gaimar's *Estoire des Engleis*, written between 1135 and 1140; the *Lai d'Haveloc*, composed around 1190–1220; the anonymous Anglo-Norman *Brut*, completed shortly after 1272; and the Middle English romance *Havelok the Dane* from around

1290–1309. Although I will only investigate the Middle English text here, it is important to note that in the Anglo-Norman versions, the female character is equally central. In the Anglo-Norman texts, Haveloc's wife, Argentille, is decisive and resourceful, often dominating her naïve and sometimes passive husband. She is the one, for instance, who urges Haveloc to go to Denmark after her prophetic dream. In the Middle English version, however, he is the one who has the dream and makes his own decisions.[52] More to the point is the emphasis placed on the woman's right of inheritance. Richard J. Moll has noted that Argentille is described as the "right inheritor" of her father's lands in the Lambeth *Brut* and the stream of light indicating a rightful ruler comes from the sides of both Haveloc and Argentille.[53]

In the Middle English version, Argentille becomes Goldeborw, and we again see an emphasis on her right to her father's throne with the words "Of his body he had no heir, / but a maiden very fair" (l.111). When King Athelwold is dying, he says to his barons:

> But nov ye sen Þat I shal deye,
> Nou Ich wille you alle preye
> Of mi douther, Þat sha be
> Yure leuedi after me,
> Wo may yeme*n* hire and Engelonde,
> Til Þat she [be] wman of helde,
> And Þha[t] she mowe [hir] yeme*n* and welde?[54] (168–175)
>
> [But now you see that I shall die,
> Now I will you all pray
> About my daughter that she be
> Your lady after me,
> Both her and England,
> Till she be a woman of age,
> That she can govern and rule?]

As in *La Manekine*, her success is thwarted. After the king's death, Earl Godrich of Cornwall takes charge. He swears to give her the best man that lives as a husband and then deliver England into her hands. But Godrich gets jealous and wonders why she should get the kingdom, uttering, "She shall never have it. / Should I give to a fool, a girl, / England, though she desires it?" ("Shal sho it neuere more haue. / Sholde Ic yeue a fol, a Þerne, / Engelond, Þou sho it yerne?") (297–299). Goldeborw is put in prison, so that Godrich's son can be king.

As in our previous examples, the story begins with Goldeborw's loss of inheritance. It is only after her dispossession that we get Havelok's story, in which an equally deceitful guardian, Godard, sends him off to be drowned by Grim, the fisherman. But Grim and his wife notice a ray of light coming from his mouth and a cross on his shoulder and spare him. The family sets off for England, where Havelok gets work in Godrich's kitchen, where he is deemed the strongest man in the land. Interpreting King Athelwold's command that Goldeborw be given to the best man that lives, Godrich marries her off to Havelok. They flee Godrich, and Goldeborw sees the same light and gold cross. An angel speaks to her and tells her Havelok is a king's son and heir and must go to Denmark. Once there, the Danish knights see the same light and cross and pledge allegiance to him. Havelok is made king and returns to England with an army to fight Godrich, telling him to "give her the land, for that is right" ("Yeld hire Þe lond, for Þhat is rith") (2718). He refuses, but the English knights recognize that Goldeborw is the rightful heir (2767–2770). She is mentioned two other times as the rightful heir (289, 2540), and three times as heir (110, 1096, 2086).[55]

It is Havelok, however, not Goldeborw, who gets crowned. Just as in *La Manekine*, the woman's property becomes her husband's. For all of her accomplishments (and Argentille's in the Anglo-Norman versions), she does not regain power herself; she uses them to help Havelok regain his rightful crown of Denmark, and through marriage, hers.[56]

Can this story, then, of joint loss of inheritance, be used to make the case that some thirteenth-century authors were concerned with women's property rights? Certainly, the fact that her story is told first in the Middle English version highlights its importance. Havelok would not have regained his throne without her, nor, of course, obtain hers. It has also been argued by K. S. Whetter that Havelok does not know of his royal birth throughout much of the poem, but that Goldeborw does, since she refuses to marry beneath her station.[57] If so, then the memory of the loss of inheritance is retained by and more keenly felt by the woman. It is her story that is central here, her double dispossession, just as in *Silence* and *La Manekine*. These three romances, authored, most likely, by men, show that only through marriage can a woman regain what is hers, which, paradoxically, can be hers only by her husband owning it.

These stories were not written in a vacuum; rather, as I will show in the next chapter, they overlap with other issues that were being debated in twelfth- and thirteenth-century Europe. Put together, they suggest that a woman's property—not only land and moveable goods, but also her own body—was part of a wider intellectual argument on her very nature.

CHAPTER 2

SILENCE, LANGUAGE, SEXUALITY

The "silencing" of Silence is a rich metaphor for the way medieval women writers chose to express themselves. As R. Howard Bloch has shown, medieval male authors associated women with verbosity and saw their language as a cover for deception. Eve, through her speech and its sexual consequences, created discord between man and God.[1] Silence, then, can be seen as the dispossession of women's voices, and it finds a parallel in other discourses in the century before *Le Roman de Silence* was written, in particular, theological debates on marriage and sexuality as well as misogynist literature. In this chapter I argue that this evidence shows a preoccupation with women's ability to own their own power and contributes to an environment in which the proper boundaries of women's roles were well-defined, whether as wife or as the bride of Christ.

As Jack Goody has explained, when women are receivers of "male" property, either by inheritance or dowry, marriage, as well as courtship and sexuality, tend strongly to be controlled.[2] As carriers of property, women's sexuality needed to be controlled in the patrilineal system of the twelfth century. If property passed through the male, then the husband had to be certain he was the father of his wife's children. In a society in which property is controlled and can be bequeathed through the woman, her sexual fidelity is of no consequence. As Georges Duby has pointed out, marriage in the early Middle Ages was an official recognition of a union between two houses (*pactum conjugale*). As such, it was an exchange that involved a woman, "or, more precisely, her anticipated motherhood."[3]

The tangled web of property, marriage, and sexuality became especially crucial in the twelfth century precisely because the legal and social landscape had changed. Marriage customs were transformed from a purely civil act to one increasingly regulated by the church, itself rapidly becoming a major owner of property. At the end of the seventh century, one-third of the productive land in France rested in ecclesiastical hands.

By the ninth century, that amount had doubled due to bequests, donations, and tithes. Although that growth began to drop off in the tenth and eleventh centuries, the church remained a significant landowner and needed to keep hold of its property.[4] Using the early church fathers as their authority, medieval clerics developed a new theory and practice of marriage, one that brought it increasingly under their control and solidified a standard of feminine behavior that mirrored the already dwindling legal rights of women.

Although marriage in the early church was a secular custom not under clerical direction, the early church fathers wrote extensively on the subject. In his *Confessiones*, written between 397 and 401, Augustine recounts his own experience and makes a distinction between wives and concubines. The former produces children, while the latter satisfies lust:

> In illis annis unam habebam non eo quod legitimum uocatur coniugio cognitam, sed quam indagauerat uagus ardor inops prudentiae, sed unam tamen, ei quoque seruans tori fidem; in qua sane experirer exemplo meo quid distaret inter coniugalis placiti modum, quod foederatum esset generandi gratia, et pactum libidinosi amoris, ubi proles etiam contra uotum nascitur, quamuis iam nata cogat se diligi.[5]
>
> [In those years I lived with a woman, not my lawfully wedded wife, but a mistress whom I had chosen for no special reason but that my restless passions had alighted on her. But she was the only one and I was faithful to her. Living with her I found out by my own experience the difference between the restraint of the marriage alliance contracted for the purpose of having children, and a bargain struck for lust, in which the birth of children is begrudged, though, if they come we cannot help but love them.]

He tempers this somewhat in *De bono coniugali*, written the year he finished his *Confessiones*, by making commitment, not sex, the decisive factor in marriage:

> Et potest quidem fortasse non absurde hoc appellari conubium, si usque ad mortem alicuius eorum id inter eos placuerit, et prolis generationem, quamuis non ea causa coniuncti sint non tamen uitauerint ut uel nolint sibi nasci filios uel etiam opere aliquo malo agant ne nascantur.[6]
>
> [It is not absurd perhaps to call this a marriage provided they maintain the arrangement until the death of one of them, and provided they do not avoid having children either by being unwilling to have children or even by doing something wrong to prevent the birth of children.]

Dyan Elliott points out that the Old Testament's reproductive function of marriage, "increase and multiply" (Gen. 1:28), becomes transformed by Paul. Advocating the avoidance of all sex (1 Cor. 7:1), he allows that men and women may have one partner if sexuality cannot be completely avoided (1. Cor. 7:2 and 9).[7] The early church fathers, Elliott contends, had "a growing awareness that marriage and procreation were best defended if they were admitted as a part of God's original plan."[8] Similarly, Augustine distinguishes three levels of guilt in intercourse. If the purpose of sex is procreation, there is no sin. If intercourse is performed with a spouse to satisfy lust, then it is only a venial sin. However, sex with someone to whom you do not have a commitment (his definition of marriage) is adultery or fornication and therefore a mortal sin. Abstinence, he stresses, is preferable to any of these.[9] Augustine argues that something good comes out of the evil of lust:

> carnalis uel iuuenalis incontentia, etiamsi uitiosa est, ad propagandae prolis redigitur honestatem, ut ex malo libidinis aliquid boni faciat copulatio coniugalis, deinde quia reprimitur et quodam modo uerecundis aestuat conupiscentia carnis, quam temperat parentalis affectus.[10]
>
> [carnal or youthful incontinence, which is admittedly a defect, is applied to the honorable task of begetting children, and so intercourse within marriage engenders something good out of the evil of lust. Moreover, the lustful tendencies of the flesh are kept in subjection, and their hot passion becomes more seemly, for parental love contains it.]

Marriage, in fact, becomes a safeguard against fornication and adultery, a legal way to contain lust: "nuptiae tamen ab adulterio seu fornicatione defendunt."[11] To protect one's spouse from sin, St. Paul in 1 Corinthians 7.3 ("uxori uir debitum reddat") created what became the "marriage debt," the binding obligation to satisfy the other's sexual needs. This idea predominates in *De bono coniugali*. Augustine sees the purpose of marriage as not only to procreate, but also to bear responsibility for each other's sins of the flesh:

> Debent ergo sibi coniugati non solum ipsius sexus sui commiscendi fidem liberorum procreandorum causa, quae prima est humani generis in ista mortalitate societas, uerum etia informatis inuicem excipiendae ad illicitos concubitus euitandos mutuam quodam modo seruitutem …
>
> [So married couples owe fidelity to each other not merely in performance of the sexual act to bring forth children—and this is the primary compact between the human species in this mortal life of ours—but also in ministering, so to say, to each other, to shoulder each other's weakness, enabling each other to avoid illicit sexual intercourse …]

For Augustine, a spouse must consent to intercourse, even if the demand appears to be too great: "in eo ipso sibi inuicem coniuges debitum soluunt, etiamsi id aliquanto intemperantius et incontinentius expetant, fidem tamen sibi partier debent" ("in the very act, in which married partners pay the debt they owe to each other, even if they demand this too passionately and too lustfully, they owe equal fidelity to each other").[12] These theological discussions, however, were quite separate from the actual ritual of early medieval marriage, which was essentially a pact between two families, not two individuals. As described by Duby, the ceremonial sealing of this agreement was split in two. The first part was the marriage, essentially a business meeting: "a ritual of faith and pledge, verbal promises, a show of disinvestment and of assumption of possession, the handing over of pledges, the ring, the deposit, the coins, and finally the contract."[13] Then came the wedding, which was the meal, the sexual consummation, and the morning gift, "the present expressing the gratitude and hope of the man whose dream it was already to have embarked upon his legitimate paternal role by impregnating his wife."[14]

Beginning in the ninth century, according to Duby, the church began to insinuate itself into the secular model of marriage, gaining full strength in the eleventh and twelfth centuries. Prior to this time, the church used its powers of excommunication to intervene in marriages that were considered scandalous, but it did not have any clear-cut matrimonial jurisdiction.[15] By the mid-twelfth century, three distinct views on marriage were held by Western jurists. The Italian school, led by Gratian, believed that the process began with consent and was completed with physical consummation. Without sexual intercourse, no binding marriage contract existed. Peter Lombard, the leading advocate of the French school, decreed that sexual consummation had no relevance and consent alone created marriage. A third group, composed of Master Vacarius and the anonymous author of the *Summa coloniensis*, wrote that the neither of these was essential to the marriage. The physical delivery of the bride to the groom (*traditio*) was the key element. This view, however, soon faded. In 1180 Pope Alexander II in his decretal *Veniens ad nos* resolved the issue and agreed with the French that consent was the key determinant in marriage. This remained the rule until the Council of Trent in 1563.[16]

Consent was fundamental to the ecclesiastical model of marriage, since the church could use lack of it as an argument against marriages arranged by heads of households. In the writings of the early church fathers, parental consent was important. In the 600 years between the collapse of the Roman Empire and the eleventh-century reforms, the head of the household had the responsibility to arrange his children's marriages, in both Germanic practice and ecclesiastical teaching. As Charles J. Reid, Jr., has described it: "This basic tension between the freedom of consent, on the one hand, and the need to retain some institutional and parental control over the celebration of marriage remained a constant feature of high and late medieval law and life."[17] By stressing consent of the two parties, canon lawyers in essence gave approval to marriages of which parents disapproved.

The church's increasing control over marriage, however, was not only to regulate sexuality, but also to maintain its own vast property and wealth. Audrey B. Davidson and Robert B. Ekelund, Jr., have convincingly argued that the church produced profits and rent streams by manipulating doctrine and policy. In particular, as it gained control over marriage, it earned significant income by providing exemptions to its rules on consanguinity, clandestine marriages, and marriage dissolution.[18] One way to ensure its hold on land was to prohibit clerical marriage: most clergy in the early church were married, and although the debates on this issue began in the fourth century, clerical marriage was not prohibited until the Second Lateran Council in 1139.[19] Pope Gregory VII's enforcement of clerical celibacy in 1074 insured that their property would not be passed to descendants or into lay hands.[20]

According to Neil Cartlidge, the establishment of clerical celibacy may have fostered the development of antimatrimonial and antifeminist literature in this period.[21] It certainly increased the divide between the clergy and laity. In the words of Dyan Elliott, "a clerical celibate elite requires a copulating laity."[22] Similarly, Jo Ann McNamara has noted that arguments for segregating the clergy were buttressed by the belief that women had uncontrollable sexual urges.[23] By labeling the female body as dangerous, clerics could make the case that women's sexuality had to be controlled, further differentiating between the good woman and the evil one.

The roots of medieval misogyny go back to ancient Judaic law and early Greek texts. Already in Hesiod, woman was identified as the plague of man. In addition, women were seen as more lustful than men and associated with the material rather than the spiritual.[24] The idea that women and men differ significantly and that men are superior was first formulated, according to Prudence Allen, in Aristotle, who argued that women have a passive role in generation. St. Augustine later developed this idea into the belief that woman is the helpmate to man for the activity of generation and is not in the image of God.[25] As E. Ann Matter has pointed out, this Augustinian tenet that women qua humans were created in God's image but women as specifically female were not was virtually unopposed in the Middle Ages.[26] Although Aquinas softened Augustine's belief that women were defective men, he agreed that they had inferior rational capacities, mainly because of the weakness of their bodies.[27]

Gradually, as R. Howard Bloch has noted, sex became identified with evil, and Eve's sin identified with its cause.[28] In both Latin satires and vernacular literature, women are portrayed as domineering, disobeying, neglectful, and demanding creatures who use sex as a way to get their wishes.[29] Walter Map, for example, in *De nugis curialium*, blames Eve for first disobeying God. Because of her disobedience, all women carry this sin. Note the many times the word "first" is used in this passage:

> Prima primi uxor Ade post primam hominis creacionem primo peccato prima soluit ieiunia contra preceptum Domini. Parentauit inobediencia, que citra mundi terminum non absistet expugnare feminas, ut sint semper indefesse trahere in consequenciam quod a matre sua traxerunt.[30]
>
> [The first wife of the first Adam after the first creation of man, by the first sin broke the first fast against the precept of God. Disobedience parented this, and on this side the end of the world, it will never cease to lay seige to women, that they may be ever unwearied in carrying out what they have derived from their mother.]

Women ensnare men by their beauty, which masks a monster:

> Desiderio tuo totus inflammaris, et speciosi nobilitate capitis seductus, chimeram miser nescis esse quod petis; sed scire deuoues quod triforme monstrum illud insignis uenustetur facie leonis, olentis maculetur uentre capri, uirulente armetur cauda uipere.[31]
>
> [You are all inflamed by your desire, and seduced by the nobility of a beautiful head, you are not able to know, poor man, that what you seek is a chimera; but you refuse to learn that a three-formed monster is adorned with the face of a extraordinary lion, polluted with the body of a stinking goat, and armed with the tail of a virulent viper.]

Citing biblical and classical examples, Map shows how men succumbed to women and sinned. Even David fell prey to a woman's innate sinful nature:

> Veritas que falli non potest ait de beato Dauid "Inueni uirum secundum cor meum." Hic tamen egregie precipitatus est amore mulieris ab adulterio in homicidium, ne umquam sola ueniant scandala.[32]
>
> [The truth which cannot err says of the blessed David, "I have found a man after my heart." Nevertheless, he was felled by the love of a woman notably from adultery to murder, lest offences never come singly.]

Petrus Alfonsi, the twelfth-century Jewish convert to Christianity, expressed his negative views on women through parables in his *Disciplina clericalis*. Although the aim of this text was not specifically misogynist, its goal was didactic and meant to impart a moral education. A "tremendous success," in John Toland's words, it survives in seventy-six medieval manuscripts.[33] It was adapted by countless medieval writers, including Chaucer, who refers to Alfonsi five times in the *Tale of Melibee*.[34] His main theme is that women are lascivious and unfaithful. In Exemplum XIV, "De puteo" ("Of the well"), he recounts how a young man who had spent much time learning the wiles of women decided to marry. He went to a wise man to ask how he could best prevent his wife from deceiving him. The man told him to build a house with high walls and only one window and one door and to keep her locked in with only minimum food and clothing. One day the wife, looking through the window, saw a handsome young man and immediately fell in love with him. Getting her husband drunk every night, she stole the keys and went out to meet her lover. One night the husband caught her and locked her out of the house. She cried and told him she would throw herself in the well, and he would be responsible for her death. Hearing a sound of something falling into the well, he ran out of the house. The wife, who had merely thrown in a stone, ran into the house and locked her husband out. She blamed him for her infidelities and told his parents about his nightly visits to prostitutes. Petrus Alfonsi describes how his life was ruined:

> Parentes uero hec audientes atque uerum esse existimantes increpauerunt eum. Et ita mulier illa liberata arte sua flagicium quod meruerat in uirum retrusit. Cui nichil profuit, immo obfuit mulierem custodisse: nam iste eciam accidit cumulus miserie quod existimacione plurimorum quod paciebatur meruisse crederetur. Unde quidem bonis compluribus pulsus, dignitatibus exutus, existimacione fedatus ob uxoris maliloquium incestitatis tulit supplicium.[35]
>
> [In fact, hearing this and deeming it to be the truth, his parents rebuked him. And so through her guile, the woman freed herself from the opprobrium she had deserved and thrust it on the man. It benefited him nothing to have kept watch over his wife; on the contrary, it harmed him: for this mass of miseries happened to him and, in the estimation of many, he was believed to have earned what he suffered. Thus removed of his many goods, stripped of his dignities, his reputation soiled by the bad words of his wife, he suffered punishment for his unchastity.]

Even good women, according to Walter Map and Petrus Alfonsi, must be feared. In Alfonsi's "De canicula lacrimante" ("The Crying Bitch"), a teacher tells his pupil how a chaste and faithful wife is duped by an old hag into sleeping with a young man who has fallen in love with her. Attributing this episode to black magic, the pupil exclaims, "Spero quod siquis homo tam sapiens erit ut semper timeat se posse decipi arte mulieris" ("I hope that any man will be so wise that he may fear the possibility of being deceived by a woman's tricks").[36] Map declares that even the best woman, who is "rarer than a phoenix" ("rarior est fenice"), must be feared.[37] Even a chaste woman can become evil in sleep: "Amice, ecce quam illibatam seruauerunt uigilie, deflorauit illusio per sompnium, ut semper omne rosarium aliquo turbine sua purpura spolietur" ("Friend, behold that one whom they had observed as virginal [literally, 'intact'], the illusion withered in sleep, as when the redness of a rose bed is always despoiled by some wind").[38]

Not only women, but the institution of marriage itself must be avoided. Using the example of Cicero, who divorced Terentia and then refused to remarry, Map declares that a man cannot have time for both a woman and philosophy.[39] Furthermore, marriage prevents happiness: "Amice, utinam tu semel maritus fueris et non sis, ut scias quid felicitatem impediat" ("Friend, would that you once should be and not be a husband, so that you may know what impedes happiness").[40]

According to Katharina M. Wilson and Elizabeth M. Makowski, "misogamy occurs in literature only when there is a certain level of civilization, order, and urbanization in a society and when women attain a certain level of economic or legal independence." When women are dependent on men, however, misogamy is absent.[41] It too had an economic component, they argue; it was a "potent propaganda tool in the hands of Gregorian reformers devoted to clerical celibacy as a means of 'husbanding' finite resources of landed wealth and public influence."[42]

Despite this pervasive misogamy, other monastic authors wrote positively about the attributes of wives. As Sharon Farmer has shown, authors such as Thomas of Chobham heralded women who influenced the economic decisions of their husbands to support monastic institutions.[43] Although excessive gifts of charity were seen as disobedient and unreasonable acts, according to P. H. Cullum, they "could be forgiven, indeed lauded, because the giving was in the service of a higher calling, by which they demonstrated their victory over their inherent weaknesses as women."[44] In the emerging money economy, wives were encouraged to give alms secretly on behalf of their greedy husbands.[45] That these gifts contributed to the wealth of the church played no small role in why generous women were seen as exemplary.

In addition, the peacekeeping and nurturing qualities of women were also stressed.[46] As Alcuin Blamires has shown, this "case for women" often drew on the paradox of women's strength in their inherent weakness, rising from St. Paul's belief that "power comes to its full strength in weakness" and continuing through Fortunatus, Peter Venerable, and

Peter Abelard.[47] Nonetheless, Blamires calls this "misogyny in disguise" since maleness is the standard, and women's softness is perceived only in relation to men.[48]

Clearly, medieval male writers took women's inherent weaknesses and polarized them into two clearly defined images: Eve, the "bad" woman who transgresses and brings down her husband with herself, and Mary, the "good" woman who transcends her bodily state and nourishes her child. Marbod of Rennes in his *Liber decem capitulorum* differentiates between these two kinds of women. As we have seen earlier, he is vitriolic in his condemnation of one sort of woman, but sees an opposite kind as well, one for whom Mary's virginity is the model:

> Et sub lege nova postquam laus integritatis
> Virgineo partu mundo celebrata refulsit,
> Innumerabilibus sunt tempora plena puellis
> Quae vitae damno comprensavere pudorem...[49]
> [But under the new law, after the glory of purity
> Shone brightly by the virgin birth, honored in the world,
> Time has been full of innumerable girls
> Who embraced chastity by the loss of life.]

In *De virginibus* Ambrose defines a virgin as one who is free from sin: "Quid autem est castitas virginalis nisi expers contagionis integritas?"[50] "Contagio" underscores the notion of a virgin as standing alone—whole, untouched and untouchable. Christianity is a prerequisite for a true virgin, in Ambrose's mind; he catalogues pagan virgins who do not deserve that name, who are immodest, overcome by lust or need to be chaste only for a short period of time. He concludes:

> Quanto nostrae virgines fortiores, quae vincunt etiam quas non vident potestates, quibus non tantum de carne et sanguine, sed etiam de ipso mundi principe saeculique rectore victoria est![51]
>
> [How much stronger are our virgins, who conquer even those powers which they do not see, to whom the victory is not only over the flesh and blood but also over the very prince of the world and ruler of the age!]

Pagan virgins, in the end, seem to give themselves up to lust. Recounting a Pythagorean virgin who bit off her tongue rather than reveal a secret to a tyrant, he denigrates her because in the end, she was overcome by passion.[52]

Medieval writers appropriated the notion that the "good" woman values her virginity above all else and is willing to martyr herself to maintain it. It permeates the *Legenda aurea* (1275), the extremely popular medieval catalogue of saints. Jocelyn Wogan-Browne has described the typical profile of the female virgin martyr: The girl is young, beautiful, rich, and noble and is secretly a Christian. Her father is a pagan, or absent. There is a pagan suitor or judge. She is approached for marriage, seduction, or rape and is persecuted by the father/suitor/judge. She is threatened, incarcerated, stripped naked, publicly flogged, lacerated, burnt, boiled, or dismembered. Her conduct is so impeccable that she converts the tyrant's populace. Her formal execution comes by beheading. She rises to heaven with doves and angelic hosts "to be welcomed into the bower of the greatest and most handsome of bridegrooms."[53]

Sexuality, or rather the absence of it, is a key determinant in the definition of a good woman. Married women who appear in the *Legenda aurea* usually are forced into marriage, but manage to keep chaste through various devices that tend to appear with the help of divine intervention.[54] This tendency, as Glasser articulates, was buttressed by the church's decision to make consent, not consummation, the key determinant of marriage. An unconsummated marriage in the eyes of some medieval theologians made its sanctity even greater.[55] John W. Baldwin has pointed out that the division of sexuality into *coniugate*, *continentes*, and *virgins* was more pervasive that the better-known social classification of *oratores*, *bellatores*, and *laboratores*.[56]

The example of the Holy Family became an important, if complicated, motif. Early church writers, such as Tertullian, believed that since Joseph and Mary produced other children after Jesus's birth, they necessarily had sexual relations. This view was vehemently denounced by Jerome, among others, who argued for their chaste marriage, describing Jesus's brothers as part of a spiritual family.[57] The arguments about what exactly constitutes marriage—consent or consummation—were complicated by the case of Joseph and Mary. Resnick explains:

> If the absence of sexual intercourse were to invalidate the marriage bond between Joseph and Mary, then Mary would suddenly appear as an unwed mother—a conclusion unacceptable to the twelfth or thirteenth centuries...But if their relationship resulted in a chaste spiritual marriage, and if lay people were encouraged to realize this model too, then the distinction between a celibate clergy and the laity would be threatened.[58]

This high standard of what women needed to do to overcome their evil nature, inherited from their mother Eve, was an unrealistic option for most women. Those who did accept virginity as their highest calling entered female monasteries. Women such as Hildegard of Bingen and Catherine of Siena, according to E. Ann Matter, found ways to use to their own advantage the accepted belief that, although inferior, women had special nurturing and spiritual qualities.[59] They did not, however, necessarily believe that their role related directly to their sex.

Hildegard, in particular, saw herself as the transmitter of the holy light. In her letters she refers to herself as a "paupercula," a poor little woman. As Barbara Newman has pointed out, this idea of "feminine frailty" actually validated her authority: because God is perfected in weakness and the humble are the most exalted, human impotence could be seen as divine empowerment.[60] Furthermore, as a self-proclaimed "indocta" (unlearned one) who spoke such words of wisdom, she could be explained "only as a living intimate of the divine Spouse, a dwelling-place of the Spirit."[61] In a letter to Eberhard, bishop of Bamberg, she says that she, a "paupercula," has looked to the true light and is sending him a "vera visio" that has been shown not in her words but in those of the true light:

> Nunc autem, o pater, ego paupercula forma ad uerum lumen prospexi, et, secundum quod ibi in uera uisione uidi et audi, quod tibi exponi petisti ita expositum non uerbis meis sed ueri luminis, cui numquam ullus defectus est, in hunc modum transmitto.[62]
>
> [Now, however, O father, I, a poor little womanly form, have looked out to the true light, and, according to what I have seen and heard there in a true vision, convey to you in this manner that which you sought to be explained to you, not in my words but in those of the true light, which never has any imperfection.]

As Barbara Newman has noted, Hildegard's biographers describe her as the bride of Christ, a description that she herself rejects.[63] She sees her authority as being a higher one, a direct link to God through the "living light." When her correspondents use lengthy Song of Songs references, she responds in a haughty and accusatory fashion. She does not specifically confront their use of the nuptial theme; instead, she makes clear exactly why she should be listened to. For example, Odo of Soissons seeks her prayers as the bride of Christ ("Hildegardi sancte ac Dei amice, sponse Christi"): "Obtestor uos per pretium sanguinis Iesu Christi; dilecti sponsi uestri, de cruce fluentis, per quem uos subarrauit et sponsam assumpsit" ("I beseech you through the value of the blood of Jesus Christ, your beloved spouse, flowing from the cross, through which he paid your dowry and accepted you as his spouse").[64] Hildegard responds to him, not as the bride of Christ, but instead says: "In uera uisione mysteriorum Dei scribo, uidendo et audiendo et sciendo in uno modo" ("I write in a true vision of the mysteries of God, to be seen and heard and understood in one way").[65] Her link is directly to God, as she tries to make clear to Odo. He writes her again in the same year, calling her the bride of God:

> Quia tu, domina, ancillam te fecisti Christi, ipse te super te eleuauit et secreta tibi uirginalis thalami adhuc in carne posite reuelasse ex parte creditur, ut una ex his credaris de quibus canitur: Introduxit me rex in cubiculum suum.[66]
>
> [Because you, lady, have made yourself the handmaid of God, he has elevated you beyond yourself and has trusted to reveal to you the secrets of the bridal chamber while you are placed in the flesh so that you may be believed to be one of those about whom it is sung: the King has brought me into his bedroom.]

Odo then interjects what can be interpreted, given their exchange, as a barb: "cum nihil horum didiceris" ("although you have studied none of these things").

In her response, Hildegard talks about the nature of the divine and ends by referring back to where she gets her authority: "Nunc iterum audi, o homo, pauperculam formam in Spiritu tibi dicentem" ("Now *again* hear the poor little womanly form speaking to you in the Spirit" [emphasis added]).[67] With this juxtaposition of the "paupercula" speaking as the Spirit, Hildegard asserts both her direct connection with God, not as spouse, but as his representative and her knowledge of the divine one in spite of being "indocta." It is as if she is telling Odo that only she can call herself unlearned. Hildegard, clearly, refuses to be silenced and marginalized.

The "bride of Christ" idea came directly from Origen's interpretation of the Song of Songs, in which he identified the bride with the perfected soul. This allegorical interpretation became the basis, according to Ann W. Astell, of all subsequent medieval writings on the Canticles.[68] Filled with longing and sexual imagery, the Song of Songs, if read literally, recounts the longing of a lover for his beloved. Stephen D. Moore has noted that a literal interpretation of the erotically charged book would have been "unthinkable."[69] The Song of Songs, he writes, "was a ticking time bomb within Scripture itself, an occasion for sin just waiting to happen, which only the ingenuity of the allegorist could successfully defuse."[70]

It was, as E. Ann Matter points out, "the most frequently interpreted book of medieval Christianity."[71] The relationship between the lovers was seen as the love between God and his church or, especially in the twelfth century, between God and the individual soul.[72] The most celebrated commentator was the Cistercian abbot Bernard of Clairvaux, whose *Sermones super Cantica Canticorum* emphasize the union of the soul with God only in heaven.[73] Bernard deconstructs the language of the Song of Songs in order to strip it of any sexual or even physical meaning. Astell notes that his allegorical reading "deliteralizes" the Song.[74] I would argue that this deliteralization is, in itself, a kind of dispossession of women's sexuality, a silencing of the female body, akin to silencing of women's voice. By using the vocabulary of sex, but confining it to the discussion of Christ's love for his bride, here distinctly *not* a real woman, Bernard is defining the perfect marriage as allegorical. His bride is unattainable in any physical sense, further polarizing women by making the possibility of being a good one even more impossible to achieve.

In his first sermon, Bernard emphasizes that the Song of Songs was meant to be read allegorically. Solomon gave us the bread, which is the Song for us to break and eat: "Est panis apud Salomonem, isque admodum splendidus sapidusque, librum dico, qui Cantica canticorum inscribitur: proferatur, si placet, et frangatur" ("There is bread in Solomon, wholly splendid and delicious, I mean the book which is entitled the Song of Songs: Let it be offered, if you please, and let it be broken").[75] Two evils are enemies of the soul: "namely, an empty love of the world and an excessive love of self" ("vanus scilicet amor mundi, et superfluus sui").[76] Continuing to detach the Song from any kind of physical interpretation, he exhorts his listeners to tame the flesh and free their spirits:

> Alioquin ante carnem disciplinae studiis edomitam et spiritui mancipatam, ante spretam et abiectam saeculi pompam et sarcinam, indigne ab impuris lectio sancta praesumitur.[77]
>
> [In general before the flesh is tamed by the zeal for knowledge and is given up to the spirit, before the ostentation and burden of the world are despised and cast aside, it is unworthy that the holy teaching be taken up by impure ones.]

Only when the soul is purified can the Song be heard because it is a marriage song of chaste souls: "Est quippe nuptiale carmen, exprimens castos iucundosque complexus animorum..." ("It is certainly a marriage song, expressing the chaste and delightful embraces of souls...").[78]

In Sermon 7, Bernard develops his notion of the bride as the soul thirsting for God ("anima sitiens Deum"): "Si ergo amare sponsis specialiter principaliterque convenit, non immerito sponsae nomine censetur anima quae amat" ("If therefore it befits brides especially and principally to love, it is not unfitting that the soul which loves be called by the name of bride").[79] That bride will want a kiss, which is all that she desires: "Osculetur me, ait, osculo oris sui" ("Let him kiss me, I say, with the kiss of his mouth").[80] This kiss of the mouth is the subject of Sermon 8. Bernard distinguishes between the kiss of the mouth and the kiss of the kiss. The Father kisses, the Son receives the kiss, and the Holy Spirit transmits the kiss, which becomes the kiss of the kiss: "Filius osculatus accipitur, non erit ab re osculum Spiritum Sanctum intelligi, utpote qui Patris Filiique imperturbabilis pax sit, gluten firmum, individuus amor, indivisibilis unitas" ("The son accepts the kissing, the kiss will not be understood as from the Holy Spirit, seeing that it is the calm peace of the Father and the Son, firm glue, undivided love, indivisible unity").[81]

The long dissection of the kiss separates it from any carnality. Not only allegory is at work here, but also a hierarchy of worthiness. By taking place between the Father and Son, the primary kiss becomes redefined as something sacred. The bride, that is, the soul, cannot receive this kiss, but only the "kiss of the kiss" communicated through the intervention of the Holy Spirit.

This disembodiment of potentially sexual imagery continues in Sermon 9, in which Bernard analyzes the breasts of both the bride and the bridegroom. Since breasts are a central sensual feature of the Song of Songs, he cleverly uses them to his advantage. Not ignoring the arousal associated with them, he shows how when the kiss is received, the bride's breasts grow large as if in pregnancy, which for him is the sign of grace: "Tantae nempe efficaciae osculum sanctum est, ut ex ipso mox, cum acceperit illud, sponsa concipiat, tumescentibus nimirum uberibus, et lacte quasi pinguescentibus in testimonium" ("Truly the holy kiss is so efficacious, that as soon as she receives it, the bride conceives, her breasts swelling with conception, as if growing fertile by her milk in testimony"). To separate the image further from any carnal meaning, Bernard says that those who pray frequently will understand: "Quibus studium est orare frequenter, experti sunt quod dico" ("For those for whom the zeal to pray is frequent have understood what I say").[82]

Just as the Song of Songs associates breasts with wine, so does Bernard. But he stresses how wine, which he associates with sensuality, is inferior to the milk of the breasts. Once a grape is pressed, he says, it can never produce any more wine; this is exactly the fate of sensuality:

> Ut enim uva expressa semel non habet iam quid denuo fundat, sed perpetua ariditate damnatur, sic caro in pressura mortis ob omni prorsus sua delectatione siccatur, nec ultra revirescit ad libidines.[83]
>
> [For the grape, once pressed, is not able to flow a second time, but is damned to eternal dryness. Thus the flesh in the press of death is utterly drained of its pleasure, and never again revives towards its longings.]

The breasts of the bride, however, flow forever:

> Merito proinde meliora carnis saeculive amore asseruntur ubera sponsae, quae nullo umquam lactentium numero arefiunt, sed semper abundant de visceribus caritatis, ut iterum fluant.[84]
>
> [Therefore, by right, the breasts of the bride are claimed to be better than worldly or carnal love. The breasts of the bride which never become dry from the number of those drinking from them, but always well up from the inmost heart of love, so that they flow again.]

By feminizing the text of the Song of Songs, as Ann Astell has pointed out, Bernard "immunizes" his monks "against lustful desires for the feminine exteriorized and objectified in sexual fantasies."[85]

The Bride, according to Astell, is associated with female characteristics: need, frailty, endurance, contemplation, compassion, and nurturing.[86] Matter explains that because *ecclesia* and *anima* are both feminine nouns in Latin, it was easy to have the church or the soul speak the words of the bride. Nonetheless, the bride of Christ became more and more closely identified with a human woman, the Virgin Mary.[87] The *Sigillum Beatae Mariae*, written right at the beginning of the twelfth century by Honorius Augustodunensis, signals the growing cult of the Virgin Mary.[88]

Mary, however, has little biblical authority. She is mentioned in fewer than a dozen passages in the New Testament. Jaroslav Pelikan characterizes her biblical account as "tantilizingly brief."[89] The Gospels of Matthew and Luke state that Mary was a virgin when she conceived Jesus, but the rest of the New Testament is silent on this, even St. Paul.[90] As Peter Brown has commented, in late antique literature Mary is portrayed as the "enclosed child," one who grew up "in total isolation from the profane world." In the second-century *Protoevangelium* of James, as Brown relates, Mary was presented "as a human creature totally enclosed in sacred space," controlled not by any male guardian but only by the "holy thought" that was inside her.[91] This idea stresses the early belief in Mary's importance in her own right, as opposed to her role in the Later Middle Ages as the immaculate conceiver of Christ. Bernard, for example, did not have much interest in Mary. As Rachel Fulton has point out, she is the protagonist only once in his *Sermons on the Song of Songs* (Sermon 29), where she is seen as the mediator to Christ.[92] Other twelfth-century commentators, she argues, see her as a compassionate symbol in her identification with Christ's pain.[93]

What, then, is the significance of all of these threads in looking at women's views of marriage in the twelfth century? Alongside a challenge to women's inheritance rights, a written discourse developed that divided women into two opposing stereotypes, Mary and Eve. Authority for these polarized images came from biblical and early church sources and conspired to marginalize women both spiritually and morally, adding to their already diluted economic position. Concurrently, the church managed to wrest authority over marriage away from what had been a civil custom and narrowly defined it so as to increase its own political, religious, and financial power. Marriage, the act by which women became the property of their husbands, was now in the hands of an institution that saw them as dangerous beings if they were not properly controlled.

In the next chapter I turn to women's narratives, which, although not dealing with the inheritance issue directly, instead question the institution of marriage. Unlike the romances analyzed in chapter one, these writers do not confront the loss of property, but rather their loss of independence. However, the economic issue is not far from their minds.

CHAPTER 3

MEDIEVAL WOMEN REJECT MARRIAGE: HELOISE AND MARIE DE FRANCE

In her first letter to Abelard, Heloise equates marriage with chains, preferring instead to be his concubine.[1] Her rejection of wedlock was not unusual. Marriage, for many medieval women, was a state to be avoided. In this chapter and the next, I examine four women writers of this period who critique the institution in terms that are economic, either literally or metaphorically. They object on many fronts, but have in common the idea that once wed, women lose their freedom.

In this chapter I consider Heloise and Marie de France, who have vastly different approaches to the marriage issue. In Heloise, we have a very real woman who writes in the epistolary genre. Her letters, along with Abelard's, are dialogic: the reader can see both sides of the arguments in which they engage. Despite their concessions to the letter-writing style of the time, Heloise, especially, does not seem constrained in her language. Her emotions refuse to be silenced either by Abelard's ignoring them or by the conventions of style. Quite simply, through her writing she tests the boundaries that as a nun have limited her experience. Heloise directly attacks marriage, criticizing both its economic and psychological chains.

Although not all of the women in Marie de France's *lais* reside in unhappy marriages, they do live in a world in which they are constrained. In two of the stories I examine, *Yonec* and *Guigemar*, women are imprisoned by their elderly husbands and try to find means of escaping their ownership and control. In the third, *Lanval*, Marie constructs a fairy tale in which the power is reversed: it is the woman who owns and dispenses property. All three, I argue, entail adventures in which boundaries are transgressed and transformation occurs—but only for the male characters. In this way Marie places her women on the margins rather than in the center of power; although they seemingly escape their unhappy situations, they are never fully free.

Heloise and the Conjugal Debt

Heloise is best known as the other half of a famous couple, the lover of Peter Abelard. As Peter Dronke has shown, at least two works contemporaneous with Abelard and Heloise allude to their relationship.[2] They first became popularized in literature with Jean de Meun's translation of the *Historia calamitatum* and his insertion of their story into *Le Roman de la Rose* in the early 1280s, a full century after Heloise's death. In succeeding centuries, writers such as François Villon, Alexander Pope, and Samuel Clemens, among others, referred to their relationship in their own works. Even in our own day they capture the artistic imagination: an opera, *Héloïse et Abélard* by Ahmed Essyad, was performed at the Théâtre Musical de Châtelet in 2001,[3] and since then, both a play and a musical have told their story.

A chronology added to Betty Radice's edition of the letters by M. T. Clanchy notes that we have no firm dates for the lives of Abelard and Heloise. Heloise was born either around 1090 (if she is assumed to be older than Peter the Venerable) or 1100/1101, the traditional date of her birth.[4] This uncertainty has a serious impact on how we view Heloise when she meets Abelard around the year 1115; she was either a teenager or a woman in her mid-twenties. She was by all accounts a learned young woman, receiving her education at the convent at Argenteuil. Not only could she read Latin, but Abelard mentions in his Letter to the Paraclete that she knew Greek and Hebrew as well.[5] Her quick mind and erudition attracted her to Abelard and later made her one of the most successful abbesses in the medieval world. As we will see in her letters to Abelard, Heloise learned the techniques of disputation that he taught her; although they differ in their analysis of their relationship, she matches his arguments.

The letters themselves were composed between 1133 and 1138. Although their authenticity and authorship have been much disputed, it is now generally accepted that they were indeed written by Abelard and Heloise. In 1974 Ewald Könsgen published a collection of letters written in Latin between a teacher and his female student and speculated that these may have been earlier letters of the pair. This issue was not taken up again until 1999 when Constant Mews reissued the letters with the title *The Lost Love Letters of Heloise and Abelard*. Since then there has been a lively debate as to their authenticity, and the matter remains unsettled.[6]

The structure of the authenticated letters is as follows: Letter 1, usually known as *Historia calamitatum*, was written by Abelard as a consolation to an unknown friend. The letter found its way into Heloise's hands and she wrote back to Abelard; this began a correspondence, which Radice has divided into Personal Letters and Letters of Direction.[7] In this chapter, I will refer mainly to the first group of four letters (five counting the *Historia calamitatum*) since in those letters Heloise takes a firm position on marriage and sexuality.

"Perpende, obsecro, quae debes," she writes in her first letter to Abelard, reminding him of the debt that he owes her. She has just received a copy of his *Historia calamitatum* and is incensed not only because he has not written her, but also because he has omitted her side of the story in his consolation letter to his friend. What is this debt that Heloise believes Abelard owes her, and why does he have this obligation? To a twelfth-century reader, as Glenda McLeod has noted, the word "debitum" would have implied the "marriage debt."[8] Taken from St. Paul in 1 Corinthians 7.3, "uxori uir debitum reddat," this conjugal sexual obligation, as Peter Dronke has pointed out, is permanently binding and prohibits either partner from making a unilateral declaration of continence.[9] Once a marriage was consummated, each partner had the unlimited right to demand sexual intercourse; the wronged party could go to an ecclesiastical court if the debt was not fulfilled.[10]

In addition to Paul, Augustine was also frequently cited as an authority to support the concept of the conjugal debt. As we have seen in chapter two, in his *Confessiones* he distinguishes between love, which can only happen in marriage, and lust, which satisfies sexual needs. In *De bono conjugali*, he differentiates between two types of sexual intercourse in marriage: the procreative (which was blameless), and sexual satisfaction under the marital debt (which was a pardonable wrong).[11] In other words, marriage provided a "remedy for lust," as Philip Lyndon Reynolds has termed it, an outlet for a sexuality that was not merely for procreative purposes.[12] Reid argues that by the thirteenth century, marriage became the only legitimate outlet for sexual expression. As a result, children who were born outside of wedlock were deemed illegitimate and unable to claim inheritance rights.[13]

It should be emphasized that the marital debt applied to both men and women. As James A. Brundage has pointed out, medieval canon law placed women in an inferior position to men except in matters of sex, where they were equal in committing sexual offenses.[14] Given the importance of the marital obligation in the twelfth century, it is likely that Heloise makes use of the concept, albeit in a different way. Her reference to Abelard's debt to her can be seen as a legitimate invocation of his marital responsibilities, which, although impossible for him to fulfill on the physical level, is still required on an emotional level.[15]

Indeed, the concept of debt is one of the central features of Heloise's first letter to Abelard. At first it appears as if she is simply asking for some word from him. He has discharged his debt to friendship by writing the *Historia calamitatum* as a solace to his friend. It is a greater debt, she contends, that binds him to her and her nuns,

> quas non tam amicas quam amicissimas non tam socias quam filias convenit nominari vel si quod dulcius et sanctius vocabulem potest excogitari. Quanto autem debito te erga eas obligaveris non argumentis non testimoniis indiget...[16] (Heloise to Abelard, Letter 2)
>
> [whom it is fitting to be called not friends as much as dearest friends, not comrades but daughters, or a name sweeter and holier that can be devised. How great the debt, moreover, by which you have obligated yourself to us needs neither argument nor testimony...]

By using "we" she refers not only to her nuns, but also, more importantly, to herself. McLeod has argued that when she uses the first-person singular, Heloise speaks in her private role as Abelard's wife, while the second-person plural indicates her public role as an abbess.[17] I would suggest, rather, that here, as in the succeeding letters, Heloise often conflates the two, allowing her an easier transition into speaking of her private heart. This is clear when she segues into the use of the singular "I":

> Qui tanta hostibus largiris quid filiabus debeas meditare. Atque, ut ceteras omittam, quanto erga me te obligaveris debito pensa ut quod devotis communiter debes feminis unicae tuae devotius solvas. (Heloise to Abelard, Letter 2)
>
> [You who give so abundantly to your enemies, consider what you owe to your daughters. Apart from everything else, repay the debt you owe a community of devoted women by discharging it more dutifully to her who is yours alone.]

In other words, Heloise tells Abelard that he should repay his debt to the nuns by discharging his debt to her. He is bound to her by the tie of marriage but he is also deeper in her debt "because of the love by which I have embraced you, an unrestrained love, as is clear to all" ("quo te semper ut omnibus patet immoderato amore complexa sum"). She argues that the bond of love is more important than the bond of marriage. He is even more in her debt, she continues, because she obeyed his orders to become a nun, and in doing so, she has allowed him to own both her body and her spirit:

> Et solus es qui plurimum id mihi debeas et nunc maxime cum universa quae iusseris in tantum impleverim ut cum te in aliquo offendere non possem me ipsam pro iussu tuo perdere sustinerem. Et quod maius est dictuque

> mirabile, in tantam versus est amor insaniam ut quod solum appetebat, hoc ipse sibi sine spe recuperationis auferret, cum ad tuam statim iussionem tam habitum ipsa quam animum immutarem ut te tam corporis mei quam animi unicum possessorem ostenderem. (Heloise to Abelard, Letter 2)
>
> [And it is you alone who owes me a higher debt, greater now when I have satisfied all that you ordered, so that when I could not oppose you in anything, by your order I found strength to ruin myself. And what is more, strange to say, my love turned to such madness that immediately on your order I changed my clothing and my mind so that I might show that you alone possessed my body as well as my soul.]

Heloise, however, did not want to marry Abelard. In what is perhaps the most widely discussed discourse in the letters, she distinguishes between marriage and concubinage. She is angry because he omitted from the *Historia calamitatum* the reasons for her refusal to marry, or in her words, "for preferring love to wedlock and freedom to chains" ("sed plerisque tacitis quibis amorem coniugio libertatem vinculo praeferebam"). She vehemently rejects marriage:

> Non matrimonii foedera, non dotes aliquas expectavi, non denique meas voluptates aut voluntates sed tuas, sicut ipse nosti, adimplere studui. Et si uxoris nomen sanctius ac validius videtur, dulcius mihi semper exstitit amicae vocabulum aut, si non indigneris, concubinae vel scorti. (Heloise to Abelard, Letter 2)
>
> [I did not expect a compact of marriage, no marriage portion, and further I sought to satisfy not my pleasures or wishes but yours, as you know. And if the name of wife seems more holy or powerful, sweeter to me always will be the word friends, or if you are not offended, concubine or whore.]

In the *Historia calamitatum* Abelard has only used the word "amica." It is obvious that Heloise means far more than that. As Claire Nouvet has persuasively argued, by preferring to be Abelard's whore, she is demonstrating "a disinterested love which attempts to 'unbind' itself from the conjugal notions of possession and contractual obligation."[18] The use of the word "whore" is, however, more than this. Heloise takes a longstanding custom, that of the clerical concubine, and privileges it over marriage. As we saw in the first chapter in the discussion on clerical misogamy, by Abelard and Heloise's time the church was consolidating its formal control over marriage, which had previously been a civil act, and, as part of the reforms, had forbidden priests to marry. Nonetheless, priests continued to have concubines, as discussed in chapter one. By confining the sexual act to marriage, the church reinforced Augustine's distinction between wife and concubine. Thus Heloise, in insisting that she does not want to be his wife, denies the notion of the *marital* debt, preferring instead a debt based on "love freely given." In this, she stands in defiant opposition to church doctrine. Although Abelard can no longer provide a sexual outlet for Heloise, her understanding of their debt to one another implies an emotional commitment central to the medieval notion of concubinage. Having both taken holy orders, she can provide solace to him and believes she has every right to demand it back from him.

Marriage, for Heloise, appears to be an economic not a sacred arrangement. In a bold critique of the "good" marriage, she writes:

> Nec se minime venalem aestimet esse quae libentius ditiori quam pauperi nubit et plus in marito sua quam ipsum concupiscit. Certe quamcumque ad nuptias haec concupiscentia ducit, merces ei potius quam gratia debetur. Certum quippe est eam res ipsas non hominem insequi et se, si posset, velle prostituere ditiori. (Heloise to Abelard, Letter 2)
>
> [And if she marries a richer man more readily than a poor one, and covets her husband more for his possessions than for himself, she deems herself not least of all to be on sale. Certainly any woman who comes to marry through these desires deserves pay rather than gratitude. Certainly she is pursuing these things rather than the man, and she would, if possible, prostitute herself to a richer man.]

This connection that she makes between marriage and property, so central to the reality of life in twelfth-century France, is startling, to say the least. By equating marriage to prostitution—different from concubinage in Heloise's eyes—she attacks the secular idea of wedlock. She describes her desire in words (*concubina* and *scortum*) that are deliberately bold and provide a stark contrast to "wife" (*uxor*). In describing marriage she uses an equally graphic word (*prostituere*). Although the three may seem to be related, Heloise actually makes a clear distinction. Concubinage was an established tradition and presumed monogamy. In even using the word "*scortum*," she is calling herself *Abelard's* whore. The relationship is based on mutual love and cannot be limited by what she sees as the restrictions of marriage. As Ruth Mazzo Karras has observed, priests' concubines were often referred to as whores, which could simply have meant a sexually active single woman.[19] A prostitute, in Heloise's model, is promiscuous and sells her services to the highest bidder. In this discourse, it is the wife who is the prostitute. This formulation allows her to argue that her relationship with Abelard is justified only outside the bounds of marriage.

She extends the financial metaphors when she accuses him of holding her "cheap" (*vilitatem*). Because he has ignored her, she questions his motives for their relationship, again referring to Augustinian distinctions between lust and love:

> Dic, inquam, si vales aut ego quod sentio immo quod omnes suspicantur dicam. Concupiscentia te mihi potius quam amicitia sociavit, libidinis ardor potius quam amor. Ubi igitur quod desiderabas cessavit quicquid propter hoc exhibebas pariter evanuit. (Heloise to Abelard, Letter 2)
>
> [Tell me, I say, if you can, or I will tell you what I think or rather what everyone suspects. Desire, rather than friendship bound you to me, the heat of lust rather than love. When, therefore, what you desired ended, any show of feeling you used to show vanished at the same time.]

Lust thus becomes equated with holding her "cheap," making her an object of exchange. She uses this kind of language at the end of her first letter: "Consider your injustice, if when I deserve more you give me less, or rather, nothing at all..." ("Quae vero tua sit iniquitas perpende si merenti amplius persolvis minus, immo nihil..."). She has become the prostitute who has not even been paid. She concludes with "I beg you, think what you owe me..." ("Perpende, obsecro, quae debes..."). Thus this letter both begins and ends with the idea of debt, and the discourse in the middle about being Abelard's "whore" redefines the conjugal debt as based not on marriage, but on consent freely given and unencumbered by external forces. He "owes" her because she has selflessly given him her love, expecting only his—her version of the marital debt—in return.

The tone of Abelard's reply to her first letter is detached and completely ignores her discourse on debt and marriage. He tells her that she herself has the God-given power to comfort her nuns and doesn't really need him at all. But, he says, if she really needs his instruction in matters pertaining to God, she should write him and he will reply as God permits ("prout mihi Dominus annuerit"). In this fashion, he carefully circumscribes the terms under which he will communicate with her. Peggy Kamuf has called his tone "too-reasonable." He is, she says, responding selectively to Heloise's request for communication in order to avoid being drawn into her "flagrant transgression of conceptual limits," what he sees as inconsistencies in her logic.[20] Martin Irvine has taken this reading a step further: by deflecting desire onto a "love triangle formed of Abelard, Christ, and Heloise," Abelard actually continues desire through a divine source.[21] Although this interpretation is intellectually seductive, it has Heloise arguing from her body, thus trapping her in her own passions and dichotomizing feminine irrationality with Abelard's rational thinking. As Catherine Brown has boldly pointed out, this comes "perilously close to reinscribing previous generations' naïve oppositions without challenging their ideological underpinnings."[22]

I would suggest that the dichotomy is between Heloise's insistence on a personal relationship with Abelard and his insistence that Christ be the mediator. In preserving a direct line to Abelard, she keeps open the emotional interpretation of the marital debt, while he asserts their relationship only has validity because of their common denominator, Christ. By inserting Christ, Abelard frees himself from any direct obligation to Heloise. This opposition is clear in the salutations of the letters. In her first letter Heloise writes: "Domino suo immo patri, coniugi suo immo fratri, ancilla sua immo filia ipsius uxor immo soror, Abaelardo Heloisa" ("To her master, rather father, her husband, rather brother, his handmaid, rather daughter, his wife, rather sister; to Abelard, Heloise"). In line with the conventions of medieval letter-writing, Heloise puts Abelard's name before her own, but only after she recounts the various roles they have played in each other's lives. This salutation links their private and public roles, but ultimately stresses their intimate connection. Abelard responds in his *salutatio*: "Heloisae, dilectissimae sorori suae in Christo, Abaelardus, frater eius in ipso" ("To Heloise, his most beloved sister in Christ, Abelard, her brother in him"). Clearly, Abelard is correcting her. They are only brother and sister, connected by their relationship to Christ. Although he puts Heloise's name first in the salutation, which denotes that she is his superior, he puts her in that role only in the circumscribed situation of their common bond in Christ.

In her second letter, Heloise skillfully manipulates his use of Christ: "Unico suo post Christum unica sua in Christo" ("To her one and only after Christ, she who is his one and only in Christ"). Peter Dronke reads this phraseology to mean that she confirms that he follows Christ in her heart, while acknowledging that it contradicts the rest of the letter.[23] She is, however, positing two separate relationships to Christ: by the use of "post" for her and "in" for him, she says that her love for Abelard stands quite apart from her love of Christ, while for him, they are tied.[24]

She excludes Christ even further in the first line of this letter in which she calls him "unice meus" ("my only one"). Abelard's response again stresses that they are related only through Christ: "Sponsae Christi servus eiusdem" ("To the bride of Christ, his own servant"). He continues to place her title before his own in the salutation and proceeds to tell her why: "Te vero extunc me superiorem factam intelligas quo domina mea esse coepisti Domini mei sponsa effecta" ("You must understand that you were made my superior, from that point when having been made the bride of my Lord, you began to be my lady") (Abelard to Heloise, Letter 5). But marriage for Heloise does not carry the spiritual significance that it does for Abelard. Rather, marriage has doomed them:

> Dum enim solliciti amoris gaudiis frueremur et, ut turpiore, sed expressiore vocabulo utar, fornicationi vacaremus, divina nobis severitas pepercit. Ut autem illicita licitis correximus, et honore coniugi turpitudinem fornicationis operuimus, ira Domini manum suam super nos vehementer aggravavit, et immaculatum non pertulit torum qui diu ante sustinuerat pollutum. (Heloise to Abelard, Letter 4)
>
> [For while we enjoyed the delights of an uneasy love and, to use a fouler but more expressive word, abandoned ourselves to fornication, divine sternness spared us. However, when we reformed our illicit acts with licit ones and covered the disgrace of fornication by the honor of marriage, the anger of the Lord laid his hand heavily upon us and did not bear a chaste union though he had tolerated an unchaste one for so long before.]

After blaming Fortune for her woes, she then blames herself, as his wife, for his: "Quod fornicatoribus suis adulterae, hoc propria uxor tibi contulit" ("what adulterous women brought upon their paramours, your own wife brought upon you"). As a wife she is responsible for his downfall; they were protected from the devil when they were lovers:

> Et callidissimus tentator hoc optime noverat quod saepius expertus fuerat, virorum videlicit ruinam in uxoribus esse facillimam...Qui denique etiam usque ad nos consuetam extendens malitiam, quem de fornicatione sternere non potuit, de coniugio tentavit. (Heloise to Abelard, Letter 4)
>
> [The cleverest tempter knew well what he had often experienced, that clearly the easiest ruin of men is from their wives...At last, extending his usual malice even to us, he was not able to destroy whom through fornication he attacked though marriage.]

By the time he was castrated, she points out, they were married and living relatively chaste lives. Although Heloise here appears to accept the medieval misogynistic and misogamistic ideas that I discussed in the first chapter, I would suggest that she actually turns these beliefs to her own ends. Similarly, to support her own desires, she uses the fact that marriage for a cleric like Abelard is worse than fornication. As his wife, she has ruined him, she argues, thus implying that if they had never married, things would have turned out differently.

She further rebels against medieval ideas of marriage by admitting that her mind still retains the will to sin and is on fire with its old desires. She cannot let go of them, even when she is supposed to be praying:

> Quocumque loco me vertam, semper se oculis meis cum suis ingerunt desideriis. Nec etiam dormienti suis illusionibus parcunt. Inter ipsa missarum

> solemnia, ubi purior esse debet oratio, obscena earum voluptatum phantasmata ita sibi penitus miserrimam captivant animam ut turpitudinibus illis magis quam orationi vacem. (Heloise to Abelard, Letter 4)
>
> [Wherever I turn they always thrust themselves before my eyes. And they do not spare me from illusions even in sleep. During the very celebration of the Mass, when prayer ought to be purer, those obscene fantasies of pleasure so captivate my most unhappy soul that I apply my mind to those disgraces rather than to prayers.]

She refuses to allow her sexuality to be contained by religious doctrine. She remains Abelard's "whore," if only in thought.

In his letter in response, Abelard acknowledges their personal relationship more fully and tries to explain why God punished them when they were married:

> Nosti post nostri foederationem conjugii cum Argenteoli cum sanctimonialibus in claustro conversareris, me die quadam privatim ad te visitandam venisse, et quid ibi tecum meae libidinis egerit intemperantia in quadam etiam parte ipsius refectorii, cum quo alias videlicet diverteremus, non haberemus. Nosti, inquam, id impudentissime tunc actum esse in tam reverendo loco et Summae Virgini consecrato. Quod, et si alia cessent flagitia, multo graviore dignum sit ultione. (Abelard to Heloise, Letter 5)
>
> [You know that after our marriage, when you were living in the cloister with the nuns at Argenteuil, I came one day to visit you privately, and what the intemperance of my desire did with you there, actually in a corner of the actual refectory, since we had nowhere else to go. I repeat, you know how shamelessly we behaved then in so revered a place consecrated to the most high Virgin. And if our other shameful behavior ended, this one deserved much graver punishment.]

Castration, he declares, was a fitting punishment for him.

He also uses the medieval misogamistic argument that marriage and children distract men from their higher duties to persuade Heloise that their marriage was a good thing and even better now that they are separated:

> Si enim mihi antea matrimonio non esses copulata facile in discessu meo a saeculo vel suggestione parentum vel carnalium oblectatione voluptatum saeculo inhaesisses... Quam lamentabile incommodum, si carnalium voluptatum sordibus vacans paucos cum dolore pareres mundo, quae nunc multiplicem prolem cum exsultatione parturis coelo! Nec esses plus quam femina nunc etiam viros transcendis et quae maledictionem Evae in benedictionem vertisti Mariae. (Abelard to Heloise, Letter 5)

> [For if you had not been previously joined to me in matrimony, you might have easily clung to the world in my withdrawal from it, either at the suggestion of your relatives or in enjoyment of carnal delights. What lamentable trouble if abandoning yourself to the defilement of carnal delights, you had brought forth in suffering a few children for the world, when now you have delivered in exultation numerous progeny for heaven! And you would not have been more than a woman, whereas now you rise above men, and have turned the curse of Eve into the blessing of Mary.]

He also finally acknowledges their intimate relationship, but sublimates it into a spiritual one. He takes Heloise's physical longing for him and transforms it into a long digression on the Song of Songs, thus continuing the theme in his salutations. He writes: "It was a happy transfer of your married state, for you were previously the wife of a poor mortal and now are raised to the bed of the King of kings." As mentioned in the first chapter, the early church fathers needed to desexualize a text that makes no direct mention of God and instead, as Ann W. Astell has termed it, "celebrates the passionate joys and sorrows of unnamed lovers."[25] The lover in the Song of Songs becomes in the twelfth century the "bride of Christ." Such nuptial imagery was not only an ungendered description of the relationship of the church with God, but also a common description of a religious woman. In transferring his own wife's allegiance to God, Abelard, in effect, rejects her.

By using the word "commercium" (whose many meanings in Lewis and Short's *A Latin Dictionary* include "trade," "traffic," "commercial intercourse," "a mercantile right," and more interestingly, "forbidden intercourse, illicit commerce"),[26] Abelard "trades" her to Christ, thus once again placing Christ between them. Heloise's salutations to Abelard, as detailed earlier, make clear that she rejects the name of "bride of Christ," as well as anything but a personal relationship with Abelard. Does Abelard use the word "commercium" precisely because of its multiple meanings? It appears in his *Theologia Scholarium* to describe the intercessory nature of prayer, which, he notes, is the only connection between God and man.[27] However, "carnale commercium" was widely used to denote sexual intercourse. This passage, in which the exchange is from Abelard, the human male, to Christ, the divine male, is thus cloaked in ambiguity.

He insists that God has bound them in marriage so that He could save the two of them together:

> ipse, inquam, clementer disposuit in uno duobus consulere quos diabolus in uno nitebatur extinguere. Paululum enim antequam hoc accideret, nos

> indissolubili lege sacramenti nuptialis invicem astrinxerat... (Abelard to Heloise, Letter 5)
>
> [He, I say, gently arranged to take care of two people in one, the two whom the devil tried to destroy in one. For a little while before this happened, he had mutually bound us by the indissoluble law of the marriage sacrament...]

By joining their salvation together, Abelard once again returns to the theme of Heloise as the bride of Christ. She should always think of Him, not Abelard, as her true spouse: "Hunc semper, soror, verum tuum et totius Ecclesiae sponsum prae oculis habe, mente gere" ("Bear in mind, sister, Him as your true spouse and the spouse of the whole Church"). Through their marriage he can share in her closeness to Christ: "Unum quippe sumus in Christo, una per legem matrimonii caro. Quidquid est tuum, mihi non arbitror alienum" ("For we are certainly one in Christ, one flesh through the law of matrimony. Whatever is yours I do not judge alien to me"). The "one flesh" comes curiously close to a sexualized union, not between the two of them, but with Christ as the mediator of their desire. The marital debt is paid only by the presence of a third party. He asks her to become his intercessor to Christ, for through her, Christ's bride, he can receive that which he cannot get on his own ("Unde et de tuo nobis apud ipsum patrocinio amplius confidimus ut id obtineam ex tua quod non possum ex oratione propria"). He has enacted his own "commercium": no longer the husband of Heloise, he is now triangulated into a divine relationship with Christ.

The last letter in which there is any kind of personal correspondence is letter five, from Heloise to Abelard, and in this letter the tone changes significantly.[28] She still attests to the primacy of her emotions, but they are now longer part of what she seeks from him: "Revocabo itaque manum a scripto in quibus linguam a verbis temperare non valeo. Utinam sic animus dolentis parere promptus sit quemadmodum dextra scribentis" ("I will therefore call back my hand from writing that which I cannot control my tongue from speaking. Oh, that a grieving heart would be prompt to obey the way of a writing hand!").[29] She will now focus her attention on other things, the care of her nuns. She asks Abelard for two things: a history for the authority of their order and a Rule suitable for women. The continuing correspondence between Abelard and Heloise after these letters show a continuing devotion to each other.[30] Her relationship to him becomes translated through the community of nuns of which she is a part. Heloise has, in effect, chosen silence—it has not been demanded of her. Indeed, it can be argued that by "institutionalizing" her relationship with Abelard, she is less marginalized from a public perspective: as nun and monk, their relationship is legitimate. She now speaks in his language and does not give voice to her private emotions.[31]

Does this mean, then, that Abelard has paid his debt? I would suggest that, in a sense, Heloise has gotten what she wants—a response to her pleas for attention, a fulfilling of the emotional component of the conjugal debt. Although their views on their marriage differ—she will always see it as both disgraceful and degrading—he finally acknowledges what has passed between them. Her grieving heart will not obey her writing hand, but having received Abelard's acknowledgment and recognition, it can allow itself silence.

Marie de France and the Aventure

Marie de France and Heloise were both twelfth-century women who examined the subordination of women to men, viewed marriage as imprisonment, privileged illicit love, and used economic metaphors in their writings. Marie's *lais*, as fiction, differ generically from the very real letters that Heloise wrote to Abelard. Nevertheless, there is a marked correspondence in the themes they discuss.

As with Heloise, there is a debate about what Marie actually wrote, compounded further by the problem that we do not really even know who she was. In his thorough study of this issue, R. Howard Bloch explains that in spite of naming herself three times in her works, the name "Marie de France" remains vague. She has been identified with Marie de Champagne, Marie de Compiègne, a nun named Marie who wrote *Vie de sainte Audrée*, and Marie de Boulogne, among others. The "de" in her name most likely means that she was born in France, but probably did not live there at the time she was writing. Thus, rather than denoting nobility, the "de" most likely refers to the fact that she was from France.[32]

Marie's *lais*, which were written in the second half of the twelfth century, drew ultimately on both Celtic oral tradition and French written sources.[33] Many scholars have argued that her characters are those of populations marginalized in her time—women, bachelor knights, that is, sons unable to inherit due to primogeniture, and those dispossessed by new modes of economic production.[34] Bloch himself, although arguing against an analysis of Marie's work restricted solely to matters of gender, identifies her crucial issue as "how language might negotiate relations between individuals in a world that is less and less defined by military might and increasingly ruled by models of mediated social exchange."[35]

The idea that Marie is "a voice from the edge," in Dolliann Margaret Hurtig's words,[36] is a fitting one. It allows us to examine the *lais* as highly popular literature ("mainstream" in today's language), but written by a woman about marginalized characters. By using the *aventure*, the personal quest in which boundaries are tested, Marie allows her characters to confront their own marginalization. The success of the *aventure*, I will argue, has everything to do with gender and the question of who controls the destiny of another person. This is at the very heart of the idea of possession: when one is possessed, one cannot take possession of one's own life.

In her influential essay "Women's Stories, Women's Symbols: A Critique of Victor Turner's Theory of Liminality," Caroline Walker Bynum argues that women's life narratives are more about continuity than about sharp change. Using Turner's concept of "social drama," she contends that women do not experience his four stages of development: breach between social elements, crisis, adjustment, and reintegration into the social structure (or recognition of irreparable breach). It is the third stage, "liminality," that is particularly foreign to women's social experience, she notes. Borrowing this term from Arnold van Gennep, she defines liminality as "a moment of suspension of normal rules and roles, a crossing of boundaries and violating of norms, that enables us to understand those norms, even (or perhaps especially) where they conflict, and move on either to incorporate or reject them."[37]

Bynum's analysis provides a key structure in which to analyze gender differences in the experience of the *aventure* in Marie's *lais*. The liminal stage in these works, I contend, is different for men than it is for women. Men go from the center, from the state of privilege, to the edge, the margins, and then back to the center. Women, on the other hand, are already in the margins; they approach the center only through their contact with men, but are then forced back to the edge. Bynum contends that women are liminal not in themselves but for men:

> The woman is thus, to the man, a retreat from the world into inner, often mystical repose. What she says...and what she is, is a criticism of male power and an alternative to it. Contact with her is, for the male, an escape from the world; after recourse to her he returns to that world girded with information and consolation.[38]

The three *lais* that I analyze (*Guigemar*, *Yonec*, and *Lanval*) share common elements: they involve journeys in which male characters come full circle, wondrous creatures appear, and, in their fairy tale "Otherworld" belief is suspended. In *Guigemar*, it can be argued, both the man and the woman cross thresholds into new worlds that change them. Yet their experiences of the journey differ substantially. *Yonec* invites us to see a woman's escape from a locked tower, following her wounded lover to a city of silver, only to return again to her husband's castle and ultimately to restore legitimacy to her son. In *Lanval* the fairy woman saves the man and restores the wealth he lost. In all three, however, the male journey is the privileged one, the one in which a choice is made between incorporating or rejecting change—liminality, in van Gennep's sense.

This approach is, by its very nature, one-dimensional. By focusing on a single element, gender, I do not mean to discount the work of scholars who have argued that twelfth-century French literature is more complex. Bloch, for example, characterizes the *aventure* as caught between the subjective individual and the objective communal understanding: it both "concretizes, fixes, immobilizes that which is imagined to be beyond language, experience, and the body" and also "serves as a reminder that no matter how much one tries to pin meaning down, it remains, even in fixed form, uncontrollable, risky, undisciplined, excessive..."[39]

In a similar fashion, Sarah Kay has argued that contradiction was central to courtly texts in general, as well as to Marie's: "Paired contraries," as she calls them, or "major paradoxes," figure prominently in twelfth-century theology as well as literature.[40] The trap of contradiction, however, is one of binary opposition: "The temptation to identify two contrary positions which between them define a total field of possiblity is a strong one and risks fettering interpretation by the very gesture which appears to free it up."[41] Michelle Freeman argues that Marie's *lais* are themselves ambiguous, what she calls "a poetics of silence." They do not describe "the private confrontation between two different worlds that gives rise to the object that symbolizes it." Marie omits things that are essential, choosing instead to wrap the discourse in darkness. The result, according to Freeman, is "the paradoxical absence-presence that brings forth, that gives birth to and speaks the poem before us."[42]

All three of these critics stress the difficulty of—even the aversion to—seeing Marie de France as one-dimensional. Keeping this in mind, it is important then to acknowledge the ambiguity and paradoxes in the *lais* while continuing to read deeper in order to understand that, at bottom, there may be a place, as Kay has described the medieval religious tradition, in which the contradictions are reconcilable, a deeper message beneath the seeming opposites.[43]

Guigemar is portrayed as a young knight whom no one can equal in prowess, but who lacks the desire to love: "De tant i out mespris Nature / Ke unc de nule amur n'out cure" (57–58) ("But in forming him nature had so badly erred / that he never gave any thought to love").[44] His call to adventure comes from a white deer, who curiously has the physical characteristics of both male and female sexes and who is accompanied by a fawn. The asexual Guigemar has wounded her and has himself become injured when the arrow rebounds. Frederick Hodgson has called this "the arrow of Guigemar's aggression…reinforcing the solitary focus of his *malaise* which is dramatized in his journey."[45] Bloch also seizes on the importance of the arrow; it is, he says, a "dismemberment," a quest for health.[46] In this search, he believes, Guigemar's desire originates. As someone who is "sexually undefined, foreign to desire," he depends on no one.[47] To heal himself, he must seek out that which has previously been denied to him, a woman's love.

Jamais n'aies tu medicine,
Ne par herbe, ne par racine!
Ne par mire, ne par poisun,
N'avras tu jamés garisun,
De la plaie k'as en la quisse,
Di si ke cele te guarisse
Ki suffera pur tue amur
Issi grant peine e tel dolur
K'unkes femme taunt ne suffri,
E tu referas taunt pur li. (109–118)
[May you never have medicine,
Neither herb nor root,
neither physician nor potion,
will cure you
of that wound in your thigh,
until a woman heals you,
one who will suffer, out of love for you,
pain and grief
such as no woman ever suffered before.
And for her, you'll suffer as much.]

This defines his *aventure*, the entrance into the world of sexuality, in which a woman must not only be his guide, but must also bear the pain of his transformation. He proceeds to a cliff and sees a magical ship of gold and ebony with silk sails. He knows that he is entering into an unknown world because ships cannot go into the harbor:

Li chivaliers fu mult pensis:
En la cuntree n'el païs
N'ont unkes mes oï parler
Ke nefs i peüst arriver. (161–164)
[The knight was troubled;
he had never heard it said
anywhere in that region
that ships could land there.]

This is the point of liminality in Turner's paradigm at which normal rules are suspended and boundaries are crossed. It also invites a suspension of belief, the entry into a fairy tale world in which nothing is familiar. Guigemar goes on board the ship and falls asleep, but when he tries to leave he finds that he is already at sea. He is frightened because he is out of his known world, but he understands that he must continue on the *aventure*:

> Mult est dolenz, ne siet ke faire.
> N'est merveille se il s'esmaie
> Kar grant dolur out en sa plaie.
> Suffrit le estuet l'aventure. (196–199)
> [He was very upset; he didn't know what to do.
> It's no wonder he was frightened,
> Especially as his wound was paining him a great deal.
> Still, he had to suffer through the adventure.]

The ship reaches a city in which the lord, an old man, jealously guards his young wife in a tower. Although she is watched by the old man's niece, the woman can miraculously cross the threshold to go and explore Guigemar's ship and then recross to bring him back with her. This is the beginning of the second *aventure*, that of the woman. The chapel at the entrance to her room is painted with a picture of Venus throwing Ovid's *Remedia amoris* into the fire. Here again is a suspension of belief: a woman is imprisoned in a tower whose entrance picture chastises those who try to control their love. Like Heloise, Marie equates marriage with chains and love with freedom. The tower has a triple symbolism according to Bloch: it is meant both to contain the young wife and to constrain her desire; it is also, he notes, the scene of the adultery.[48] Miléna Mikhaïlova has described the room as serving as an asylum where the woman can receive her love, a revenge against being trapped.[49] For the woman, the space confines her not inside, but outside; it is, paradoxically, an imprisonment at the margins. Guigemar spends a year and a half with her in this room, which for him is his liminal space. It is the place where he has his *aventure*, which is his initiation as a sexual being.

One day, the woman has a premonition that she will lose him. She ties a knot in the tail of his shirt and gives him permission to love any woman who can untie it. In return, he gives her a corresponding locked belt that fits tight around her flanks and tells her that she may love any man who can open it. Both of them are tied or locked into one another in a bond that no one else can penetrate. For the woman, these tokens of possession also signal the transfer of her allegiance from her husband to

Guigemar. As H. Marshall Leicester, Jr., has noted, Guigemar's knotted shirt is "detachable," that is, he can take it off, whereas her knotted belt is not.[50] She is thus more constrained in her actions than he is.

The husband discovers the two of them, and Guigemar is banished from the kingdom. The woman returns to the tower and lives for two more years in conditions that are even worse than before. By going outside the boundaries, she is punished even more. Her *aventure* has been put on hold; he is free to go, whereas she must suffer the punishment for their adultery. In her grief, she says that she would rather die than live like this:

> Mieuz voil hastivement murir
> Que lungement cest ma suffrir.
> Amis, si jeo puis eschaper,
> La u vus fustes mis en mer
> Mer neierai. (669–673)
> [I'd rather die quickly
> than suffer this lingering torture.
> My love, if I could escape,
> I'd go to where you put out to sea
> and drown myself.]

Miraculously, when she utters these words, the door is unlocked and Guigemar's boat is waiting. She gets transported to him and when they meet, he doesn't recognize her: "Bien sai que ceo n'est ele mie: / Femmes se resemblent asez" ("I know it can't be she; / women often look alike") (778–779). He knows her only when he sees the belt on her body, which, as Sarah Kay has argued, is a fetish, a replacement for Guigemar's wound.[51] The woman has become only the vehicle for his healing, not the object of his love, since his recognition is not of her (since all women look alike), but of the symbol of his tie to her.

Clearly, although both Guigemar and the woman set off on *aventures*, only his is liminal in Turner's definition. She clearly believes that she has gone on a journey:

> Ele li cunte la dolur,
> Les peines granz e la tristur
> De la prisun u ele fu
> E coment li est avenue,
> Coment ele s'enschapa.
> Neer se volt, la neif trova,
> Dedeinz entrat, a cel port vint. (825–831)
> [She told him about the grief,
> the great pains, the sadness
> of the prison where she was held captive,

and everything that had happened to her—
how she escaped,
how she wished to drown, but found the ship instead,
and how she entered it and was brought to this port.]

However, she is liminal only to Guigemar. He is the one who set out to find love to heal his wound; she is the one he found, thus love came *to her.* He is guided by a magical boat on his quest, she is transported on the same boat *to him.* He is, within the bounds of his *aventure*, in charge of his destiny, free to go where he chooses. She is the property of whichever man has claimed her. The old husband is replaced by Meriaduc, in whose kingdom she lands, who will not give her up to Guigemar: "Jeo la trovai, si la tendrai / E cuntre vus le defenrai" ("I found her and I will take care of her / and defend her against you") (851–852). Guigemar battles Meriaduc, wins, and takes the woman away: "Le chastel ad destruit e pris / E le seignur dedenz ocis / A grant joie s'amie en meine" ("He captured and destroyed the castle, / killed its lord. / He led away his mistress with great rejoicing") (879–882). But it is clear in the next line that this is Guigemar's story, Guigemar's adventure: "Ore ad trespassee sa peine!" (882). It is *his* pain that is at an end, now that he has possession of the woman. This was, as Heather Arden has phrased it, the "social reality" of the *lais*: the subordination of women to their husbands and male relatives. Men are named first in the *lais* and many of the women remained unnamed.[52] Although in this *lai* love wins out over marriage, the woman has simply been passed from one man to another. We do not know the outcome for the woman, we only know that Guigemar's pain has come to an end.

In *Yonec*, it is even clearer that the woman's journey is subordinate to that of the man. As in *Guigemar*, a young wife is locked inside a tower, guarded by her old husband's widowed sister, who, unlike the niece in *Guigemar*, is not sympathetic to the wife's misery. She has been in the tower for seven years and has produced no children. She expected to find *aventure* in the country of her husband, but instead, in her unhappiness, she has lost her beauty and prefers to die. She asks God to help her find the courtly society she once desired:

Mut ai sovent oï cunter
Que l'em suleit jadis trover
Aentures en cest païs
Ki rehaitouent les pensis.
Chevalier trovoent puceles
A lur talent, gentes e beles,
E dames truvoent amanz
Beaus e curteis, pruz e vaillanz,

Si que blasmees rien esteient
Ne nul fors eles nes veeient.
Si ceo peot estrë e ceo fu,
Si unc a nul est avenu,
Deu, ki de tut ad poëstë,
Il en face ma volenté! (91–104)
[I've often heard
that one could once find
adventures in this land
that brought relief to the unhappy.
Knights might find young girls
to their desire, noble and lovely;
and ladies find lovers
so handsome, courtly, brave, and valiant
that they could not be blamed,
and no one else would see them.
If that might be or ever was,
if that has ever happened to anyone,
God, who has power over everything,
grant me my wish in this!]

She is, quite clearly, yearning for an *aventure* of her own; by entering into this new land, she assumed she would find it. However, in *Yonec*, Marie gives us a picture of something far different. The old, rich lord needs a wife to produce children. Because she is young, beautiful, and noble, he must guard her against other men, to ensure that he is the father of any children she might have. She cannot be allowed to have any adventures of her own. The young wife curses her family who gave him to her:

Maleeit seient mi parent
E li autre communalment
Ki a cest gelus me donerent
E de sun cors me marïerent! (81–84)
[A curse on my family,
and on all the others
who gave me to this jealous man,
who married me to his body!]

This particular exchange of property turned out to be valueless, since the marriage is barren and no progeny are produced. She is also cut off from courtly society since her husband will not allow her to see other people. In this way, she is doubly marginalized: she can neither be a mother nor a lady.

One day she sees the shadow of a great bird through her narrow window. It flies in and is transformed into a handsome knight, who tells her that he loves her. As in *Guigemar*, our belief is suspended by the entrance of a fairy-tale creature who changes identity before our eyes. She only believes him when he tells her that she herself has called him to her from a distant land. The woman agrees to become his lover on two conditions: that he believe in God and that their love be truly possible. In order to prove this, he suggests that they exchange identities so that he can take communion from her chaplain. In this way, they become locked into one another, similar to the two lovers in *Guigemar*.

As in *Guigemar*, as well, the entrance of the male into the tower begins the woman's journey. Mikaïlova has shown how Marie's windows permit a transition between two worlds and, as such, become an instrument of the tragic.[53] This sense of tragedy is foreshadowed when the bird-man tells her that he will come to her whenever she pleases, but she should be careful that the old woman not discover them. If so, he will die:

> Si ceo avient cum jeo vus di
> E nus seium issi trahi
> Ne mien puis mie departir
> Que mei rien estuce murir. (207–210)
> [If that happens,
> if we are betrayed,
> I won't be able to escape.
> I shall die.]

He can fly in like a bird as long as he is not recognized. Once seen, he will no longer be able to transform himself back into a bird and escape.

This insistence on their love being kept secret, as R. Howard Bloch has noted, is a central theme in courtly literature: "love only exists to the degree that it is secret; that secret love only exists to the degree that it is revealed; and revealed, it is no longer love."[54] The danger of recognition and the need to remain hidden is paralleled in their relationship. Because she has become beautiful again through her happiness, her husband senses that she is betraying him; by becoming beautiful, she in turn betrays her lover; by causing suspicion, he is destroyed.

The husband's sister sees the lover change from a bird into a man; when she tells the old man, he orders that sharp spikes be made and inserted into the window. When the lover flies in, he is wounded and blames the woman:

Ma duce amie,
Pur vostre amur perc jeo la vie.
Bien le vus dis que en avendreit
Vostre semblant nus ocireit. (319–322)
[My sweet love,
I lose my life for love of you.
I told you it would happen,
that your appearance would kill us.]

Her very appearance has killed him—she *looks like* she has changed. Her beauty back, she has crossed Turner's threshold into liminality: she has violated norms and crossed boundaries, but unlike men, she is punished for doing so by losing the thing she loves most, the one who has engineered her transformation.

After telling her that she is pregnant with a son, whom she should name Yonec and who will avenge them both, he flies, bleeding, out the window. In a wondrous leap, in which she is not hurt, she follows him—the spikes having somehow disappeared:

Ele le suit a mut grant criz.
Par une fenestre s'en ist;
C'est merveille k'el ne s'ocist,
Kar bien aveit vint piez de haut
Iloec u ele prist le saut!
Elle esteit nue en sa chemise. (336–341)
[She followed him with loud cries.
She leapt out a window,
it's a wonder that she wasn't killed,
for it was at least twenty feet high
where she made her leap,
naked beneath her gown.]

As she leaves the confines of the castle, the woman begins a journey outside the boundaries of her existence. As in *Guigemar*, she goes outside only after love has come in to her; she follows not in a search for love, but in search of a specific lover. This is clear when, after following his drops of blood down a road, through an opening in a hill, into a meadow, and through a gate into a castle in a city, she finds three chambers: the first two have beds inhabited by sleeping knights. Only in the third does she find the bird-man, her lover. Unlike Guigemar, for whom all women look alike, she has no trouble differentiating him from others.

The bird-man tells her that she must leave or else she will be blamed for his death:

> Bele amie, pur Deu merci
> Alez vus en, fuiez d'ici!
> Sempres murai en mi le jur,
> Ci einz avrat si grant dolur,
> Si vus i esteiez trovee,
> Mut en serïez turmentee.
> Bien iert entre ma gent seü
> Que me unt por vostre amur perdu. (401–408)
> [Sweet love, for God's sake, I beg you
> go away! Leave this place!
> I shall die within the day,
> there will be great sorrow here,
> and if you are found
> you will be hurt.
> Among my people it will be well known
> that they have lost me because of my love for you.]

The woman is forced to go back to her husband, who, she fears, will kill her; she would rather die there with her lover. The bird-man gives her a ring, which, if she keeps it, will induce forgetfulness of the whole incident in her husband. He also gives her a sword to keep for their son. He tells her that when the son becomes a knight she will go with him and her husband to a festival, where the son will hear the story of his birth father's death; she should then give him the sword. Thus, armed with three tokens—the ring, the sword, and a precious robe—she returns to the tower. These three objects are protections against the past (the ring of forgetting), the present (the robe for the journey), and the future (the sword that will avenge them).

All happens as was revealed: she returns to the tower, Yonec is born, and the truth is revealed at the festival. After she tells her son about his father, she faints and dies. Yonec then kills his stepfather. Miranda Griffin has explained that *Yonec* problematizes paternity, "articularing patriarchy's anxiety that it has to rely on the body, and above all, the word of woman to guarantee its stability... *Yonec* plays on this anxiety, creating an illusion of unproblematic, clear-cut paternity."[55] In fact, as K. Sarah-Jane Murray has shown, the woman's marriage to the old man is not seen as legitimate: the fact that she is childless is a sign that it is not a truly Christian marriage. In this way, she is not committing adultery with the bird-man.[56]

Although adultery is certainly a theme of *Yonec*, it is, I believe, secondary to the fact that this *lai* is, above all, the story of a woman who journeys out, only to return back to her former situation. But a significant change occurs in her: she is pregnant with Yonec. She herself has not been changed by the experience of the *aventure*; rather, the purpose of her quest has been to bear a son. This emphasis on childbearing is highly suggestive of a literature that uses Mary as a model for womanhood. Robert W. Hanning has pointed out that the appearance of the bird-man signals both the Annunciation as well as the Crucifixion.[57] The woman in *Yonec* gets her importance not from a personal journey, not in relation to the quest of the bird-man, and certainly not from her husband. Her liminality is totally in relation to her son, who, we are led to believe, goes on to complete the journey that his true father started. It is, as Robert M. Stein has noted, the "restoration of a legitimate succession."[58] Hence the name of the *lai*: "*Yonec*."

In *Lanval* gender roles are markedly reversed: Lanval is the marginalized character. As a member of King Arthur's court, he is excluded from any of the gifts that Arthur distributes to his knights:

Femmes e teres departi,
Fors a un sul ki l'ot servi:
Ceo fu Lanval; ne l'en sovint
Ne nuls des soens bien ne li tint. (17–20)
[He distributed wives and lands,
to all but one who had served him.
That one was Lanval; Arthur did not remember him
And none of his men favored him either.]

Although he comes from a noble family, he has spent all of his wealth. Arthur, in gifting other knights, has passed over Lanval, which causes great anxiety and worry for Lanval:

De la meisnie le rei fu.
Tut sun aveir ad despendu,
Kar li reis rien ne li dona
Ne Lanval rien ne demanda.
Ore est Lanval mut entrepris,
Mut est dolent, mut est pensis! (29–34)
[He was of the king's household
but he had spent all his wealth,
for the kind gave him nothing
nor did Lanval ask.
Now Lanval was in difficulty,
Depressed and very worried!]

He is, as Laurie A. Finke and Martin B. Shichtman have pointed out, disenfranchised socially, politically, and economically and, as a result, "is pushed to the geographic margins of Arthur's kingdom."[59] He leaves the city and lies down by the bank of a river. Like Guigemar, he must go into unknown territory to begin his *aventure*. Soon two women approach him and tell him they have been sent to guide him to their lady, who is "pruz e sage e bele" (72). Again, as with Guigemar, this becomes his point of liminality, when normal rules are suspended. They lead him into a tent that is described as being sumptuous:

> Treskë al tref l'unt amené,
> Ki mut fu beaus e bien asis;
> La reïne Semiramis,
> Quant ele ot unkes plus aveir
> E plus pussaunce e plus saveir,
> Ne l'emperere Octovïan,
> N'esligasent le destre pan. (80–86)
> [They led him up to the tent,
> which was quite beautiful and well placed.
> Queen Semiramis,
> however much more wealth,
> power, or knowledge she had,
> or the emperor Octavian
> could not have paid for one of the flaps.]

Inside he finds a beautiful girl, who is dressed in costly garments. After she expresses her love for him, he vows to obey her and to leave all else behind:

> Bele, fet il, si vus pleiseit
> E cele joie me aveneit
> Que vus me vousissez amer,
> Ja n'osiriez comander
> Que jeo ne face a mun poeir,
> Turt a folie u a saveir.
> Jeo ferai voz comandemenz;
> Pur vus guerpirai tutes genz. (121–128)
> [Lovely one, he said, if it pleased you,
> if such joy might be mine
> that you would love me,
> there is nothing you might command,
> within my power, that I would not do,
> whether foolish or wise.

I shall obey your command;
for you; I shall abandon everyone.]

In return, she gives him a gift of unlimited riches:

Ja cele rien ne vudra mes
Que il nen ait a sun talent;
Doinst e despende largement,
Ele li troverat asez. (136–139)
[He would never again want anything,
he would receive as he desired;
however generously he might give and spend,
she would provide what he needed.]

This abundant wealth comes with a price of its own: he must be silent. If their love were to become known, he would never see her again nor would he ever again possess her body ("Ne de mun cors seisine aveir"). H. Marshall Leicester, Jr., has pointed out that the use of the word "seisine" here emphasizes that the lady has given him usufruct, not ownership of her body, "the possession in the sense of enjoyment, plainly extending her to the *jouissance of* herself, but plainly reserving *to* herself her ownership and final disposal."[60]

Lanval is clearly the outsider. He is allowed to enter into the realm of riches and love from which he had been excluded, but he is not free to possess it, a stunning inversion of women's economic situation in the twelfth century. By requiring his silence, the lady goes beyond the need for secrecy that we saw in *Yonec*. Instead, she transfers the danger of the woman's voice to a man. In owning his wealth and his speech, she possesses him, body and soul. She then leaves, after telling him that she will satisfy his desires whenever he wants.

Once he returns to Arthur's court and begins to distribute his newfound wealth, Lanval is received into the inner circle of knights. He is now seen as generous and courtly ("larges e curteis") and has what he desires—the social companionship of his peers and the love of the fairy woman. Lanval's silence is tested, however, by the queen, who professes her love for him. When he demurs, she accuses him of having no interest in women: "Vallez avez bien afeitiez, / Ensemble od eus vus deduiez" ("You have fine-looking boys / with whom you enjoy yourself") (281–282). Again, he is marginalized, this time with accusations of homosexuality. To defend his honor, Lanval exclaims that he loves a woman who is better in every respect that she is:

Mes jo aim e si sui amis
Cele ki deit aver le pris
Sur tutes celes que jeo sai.
E une chose vus dirai,
Bien le sachez a descovert:
Une de celes ki la sert,
Tute la plus povre meschine,
Vaut mieuz de vus, dame reïne,
De cors, de vis e de beauté,
D'enseignement e de bunté! (293–302)
[But I love and I am loved
by one who should have the prize
over all the women I know.
And I shall tell you one thing;
you might as well know all:
any one of those who serve her,
the poorest girl of all,
is better than you, my lady queen,
in body, face, and beauty,
in breeding and in goodness!]

Once the queen tells Arthur that Lanval has dishonored her, Lanval knows that he has broken his silence and lost his love. He is put on trial and told that the only way he can be found innocent is to prove the truth of his statement. In short, the fairy woman must appear. As soon as Lanval refuses, the two beautiful girls arrive and, in their wake, the fairy woman. She is judged to be the most beautiful of all and tells Arthur that the queen was in the wrong. Lanval is set free, and he and the woman ride off to Avalon on her horse and no one hears of him again ("Nul hum n'en oï plus parler").

Lanval has a number of things in common with *Guigemar* and *Yonec.* In all three, men are the ones who cross boundaries on their *aventures*, helped by women whose only purpose is to assist them on their quests for integration. *Lanval*, of course, differs because the woman is the one who has the power to effect change. It can also be argued that Lanval is never fully reintegrated into society because in the end he gets carried off to Avalon. Lanval remains a marginalized figure through the *lai*, the dispossessed male who, helped by the wealthy woman, can reenter the world of Arthurian knighthood. His disappearance at the end of the story only highlights the very real economic position of all but firstborn sons: they must actually find rich women and go to another land if they want to succeed.[61] In this sense, *Lanval* is less a story about women's marginalization than it is about men's dispossession of their property. Lanval becomes the property of the fairy lady from the moment he falls in love with her.

And yet, we cannot fully say that the woman in Lanval forms part of the center. She lives in a land that is separate, and her power can only be realized when those affected by it remain silent. *Lanval*, as Leicester has remarked, is the only *lai* that takes place at Arthur's court, which he views as a place of retreat and escape, a fantasy world of its own.[62] I would argue that Marie de France locates her only *lai* in which a woman has wealth in a real place precisely to show how much of a fairy tale it actually is. A woman with property cannot live in the real world; she must live, however successfully, on the margins of that world. In her other *lais*, women are trapped in towers, unhappy marriages, or tragic love affairs. Even in the few in which there is a "happily ever after" resolution, it always ends in marriage and always in some fictitious place. In *Lanval* she confronts the issue of property, silence, and marginalization directly by situating it in an actual place and making the woman the controlling force. The fairy woman, in effect, does not need to go on an *aventure*; wherever she goes, she is at the center and is never on the margins. But her success completely depends upon the silence of those who know about her; she cannot remain in the real world once she is identified. In requiring silence, she is both silenced and forced into the margins.

In dealing with marriage, Heloise and Marie directly confront one of the central issues of their time. Although Heloise's response is on the personal level, she has nonetheless been forced into marriage because of the expectations of her time. The alternative she preferred, "love freely given," or concubinage, as she called it, was no longer a viable option for Abelard. Furthermore, by describing her own situation, as well as marriage in general, in economic terms, she clearly saw the reality of women's lives. Heloise had the education and the confidence, however, to give voice to her opinions. Through her mastery of dialectic and letter-writing, she willingly placed herself in the margins but was able to confront the center, boldly and forcefully arguing her points.

Marie also clearly saw the marginalized economic role of women. Unlike Heloise, Marie does not argue philosophically, but rather tells her stories using fairy-tale techniques, in which the possible may be just around the corner. Her women live in the margins and interact with the center only through the men with whom they have relationships. Marie and Heloise, however, share a common critique of marriage as an institution that constricts women and inhibits love. In the next chapter, we see how women who have chosen a spiritual life carry a similar message.

CHAPTER 4

SEXUAL PURITY AS PROPERTY: *VIE SEINTE AUDREE* AND *THE BOOK OF MARGERY KEMPE*

In the previous chapter, both Heloise and Marie de France offer profound critiques of marriage using economic metaphors and analysis. In this chapter I turn to medieval England to show a different framing of the marriage critique. Using the examples of two religious women, Saint Audrey (also known as Sainte Audrée and Aethelreda) and Margery Kempe, I argue that their narratives also have an economic focus that allows them to regain control over their property, which they reconfigure in their physical selves. These women use their own sexual purity as economic capital, either "paying off" their husbands (Margery) or using their dower property to establish a safe haven for themselves (Audrée). In both cases, they are aware that their sexuality has an economic value that they can manipulate in order to be released from intercourse with their husbands or husbands-to-be. What is even more interesting, however, is that both women acknowledge their own sexual impulses, at times with men who are not their spouses. Their desire to escape marriage did not mean a rejection of sexuality, but rather a rejection of the compulsory sexuality that was necessitated by the conjugal debt.[1]

If on the continent the practice of primogeniture was not always the rule, in England there was a stricter adherence to the rule of property transmission to firstborn sons. The practice of settling family land on the bride, the *maritagium*, was replaced in England by the marriage portion, a money payment given to the father of the groom. If the wife did not produce heirs, the land would return to the family. Before the thirteenth-century Statute of Westminster, a woman had full possession of her *maritagium* and could pass it on to her younger sons or daughters, often in the form of dowry.[2] This change was detrimental not only because it replaced real property by a sum of money and prohibited women from passing it on directly, but also because it shifted the nature of the gift. Rather than being intended for the woman's support, it was seen as a payment to the groom, who, in turn, was expected to provide for his wife in case of his death. In England, this gift, the dower, developed under common law into an estate in land for the widow. She was entitled to one-third of her husband's lands for her lifetime.

When the prospective bride was an heiress, the groom's family often made jointure a part of the marriage contract. In this arrangement, certain lands were put into joint tenancy to provide a life income for her should he die first. As Ann J. Kettle has pointed out, although these practices appear to provide some future security for the bride, "they were not designed to secure the economic independence of the bride during the marriage as English law allowed few property rights to the married woman."[3] Furthermore, the husband controlled all of the lands that the wife inherited or acquired during the marriage. If she died before he did and had produced a child, the widower was entitled to a particularly English custom called "curtesy," which allowed him a life estate in all of her real property.

Any moveable property the wife had or acquired during the marriage was irrevocably owned by her husband. Because under common law married women could not own chattel in common, even the clothes on her back were considered the husband's property, free for him to give away at will.[4] She could not make a will without his consent, because legally she had nothing to leave.[5] The creation of a "use" allowed property owners to bequeath land to family members, but this rarely deprived a widow of her dower, since the common law courts upheld her right to a third of her lands and all lands in joint tenancy.[6] As for movable property, a husband could bequeath it to whomever he wished. A wife, however, could not pass even this type of property without her husband's permission. Although the church argued that a woman should be allowed to will her personal property, the courts disagreed. In a case in the Court of Common Pleas in 1311, it was declared that "no person can make a testament save he who can claim property in the chattels, but a wife cannot claim property and consequently cannot make a testament."[7] Dower, as Janet Senderowicz Leonard has termed it, "was the medieval woman's insurance policy." Nonetheless, she continues, thousands of women had to appear in court to claim their rightful dower.[8]

Compared to the rest of England, London's inheritance, dower, and dowry laws were more favorable to women. All children, male and female, could inherit equally. A father's estate was divided in three equal ways: a third to pay testator's debt and for his "soul's salvation," another third for the children's inheritance, and the final third as dower for his widow's life use, later to be inherited by the children. As a result, London did not evolve what Barbara Hanawalt calls "patrilineal social structures." Women were able to circulate wealth and thus were able to contribute to capital formation in late medieval London. Thus, they contributed to the economy not only through work, but also through transfer of wealth through marriage.[9]

Nonetheless, London's laws, although favoring women, did not give them equality. As with the rest of England, wives came under the *coverture* of their husbands. As *femes couvertes,* their husbands were responsible for their conduct and finances. A husband could control his wife's wealth and even use it for his own business, but could not permanently alienate her dower or inherited property.[10] The very word "*coverture*" implies that marriage "covered" women's legal existence. A wife who murdered her husband, for instance, was deemed to have committed petty treason.[11] Although this crime was recharacterized in 1828, until 1790 a woman could be burned at the stake if convicted.[12]

Once a widow, however, a woman was not under any man's *coverture.* She could be independent, powerful, and, as we see in Chaucer's Wife of Bath, sexually aggressive. This was not a welcome situation in such a patrilineal culture. As Hanawalt has observed, "Remarriage seemed a convenient solution to curb widows' freedoms and distribute their wealth to other males."[13] Although the Magna Carta stipulated that a widow could not be compelled to remarry, political pressure was often brought to bear upon them to do so. Widows who inherited one-third of their husbands' property were particularly vulnerable. Rhoda Lange Friedrichs, for example, has shown how Edward IV was able to control the inheritances of two fifteenth-century aristocratic sisters, Maud and Joan Stanhope, in order to give their property to his loyal followers.[14]

The traditional view of women's work during the Middle Ages is that the preindustrial world provided them with an egalitarian standing in the household. Both husband and wife worked toward the economic good of the entire family. Alice Clark's *The Working Life of Women in the Seventeenth Century*, written in 1919, concluded that men and women had separate, but equal, spheres in the premodern household economy. The woman controlled the production and selling of family goods, such as cloth and dairy products. By substituting an individual wage for a family wage, the Industrial Revolution undermined women's work. This argument was supported by Louise Tilly and Joan Scott in their 1978 book titled *Women, Work, and Family*. More recent scholars, such as Martha Howell, have moderated this view, arguing instead that the exclusions on women began earlier than the Industrial Revolution.[15]

Judith M. Bennett, in her book *History Matters: Patriarchy and the Challenge of Feminism*, contends that the medieval economy did not allow women anything approaching the equality that Tilly and Scott postulated. They did not control the value that their labor produced, but by virtue of their status as *femes couvertes*, husbands controlled all of the property, both real and personal, in the family.[16] Bennett looks beyond the production of the household to the general economy and finds that women worked in less-well-paying occupations, had only limited access to guild membership, and received wages that were roughly 75 percent of those of men.[17] Although there were certainly improvements in the status of women in the years between 1350 and 1700, she argues that these were "*changes*, not *transformations*."[18] Bennett shows evidence that the trade of brewmaking, which women controlled in 1300 when it had a low status and low profits, was perceived as "women's work." By 1600 it had become a profitable business and was largely controlled by men.[19] As Margaret R. Hunt has pointed out, women's work in the preindustrial economy was labor rather than capital intensive.[20] Thus, what could be perceived as a loss in women's status was, in reality, due to an upgrade in the status of the business itself, with male brewers usurping an industry that itself was being transformed. Although there was a tradition of the *feme sole* trader, women who could act independently of their husbands, their primary responsibility was to the household. Furthermore, although husbands were not responsible for their wives' business debts, they had disposition over all of the profits. Thus, men had the possibility of gain with none of the financial risks.[21]

As we will see with Margery Kempe, a medieval woman in business, access to financial resources is directly connected to the issue of ownership of one's body. Both Margery and Audrée use some kind of financial instrument, whether it be physical property or money itself, to free themselves from marriage. Freed from *coverture* by choosing chastity, they are able to control the outcome of their lives.

The texts also raise important issues about female authorship and ownership of one's own narrative. Audrée's life was written by a nun, and Margery's autobiography was dictated to a scribe. Can we, then, speak of these texts as female self-narrative? As Jennifer Summit has noted, the use of scribes does not mean that women were illiterate, since their employment was a measure of social status. Furthermore, for medieval women visionaries, writing was "a suspension, rather than assertion, of selfhood."[22] The situation is made even more cloudy by the fact that texts were not always signed, and authors appropriated work from others.[23]

With *Vie seinte Audree*, although the author is identified as "Marie," there is disagreement on who she actually is.[24] The Anglo-Norman account of Audrée is of particular interest because, unlike the *vita* of Christina of Markyate, for example, it was almost certainly written by a woman. Wogan-Browne identifies Marie as one of the female religious in a community dedicated to Audrée,[25] located in Chatteris, although June Hall McCash and Judith Clark Barban believe the author is none other than Marie de France. They cite the fact that this Marie has none of the humility common to a nun and point out the strong similarities of the text to *Espurgatoire Seint Patriz*.[26] Furthermore, the single extant copy appears in a codex that contains all the Old French saints' lives known to have been written by women, which indicates that it was prepared for women.[27] Virginia Blanton's recent work, which follows the cult of this saint through different historical periods, believes that *Vie seinte Audree* was likely written for a female aristocratic audience to promote religious patronage.[28] The probability of female authorship thus allows us to see how women viewed virginity, marriage, and sexual desire through what Blanton calls "narrative interruptions" about Audrée's experiences.[29]

As with our other texts, scholars have questioned the authorship of *The Book of Margery Kempe*. As Margery herself admits, there were two scribes involved in its writing, but insists that the *Book* is a reliable version of her life:

> Thys boke is not wretyn in ordyr, every thyng aftyr other as it wer don, but lych as the mater cam to the creatur in mend whan it schuld be wretyn, for it was so long er it was wretyn that sche dede no thing wryten but that sche knew rygth wel for very trewth.
>
> [This book is not written in order, every thing after another as it was done, but just as the matter came to this creature's mind when it was to be written down, for it was so long before it was written that she had forgotten the time and the order when things occurred. And therefore she had nothing written but what she well knew to be indeed the truth.][30]

John Hirsch has argued that the second scribe was the main author of the text.[31] Lynn Staley takes a different approach, distinguishing Kempe the author from Margery the protagonist, comparing this difference to the one between Geoffrey the pilgrim and Chaucer the poet.[32] The more recent dialogue between Nicholas Watson and Felicity Riddy demonstrates the complicated nature of assigning textual ownership. For Watson, there is no question that she was the author, "responsible for the *Book*'s structure, arguments, and most of its language."[33] Riddy, however, points to the difficult process of the "remembered life," arguing that we cannot use the modern idea of the author. She does not accept the dictation model nor does she know what role the scribe played in the composition of the *Book*.[34]

This chapter thus presents two different examples of women's "writing." *Vie Seinte Audree* has an author who is not the subject herself; nonetheless, it portrays a narrator speaking in a woman's voice. And although there are questions as to the verbatim transcription of Margery Kempe's life, she is, nonetheless, at least one of its authors. With these restrictions in mind, I believe there is a remarkable uniformity in the views these two women hold on marriage, demonstrated by their actions and the words used to portray these actions.

Vie seinte Audree

Vie seinte Audree, an Anglo-Norman text composed sometime between the late twelfth and early thirteenth century, is a *vita*. It details the life and miracles of the English female saint also known as Ethelreda, Aethelthryth, Audrée, Ethelred, and Audrey. As Jocelyn Wogan-Browne has noted, there are more accounts of her life than of any other English female saint.[35] Twice-married and widowed, she managed to maintain her virginity, establishing a monastery with her dower. The antimarriage theme runs throughout the text, as does the connection of property with power.

The text itself supplies us with a wealth of historical evidence about medieval women's property rights. Although Audrée wishes to remain a virgin, her parents marry her to Tonbert, and she is "given the isle of Ely as her dower" ("et de l'ydle d'Ely douee") (306). After he dies, she goes to her dower lands to live in peace (740–749). King Egfrid wants to marry her, offering her "very great riches and a large dower" (785–789), and although she refuses, her relatives insist on the marriage. As Rhoda Lange Friedrichs has shown, by the fifteenth century, widows in England, although having property, were often not able to use it to gain their own independence.[36] Those women who were not marriageable were often placed in convents by their relatives. Marie notes this fact, adding that they brought with them large endowments (212–213).

Although she shows that women had little control over their own fortune, Marie uses money metaphors and imagery through *Vie seinte Audree*. At the very beginning of the text, she indicates that Audrée gives up the riches of the world for the riches she can have in God (17–22). She believes that the tumor in her neck that eventually kills her was caused by the gold necklaces that she once loved to wear (1939–1950). Sixteen years after her death, when her tomb was opened, her body was still intact and her throat wound healed. This, says Marie, is proof that she was a virgin. Indeed, her virginity is a valuable commodity:

> Pur ce ne pout le cors suffrir
> Ke enpirer deut no blemir:
> Bonë est ceste marchandise
> Ke la virge ha de Deu conquise,
> Ke pur li danter et destreindre
> Puet a la gloire Deu ateindre. (2811–2816)
> [For this reason her body would never suffer
> deterioration or damage.
> Good is the merchandise
> which the virgin conquered for God:
> for by restraint and control of it
> she may attain the glory of God.]

She has "through her holy chastity / and virginity / made a worthy marriage / which lasts eternally" ("Par sa seintisme chasteté / Et par sa grant virginité / Parvint a noces saluables / Ky durent et sunt parmenables") (385–388). The economic language here stresses the virtues of good stewardship, the acquisition of property, and strong management of it. It is not the voice of a disempowered woman, but rather one who asserts her right to own her body as well as financial possessions.

Indeed, Marie gives Audrée great powers over money. When she founds the church at Ely, which is part of her dower lands, she is able to get financial benefits for Wilfrid, whom she placed in charge of the place:

> Sainte Audree par sa cointise
> A li purchaça grant franchise
> Des rois, de[s] ducs, de meint prudome
> Par le confermement de Rome.
> Cist yle li estoit donee
> Et par douaire confermee.
> Pur ceo purchaça tel franchise
> Qu'el la torna a Deu servise. (1657–1664)
> [Through her shrewdness Saint Audrey
> obtained for him important tax exemptions,
> approved by Rome,
> from kings, dukes, and many noblemen.
> Since the island had been given to her
> and confirmed as her dower,
> she was able to procure this type of exemption,
> and she turned it over to the service of God.]

Through her virginity, and we are led to believe, her connections, she is able to transform the marriage that she scorned into a treasure for God.

Likewise, Audrée uses her miracles to gain power, meting out punishments as well as healings. In particular, she appears to right many monetary wrongs. For example, a Norman sheriff named Picot imposed heavy taxes on her lands and then mysteriously disappeared:

Li uns distrent k'il fu raviz
Et de cors et d'ame periz
Si com Datan et Abiron
Ki alerent en Achiron.
Li autre distrent ke müez
Est en beste et transfigurez
Com Nabugodonosor fu
En qui Deu mostra sa vertu. (3019–3026)
[Some said that he was snatched away
and perished body and soul
like Dathan andAbiram
who went into the river Acheron.
Others said he was changed
and transformed into a beast,
as was Nabuchadnezzar
on whom God demonstrated his power.]

Likewise, Stephen of Eschaliers did not pay his rent on his Ely land, lying that he was too poor. Once his perjury was revealed, "For this deed Saint Audrey / did not forget to avenge herself. / Stephen suffered with his feet / and could not be cured; thus he came to a bad end" (Pur iceste ovre seinte Audree / N'a pas sa vengeance oblïee: / Estiefne de pez mahaigna, / Ne pot garir, einz mal fina" (4469–4472). His son also withheld rent money from the monks at Ely, but he begged Audrée for mercy and she granted it to him once he had paid back what he owed (4513–4544).

Audrée resisted marriage, claiming that "no one can lead a married life without sullying themselves" (401–402). She had two marriages, but both were chaste. She married Tonbert "without the consent of her heart" ("sanz volenté de son curage") (l. 802), but he agrees to live chastely. Three years later, he dies and although she was sad, "inwardly she rejoiced / to be free from the servitude / she had endured under the yoke of marriage / and from the hindrance of this world, / which blinds and confuses people" ("Son corage s'en esjoÿ / Kant delivre estoit del servage / K'ele out del jou [del] mariage / [E] de l'enpechement del mond / Ke la gent avuegle et confund") (368–372). Audrée's second husband, Egfrid, is less accommodating, pressuring her to fulfill the marital debt. But God is on her side: "Whenever the king lay / in his royal bed awaiting his pleasure, / it pleased God to have him fall asleep" ("Come le roy pur son delit / Ert cochiez en son real lit / Si com Deu plesoit somellioit / Et la roÿne se levoit") (931–933). This situation continues for twelve years, until he finally releases her to become a nun.

Audrée's emotional bonds are not with her husbands, but with two holy men, Wilfrid and Cuthbert, who are both, as Marie takes care to reiterate, chaste. She "often gave / very generously of her wealth" ("dona sovent / De son aver mut largement") (1095–1096) to Cuthbert; their love "was proper / and acceptable to God / for they were both virgins who led / chaste and holy lives" (ert covenable / Kar ele ert a Due acceptable: / Virges furent et chastement / Tindrent lur vie et seintement") (1105–1108). She has temptations of the flesh, both with her husbands and after Tonbert dies, but she overcomes them through good works.[37]

Audrée's virginity is her prime asset, one that she protects as an important commodity; she sees marriage as the primary challenge to the preservation of its value. Without denying her sexuality, she chooses not to satisfy her physical desires, since it is only in marriage that the conjugal debt is enforceable.

The Book of Margery Kempe

The precariousness of women in business in medieval England can be seen clearly in Margery Kempe, best known for her spiritual autobiography *The Book of Margery Kempe.* Completed sometime around 1438, Margery chronicles her attempts to support herself and her failures as a businesswoman. She first turns to brewing and "was one of the greatest brewers in the town of N. for three or four years until she lost a great deal of money" ("was on of the grettest brewers in the town N a three yer or four tyl sche lost mech good, for sche had nevyr ure therto" (24,44). Thinking that God was punishing her, but not yet ready to give up worldly goods, she became a miller and "thus she was confident of making her living" ("thus sche trostyd to getyn hir levyng") (25,44). This too was a failed enterprise. Margery eventually decides to go on a pilgrimage to the Holy Land, and before she leaves, asks the priest to announce from the pulpit that if either she or her husband has any debts, they should speak with her so she may settle them. The fact that she takes responsibility for her husband as well as herself is indicative not only of the prevalence of working women in fourteenth-century Britain but also the financial responsibility they assumed. By assuming her husband's debts, it is clear that she has more money than her husband. Even when she assumes religious poverty and trusts that God will provide for her, she still worries about money.

Sheila Delany's perceptive Marxist-feminist reading of *The Book of Margery Kempe* underscores Margery's "constant awareness of money" as well as "her perception of herself as property."[38] As part of the bourgeoisie, Delany notes, she is still comparatively rich despite her business losses.[39] Because of the economic imbalance between herself and her husband John, she can buy her way out of having sex with him. Religion thus becomes "Margery's way of asserting her ownership of herself."[40] In the end, however, Delany privileges class over gender, arguing that Margery's "spiritual economics" is focused on turning a profit in heaven.[41] David Aers observes that Margery "seemed compulsively driven to accumulate, always desiring more and more."[42] She wants to return to Jerusalem to purchase pardons, but God tell her that if she simply thinks about hold places, she will receive them.[43] Although Margery's class gave her access to the market, gender operated as well, he contends. She was actually in a more powerless position than lower-class wives because she did not have to work.[44]

Indeed, Margery's preoccupation with finances is evident throughout the *Book*, but it is not only with its acquisition. On pilgrimage, she does not get along with her companions, who make fun of her, and, she relates, actually withhold some of her money that she has entrusted to them (72,100). She is convinced that the ring that God had commanded her to have made, engraved with the words *Jesus est amor meus*, has been stolen. This is especially frightening to her because she considers it her wedding ring to Jesus, but she later finds it under her bed (84–85, 114–115). When Margery is in Rome, God tells her to give away all of her money and "make herself destitute for his love ("makyn hir bar for hys lofe"). She obeys, believing that "he who bade me give it away for his love will help me to pay it back" ("he that bad me gevyn it awey for hys lofe wil help me to payn it ageyn"; 96,128–129). Even when she falls into debt and has no money for warm clothes, she trusts in God and her needs are met. Rather than worry about money, God tells her:

> Daughter, don't concentrate on getting money, because I shall provide for you, but always concentrate on loving and remembering me, because I shall go with you wherever you go, as I have promised before.
>
> [Dowtyr, stody thow for no good, for I schal ordeyn for the, but evyr stody thow to love me and kepe thi mende on me, for I schal go with the wher thow gost as I have hite the beforn.] (109,143)

He later gives her enough funds to pay off her debts (109,144). This economic exchange with God is a parallel relationship to the conjugal debt. Rather than giving sex, she is required to give only love. Their marriage can thus satisfy all of her needs: she has a bridegroom without physical demands, allowing her to remain chaste.

My own reading of Margery Kempe emphasizes her similarities to Audrée, who is also described as part of an economic universe. She too rejects earthly marriage while not denying her sexuality, especially with other men. Margery differs from Audrée in that she believes that she has quite literally become the "bride of Christ," which is sealed in a ceremony and wedding night. Her chastity, however, is preserved—indeed God tells her she is a "a mayden in thi soule" (62). Margery's two business ventures, as a brewer and miller, both fail. She sees this as God's chastisement for sin and this sets her on the "wey of evyrlestyng lyfe" (25). Soon afterward, while laying with her husband in bed, she hears a sweet sound, to which she responds, "Alas, that evyr I dede synne, it is ful mery in hevyn" (26). The incident causes her to lose

> all sexual intercourse with her husband, for paying the debt of matrimony was so abominable to her that she would rather, she thought, have eaten and drunk the ooze and muck in the gutter than consent to intercourse, except out of obedience.
>
> [sche had nervy desyr to komown fleschly with hyre husbonde, for the dette of matrimony was so abhominabyl to hir that sche had levar, hir thowt, etyn or drynkyn the wose, the ukke in the chanel, than to consentyn to any fleschly comownyng saf only for obedyens.] (26,46)

Interestingly, her call to salvation happens when she is in bed with John and results in her loss of desire for him. Referring to intercourse as the marital debt further removes the act from pleasure it had always been; instead, it is something that is theologically required of her.

Although she tries to persuade her husband to become chaste with her, he refuses, saying that he will do so when God wills (47). For three years she struggles with temptations, but they do not seem to be centered upon John. Instead, she develops a desire for another man, who had proclaimed his wish to sleep with her:

> Sche lay be hir husband, and for to comown with hym it was so abhomynabyl onto hir that sche mygth not duren it, and yet was it leful onto hir in leful tyme yf sche had wold. But evyr sche was labowrd with the other man for to syn wyth hym inasmech as he had spoke to hir. At the last thorw inoportunyté of temptacyon and lakkyng of dyscrecyon sche was ovyrcomyn, and consentyd in hir mend. (29)
>
> [She lay beside her husband, and to have intercourse with him was so abominable to her that she could not bear it, and yet it was permissible for her and at a rightful time if she had wished it. But all the time she was

tormented to sin with the other man because he had spoken to her. At last—through the importunings of temptation and a lack of discretion—she was overcome and consented to it.] (50)

Fortunately, when she told the man she would consent, "he said he would not for all the wealth in this world; he would rather be chopped up as small as meat for the pot" ("he seyd he no wold for al the good in this world; he had lever ben hewyn as small as flesch to the pott"; 50,29). In other words, money could not buy Margery the sex she desired, but she is able to use it to satisfy off her marital debt when she pays off her husband's financial obligations:

> Sere, yf it lyke you, ye schal grawnt me my desyr, and ye schal have your desyr. Grawnthyth me that ye schal not komyn in my bed, and I grawnt yow to qwyte yowr dettys er I go to Jerusalem. And makyth my body fre to God so that ye nevyr make no chalengyng in me to askyn no dett of matrimony aftyr this day whyl ye levyn... (38)
>
> [Sir, if you please, you shall grant me my desire, and you shall have your desire. Grant me that you will not come into my bed, and I grant you that I will pay your debts before I go to Jerusalem. And make my body free to God, so that you never make any claim on me requesting any conjugal debt after this day as long as you live...] (60)

As Aers comments, "Margery acts as one merchant with capital to buy a commodity that had been purchased from her merchant father in the Lynn marriage market."[45] Nona Fienberg has concluded that she creates a "contractual widowhood" with John, but it is, I believe, more of a divorce, allowing her to contract a marriage with God, who gives wealth and property, allowing her to be virginal in the process.[46]

Written 250 years after *Vie seinte Audree*, *The Book of Margery Kempe* uses similar economic metaphors to free its subject from marriage. Although not a virgin, Margery values her chastity as much as Audrée protects her virginity. While not denying their sexuality, they reject the marital state in order to be in control of their physical bodies. As Heloise and Marie de France in the previous chapter, they use the language of property in order to exert autonomy. In succeeding centuries it is a power that women lose, as social and economic forces persuade them that marriage is a thing to be desired, not shunned. This is the subject of the following chapters.

CHAPTER 5

PROPERTY AND PROPRIETY IN EIGHTEENTH- AND NINETEENTH-CENTURY ENGLAND: BURNEY, AUSTEN, ELIOT

The progressive economic disenfranchisement of women from the Middle Ages through the nineteenth century was supported by changing cultural norms that transformed the woman who once could control property into a submissive, financially unstable creature. In this chapter, I look at literary representations of perfect womanhood and trace the growing opposition to women's plight, which finally resulted in the Married Women's Property Act of 1882. Finally, I analyze three women writers (Frances Burney, Jane Austen, and George Eliot) to show how they critiqued marriage while still being trapped in its economic consequences. While making the marriage plot central to their novels, they nonetheless find ways to subvert its traditional authority.

Adaptations of Property Law

Although medieval property rights did not see any significant changes until the early nineteenth century, modifications appeared as early as the sixteenth century. Jointure, a provision of land or income for the widow, developed as a substitute for dower. Under this custom, fathers bargained for a settlement for their daughters, which could be more or less than the one-third of her future husband's property that constituted dower. Because it consisted of personal as well as real property, the actual settlement to the widow could be less secure than dower.[1] The way to measure the value of an estate had also changed between 1535 and 1800: an estate's annual revenues came to be deemed a more relevant measure of its value.

During the seventeenth century, trusts became a much-utilized vehicle for passing on property. Originally they were private arrangements and therefore unenforceable by common law and were used to protect the propertied classes. Often these trusts were not in the best interests of wives. For example, a man could convey land to a friend as trustee to hold for the benefit of his widow and children. The common law courts would then see only the friend as owner and would not recognize that the wife and family had any interest in the property.[2] Trusts were also part of the separate property that could be conveyed to a woman during marriage by her family to protect their interests against her husband's common-law rights. Although this was meant to ensure that a wife had sole use of the income from this property, she was not in control of the property. Rather, a trustee, not the woman, controlled it according to the restrictions of the trust.[3]

During marriage, a wife had a separate income known as "pin money." This annual allowance was explicitly intended to be used to keep her appearance and that of the household up to the standards of her husband's social and economic position.[4] The history of legal thought on pin money in the period 1690–1834 stressed that it was for the wife's own maintenance and minimized the possibility that a woman could use this as capital. By the nineteenth century, there was widespread opposition to female control even over these small sums. Women themselves felt they could not be trusted with money, and some even refused it. Mrs. Catherine Gore's novel *Pin Money*, written in 1831, depicts the wife who spends it recklessly and incurs debt upon her husband.[5]

Virginia Duff argues that the primary writers of fiction before 1740 were women; many portrayed men's inhumane treatment in issues of marriage, divorce, adultery, rape, incest, and property issues. Around this same time, contract law, as opposed to common law, began to be applied to married women's right to own, manage, and dispose of property. As Duff explains, this change created a conservative backlash, which overturned any progress.[6] The Marriage Act of 1753 ensured that only women who had marriages that met precise rules were protected. These rules included most of what we now think of as components of a legal marriage: banns or a license, parental permission for minors, a ceremony before witnesses and authorized clergy, and recording in a marriage register. Because all of these regulations had to be followed, women who had common-law or clandestine marriages were thus excluded.[7]

Set against these conservative fears, the call for reform of married women's property laws grew more insistent. Critics such as John Stuart Mill pointed out the inequalities in the property laws. In *The Subjection of Women*, written in 1869, he traces the history of marriage and concludes that "the woman is the actual bondservant of her husband: no less so, as far as legal obligation goes, than slaves commonly so called... She can acquire no property but for him; the instant it becomes hers, even by inheritance, it becomes *ipso facto* his."[8] Even settlements do not protect the woman since she has no control over this property; their function is to prevent the husband from squandering it. Mill instead posits the solution of separate property:

> The rule is simple: whatever would be the husband's or wife's if they were not married, should be under their exclusive control during marriage; which need not interfere with the power to tie up property by settlement, in order to preserve it for children. Some people are sentimentally shocked at the idea of a separate interest in money matters, as inconsistent with the ideal of fusion of two lives into one. For my own part, I am one of the strongest supporters of community of goods, where resulting from an entire unity of feeling in the owners, which makes all things common between them. But I have no relish for a community of goods resting on the doctrine, that what is mine is yours but what is yours in not mine; and I should prefer to decline entering into such a compact with any one, though I were myself the person to profit by it.[9]

Mill, unlike earlier commentators such as John Locke and Mary Wollstonecraft, used the criterion of utility rather than natural rights to assess the institution of marriage: was it conducive to the greatest happiness for the greatest number of people? Clearly, he believed, the marriage laws were not. Conservatives, on the other hand, argued that they were for the protection of women and hence critical.[10]

The process of changing the property laws in England was a long one. Beginning in 1855, a group of feminists headed by Barbara Leigh Smith collected evidence, presented philosophical arguments in favor of reform, and circulated petitions for Parliament. Many of the women writers of the day signed, including Elizabeth Barrett Browning, Elizabeth Gaskell, Marian Evans (George Eliot), and Harriet Martineau.[11] When the petition was unrolled in Parliament on March 15, 1856, it supposedly ran the length of the House of Commons.[12] The legislation came before the House of Lords in 1857, but due to a change in government, it was not debated again for twelve years. The House of Commons bill passed 120 to 65, but then disappeared in the wake of the Divorce Bill.[13] The government was simply not interested in further reform on behalf of women.[14] In 1865 John Stuart Mill was elected to Parliament and gave a speech in favor of women's right to vote. The rise of suffrage committees coincided with a new bill, the Married Women's Property Bill, which was introduced in 1868. A number of books were published dealing with this issue, including Mill's *Subjection of Women* in 1869. A very diminished bill, the 1870 Married Women's Property Act, protected only the earnings of poor women. It was, in Holcombe's words, "emasculated by the House of Lords." Arthur Arnold called it a "legislative abortion."[15] It was not until the Liberals returned to power in 1880 that a universal bill was introduced. The Married Women's Property Act of 1882, which defined the nature of separate property as all property held before or entitled to at marriage and acquired or entitled to after marriage, was finally passed.[16]

Perfect Womanhood: Literary Representations

How was it that it could take so many centuries for women to gain access to their own property? As we saw in the previous chapters, the misogynistic discourses that paralleled women's loss of economic rights, as well as the church's increasing control over marriage, became cultural norms that supported the legal changes. In England, a similar set of norms developed. Ideas of the perfect lady, as well as responses to historical and economic developments, prevented women from claiming their rightful inheritance.

One such change was the development of credit as a vehicle of exchange. As J. G. A. Pocock has formulated, at the beginning of the eighteenth century, the idea of property went through a transformation from estate to credit. In the Western moral tradition, he explains, a citizen possessed property in order to be autonomous and therefore virtuous. "He did not possess it in order to engage in trade, exchange or profit; indeed, these activities were hardly compatible with the activity of citizenship." Money as the medium of exchange was seen as threatening the very nature of virtue. "Propriety" and "property" were therefore interchangeable terms.[17] For women, it was the very lack of property that was their propriety. With the founding of the Bank of England in the 1690s, people were able to borrow and thus live beyond their means. Nobility was once constituted by what was owned; with credit came the *appearance* of ownership. The illusion of property was now power. In Pocock's words, "in the credit economy and polity, property had become not only mobile but speculative: what one owned was promises... "[18]

Under Pocock's formulation of property and propriety, credit became the basis of the British economy—necessary and at the same time unstable. As we saw with Mrs. Gore's book on pin money, this fear that possessions could disappear in an instant was projected even onto women's small allowances. In addition, Catherine Ingrassia has shown how the instability of paper credit was identified with women. Unlike real property, which was fixed and secure, the new credit was "increasingly unreal" and "could be realized only imaginatively."[19] The new prose forms of popular fiction, she argues, were seen as distinctly feminine:

> Unlike history, which can purport to be "real," fiction by its very nature was seen as not real, a discourse of intentional deception designed in part to arouse fantasies and desires in the reader... Consequently, imagination and fantasy, unleashed emotions, and unregulated passions—all impulses distinctly gendered female—were seen as driving the engines of Exchange Alley and Grub Street.[20]

In addition, as Mona Scheuermann has pointed out, many female characters in eighteenth-century novels, such as Roxana, Pamela, and Moll Flanders, are intensely interested in money.[21] These representations of women were a vehicle for the debate about women's property, according to April London: female characters in eighteenth-century novels exercise "reformative agency" through their own industriousness, which is then relocated to men.[22]

This "reformative agency" was a characteristic of what came to be known as "perfect womanhood." As Mary Poovey has reflected, property was "the visible sign of man's inner worth" as well as "the source of present income, the measure of social prestige, the basis of political power, and the legacy that carried a man's name beyond the grave." A woman, by one act of infidelity, could "imperil both a man's present security and his dynastic ambitions."[23] The stereotype of woman as seducer that we saw in the Middle Ages became tamed in the eighteenth century; the new perfect woman was one who would not only accept her subservient role, but would enforce the civilizing of herself and her family.

As Thomas Laqueur has argued, the idea of two separate sexes was newly developed and strengthened in the eighteenth century. Rather than being a lesser form of the male body, a woman had her own distinct anatomy, and a whole new stereotype was developed:

> The assertion that women were passionless; or alternatively the proposition that, as biologically defined beings, they possessed to an extraordinary degree, far more than men, the capacity to control the bestial, irrational, and potentially destructive fury of sexual pleasure; and indeed the novel inquiry into the nature and quality of female pleasure and sexual allurement—all were part of a grand effort to discover the anatomical and physiological characteristics that distinguished men from women.[24]

Thus, a woman's very biology enabled her to become a civilizing force on men, but also kept her subordinate to them. As Laqueur notes, "What matters is the superior strength of men or, more important, the frequent incapacity of women because of their reproductive functions. Bodies in these accounts are not the sign but the foundation for civil society."[25]

Nancy Armstrong in *Desire and Domestic Fiction* argues that the very idea of female desirability changed in the eighteenth and nineteenth centuries. The domestic virtues of the middle-class woman overtook fortune and family name in literary texts. Modern domesticity became "the only haven from the trials of a heartless economic world."[26] The historic aristocratic woman became the embodiment of superficiality and idle sensuality, whereas the new middle-class woman was a paragon of frugality and thrift, modesty and sobriety.[27] She was held up as a "powerful icon of stable property" in an unstable economy, according to Tim Dolin, conceived of as a valuable property, but not an owner of property herself.[28] Her responsibility was to control not only her own actions, but the economy of the household. Thus, although she could not own property, the wife was put in charge of seeing that the family did not lose what they owned. This paradoxical situation is easily explained: if a woman's biological difference enabled her to control her own passions and her faithfulness to ensure a genuine son and heir to her husband, then surely she could keep a tight rein on the family's financial resources.

The wife was educated into the performance of this duty through conduct books. As Janet Todd has noted, they "tell us how men wanted women to see the social order and their gendered place in it."[29] The content of these books over the centuries reflected the cultural norms of their times. In the sixteenth and seventeenth centuries, they stressed marriage as the reflection of a divine hierarchy, containing women's potential wickedness within the confines of the family. With the medical revolution of the early eighteenth century, which revealed that there were two sexes instead of one, the content as well as tenor of conduct books changed. Women began to be seen as the paragons of moral judgment, and the books stressed the subjugation of their own desires in favor of the care of husbands and household. By the late eighteenth century, marriage was depicted as the most important thing in a woman's life, whereas it was only one of many pursuits for men.[30] Mary Wollstonecraft laments this inequity in *A Vindication of the Rights of Woman*:

> Men, in their youth, are prepared for professions, and marriage is not considered as the grand feature in their lives; whilst women, on the contrary, have no other scheme to sharpen their faculties. It is not business, extensive plans, or any of the excursive flights of ambition, that engross their attention; no, their thoughts are not employed in rearing such noble structures. To rise in the world, and have the liberty of running from pleasure

> to pleasure, they must marry advantageously, and to this object their time is sacrificed, and their persons often legally prostituted.[31]

This pronouncement was not the language of male-authored conduct books. Thomas Gisborne's *An Inquiry into the Duties of the Female Sex*, written in 1797, was in its eighth edition by 1810. He advised women to improve themselves through reading the Holy Scriptures, biography, history, and poetry, but not romance novels, which were "liable to produce mischievous effects" and "hence the mind is secretly corrupted." What is most interesting about Gisborne's advice is the warning that at all times the woman is being observed: "Let her remember that there is an all-seeing eye, which is ever fixed upon her, even in her closest retirement."[32] His essay "On the Duties of Matrimonial Life" is an extensive guidebook on how a wife should behave with her husband, family, servants, and the public. The married woman has an important influence over the conduct and character of her husband, he writes. The wife who is pious, frugal, and modest is the guardian of her husband's virtue: "She who, at present, appears to regard piety of heart as a matter of secondary importance knows not whether she shall not have to answer at the day of retribution for having betrayed her husband into a neglect of his external welfare."[33] A woman thus has to watch over her husband's morality as well as her own. As a moral and spiritual compass, her behavior can influence his eternal soul. She has been transformed from a creature who is feared for her sexuality into one who can control her passions as well as those of her family.

James Fordyce's popular *Sermons to Young Women*, first published in 1765, became an important text on female conduct. Fordyce stressed the civilizing effect of women's love upon men:

> Honourable love! That great preservative of purity, that powerful softener of the fiercest spirit, that might improver of the rudest carriage, that all-subduing, yet all-exalting principle of the human breast, which humbles the proud, and bends the stubborn, yet fills with lofty conceptions, and animates with a fortitude that nothing can conquer—what shall I say more?—which converts the savage into a man, and lifts the man into a hero![34]

He, too, however, warns women against frivolity and its corrupting influence. It is not only prostitutes, he says, who tempt men; women who are too forward and do not have the proper demeanor are "unspeakably hurtful to young men. Their reverence for female virtue in a great measure destroys; it even tempts them to suspect that the whole is a pretence, that the sex are all of a piece."[35] This continuum of whore and proper lady suggests that with a mere thoughtless glance, a woman can be the ruin of a man. Women's responsibility for men's morality—indeed for their very souls—is itself precarious. This is the underside of the perfect woman: one who can be lost to immorality just as the husband's property can be lost in an increasingly unstable economic world. Both need to be carefully monitored.[36]

Critics of the Marriage Plot I: Frances Burney

The responsibility for cultural stability became situated in the wife. It is no surprise, then, that marriage, and more specifically the marriage plot, becomes an important aspect of the novel. In this device, a young woman moves from her family circle into the world of her husband and from an individual into a couple. The marriage plot, in essence, has an ideological function to move women and their property from father to husband.[37] In English fiction, as Ruth Bernard Yeazell has pointed out, it has the task of equating love and marriage and married love and domestic bliss.[38] British courtship novels, according to Katherine Sobba Green, were written for women, by women, and offered women a choice: a husband should be chosen for love and on no other grounds. This was, she contends, an "ideological shift from arranged to companionate marriage."[39] The courtship novel, Green continues, was an ideal vehicle for middle-class women's values and issues in several ways. First, the "proper lady" was the central focus, whereas male characters were minimized. Second, the reader was brought into domestic settings, traditionally the domain of women. Third, the subject matter, settings, and heroines appealed directly to the middle-class woman reader. Fourth, there was an absence of sexual pursuit scenes. Finally, the courtship novels were didactic, and in this, Green argues, they were not uniform: their views of women's conduct at times replicated male-authored conduct books and at times reflected the feminism that was beginning to question women's traditional roles.[40]

Feminist critics have noted that women writers, although criticizing marriage, had to write this type of fiction because of the demands of the marketplace. Julie Shaffer has argued that within this structure they tried to show their women characters as autonomous rather than subordinate. She identifies two marriage plot conventions, the "lover-mentor," in which male behavior is the standard for female morality, and the "perfect heroine," where the domestic realm becomes the site of morality. This latter case reflects the influence of conduct books, in which women have greater access to moral behavior.[41]

We can see elements of both of these conventions in Frances Burney's *Evelina, or, The History of a Young Lady's Entrance into the World*, published in 1778. Burney herself had narrowly escaped marriage to a man she did not care for in 1775, the year before she wrote *Evelina*. Its writing was, according to Judith Lowder Newton, her way of coming to terms with the experience of the marriage market.[42]

Evelina, a sheltered young woman who has been raised in the country by her guardian, the Rev. Mr. Villars, is introduced to the complexities of life in London. Burney herself describes it in this way:

> A young female, educated in the most secluded retirement, makes, at the age of seventeen, her first appearance upon the great and busy stage of life; with a virtuous mind, a cultivated understanding, and a feeling heart, her ignorance of the forms, and inexperience in the manners, of the world, occasion all the little incidents which these volumes record...[43]

Evelina's father, Sir John Belmont, has not legally recognized her as his daughter, and thus she enters society with only the possibility of "a very moderate fortune" from Mr. Villars, who understands the problems that face Evelina: "this artless young creature, with too much beauty to escape notice, has too much sensibility to be indifferent to it; but she has too little wealth to be sought with propriety by men of the fashionable world" (63–64). Evelina is thus set up as an outsider to the world of the marriage market: she is both innocent and of very modest means, a new set of eyes on the society that is the subject of her letters.

Evelina moves back and forth from the company of London nobility to that of its middle classes, attracting male attention, committing social errors due to her naiveté, and encountering danger and violence. She is a woman without her rightful name, and although called "Miss Anville," Evelina herself cannot accept it. In her first letter to Mr. Villars, she leaves her last name blank, lamenting "I cannot to *you* sign *Anville*, and what other name may I claim?" (69). Nameless and devoid of the protection of social standing, she is thrown into situations in which she is physically violated by men, highlighting the precariousness of the woman without the legitimacy of birth. Evelina also lacks the knowledge of how she is supposed to act; this, too, is a factor in the dangerous situations in which she finds herself.

Throughout the novel, Evelina seeks advice from Mr. Villars in the letters she writes him. He continually cautions her, stressing that she is not suited to the urban life: "Alas, my child, the artlessness of your nature, and the simplicity of your education, alike unfit you for the thorny paths of the great and busy world. The supposed obscurity of your birth and situation, makes you liabile to a thousand disagreeable adventures" (161). He stresses the importance of keeping the appearance of virtue: "You cannot, my love, be too circumspect; the slightest carelessness on your part, will be taken advantage of..." (203). Echoing the language of the conduct book, he advises: "Remember, my dear Evelina, nothing is so delicate as the reputation of a woman; it is, at once, the most beautiful and most brittle of all human things" (206).

It is perhaps too easy to categorize *Evelina* as belonging to the lover-mentor type of marriage plot. In fact, Evelina does not appear to be on the marriage market at all. She dismisses the attention of all of the men who approach her, save Lord Orville, who, knowing her innocence while at the same time wanting to be close to her, asks to become her friend and take on the role of brother. She herself does not think about being in love; it is Mr. Villars who points out to her that she is actually dangerously infatuated with Orville. Believing that it is an impossible match and that she will be hurt, he advises her:

> You must quit him!—his sight is baneful to your repose, his society is death to your future tranquillity!...Could I flatter myself that Lord Orville would, indeed, be sensible of your worth, and act with a nobleness of mind which should prove it reciprocal, then would I leave my Evelina to the unmolested enjoyment of the cheerful society and encreasing regard of a man she greatly admires: but this is not an age in which we may trust to appearances, and imprudence is much sooner regretted than repaired. (343–344)

Evelina's initial compliance with this request provokes a declaration of love from Orville. Her acceptance of his proposal shifts the mentoring relationship from Mr. Villars to him when she uses her own judgment to decide her future. Although it appears that, in doing this, Evelina is following the traditional marriage plot trajectory from the protection of father to husband, Burney uses several devices that critique this outcome.

By allowing Evelina to decide for herself the wisdom of following Mr. Villars' instructions, Burney suggests that she is Shaffer's "perfect heroine" who has moral authority. Evelina shows this ethical character when she befriends the impoverished Mr. Macartney against Orville's advice. As Shaffer points out, if she had heeded Orville's warnings, she would not have been recognized by Sir John as his real daughter.[44] Burney also triangulates the father-daughter relationship: Evelina's birth father has offered no protection, although he now gives her property; Mr. Villars, while giving her advice, is an outsider to London society and gives up his authority (and protection of her) once she leaves his home. There is, in reality, *no* father.

Additionally, by using the epistolary style throughout *Evelina*, Burney can write critically. Julia Epstein has observed, "As a narrative form, letters pretend to spontaneity and absolute sincerity. But they can never be utterly sincere, as no crafted piece of writing can be without artifice."[45] Burney, she believes, uses this technique subversively. Marriage is a conventional ending, but Evelina manages to find some autonomy within it, knowing full well what she has to sacrifice to achieve security.[46] Susan Fraiman also points to the complexities of Burney's intention: "Far from being a *Bildungsroman* simply vanished into sentimental novel, *Evelina* may be a work revealingly at odds with itself, continuing to invoke and value some 'masculine' notion of linear development, even as another geometry of obstructed female development emerges."[47]

Nonetheless, Burney suggests that whatever autonomy Evelina has attained disappears when she marries Orville. Once she attains the legitimacy of her rightful name, Belmont, she gives it up for that of her husband.[48] In marrying Lord Orville, she becomes his property: "'You are now' (said he, in a low voice), 'all my own!'…I could make no reply; indeed I hardly spoke another word the rest of the evening…" (435) As Susan Fraiman has concluded, Evelina is thus silenced.[49] The novel is thus more than Evelina's education in the world: Burney shows that the movement from innocent girl who is always in danger to the protected proper wife is not without sacrifice.

Critics of the Marriage Plot II: Jane Austen

As with *Evelina*, Jane Austen's novels resolve the marriage plot with what appear to be happy endings, while at the same time criticizing the conditions of marriage. Unlike Evelina, whose protected upbringing gives her some distance from the marriage market, Austen's female characters are acutely aware of its importance and ramifications. Evelina *becomes* a woman ready to be married; we encounter Marianne and Elinor Dashwood, and Elizabeth Bennet and her sisters as women who know that marriage is expected of them. The conduct books appear to have done their work in the thirty-odd years between the publication of Burney's work and *Sense and Sensibility* in 1811. In addition, as Claudia L. Johnson has argued, England's reaction to the French Revolution centered on the preservation of the patriarchal family.[50] Women had to be prevented from having personal expectations about marriage:

> With the countryside full of Jacobin riffraff out to ruin English families by seducing women away from fond fathers and rightful husbands, female modesty—that is to say, the extent to which women do not feel, express, and pursue their own desires—is no less than a matter of national security.[51]

In order not to be associated with radical writers such as Mary Wollstonecraft, who was regarded as a Jacobin, women had to write about conservative topics. Although Austen appears to be silent on political matters, continues Johnson, she explored and exposed traditional institutions that were harmful to women.[52]

This might help to explain Austen's focus on the marriage plot in her novels. William H. Magee has noted the development of this device in her works: *Northanger Abbey* and *Sense and Sensibility* use the normal plot conventions; in *Pride and Prejudice* and *Mansfield Park*, the heroines learn from experience and struggle to free themselves from the marriage plot; and in *Emma* and *Persuasion*, women's new experience triumphs.[53] Austen's growing reliance on love in marriage, he argues, stresses women's values.[54]

Charles H. Hinnant has also shown the progression of her work. He identifies seven different models of courtship and romance in her novels. Although she "does not quite manage to escape the homogeneity inherent in the form's insistence upon closure," these models "reveal a far greater uneasiness about the premises of the courtship plot."[55] *Mansfield Park* has a Cinderella plot, *Northanger Abbey* a rescue plot, *Sense and Sensibility* and *Persuasion* involve "a drama of prior commitment," and *Persuasion* "a narrative of lost and rediscovered love." In *Pride and Prejudice* Elizabeth and Darcy have an antagonistic relationship that turns into mutual amity. *Emma*'s lovers are "just friends" and *Sense and Sensibility* has a plot of calculated seduction and betrayal followed by a second relationship.[56] In these, Hinnant believes, there are no real courtship narratives at all, rather a "non-assurance, a risk of misunderstanding is initially supposed." Austen does this so that her characters have "an opportunity to engage in face-to-face interaction without having to deal with the illusions involved in courtship, the opportunity to forge invisible but still very real bonds, the opportunity to become enmeshed in a gradually enveloping web of erotic tension."[57]

In this section, I will look at two of Jane Austen's novels—*Sense and Sensibility* (1811) and *Pride and Prejudice* (1813). The first, I argue, focuses on money as the driving force in the marriage plots. With its clear distinction between women who have property and women who do not, Austen critiques the plight of the economically marginalized female. In *Pride and Prejudice*, she turns to a broader and more nuanced indictment of a social system that places marriage—at all costs—at the center of young women's lives.

Austen populates *Sense and Sensibility* with certain models, almost caricatures, of women. We have the "controlling mother" (Mrs. Smith, Mrs. Ferrars), the "conniving woman" (Lucy), the "selfless woman" (Elinor), the "passionate woman" (Marianne), the "selfish woman" (Mrs. John Dashwood), the "empty woman" (Lady Middleton), and the "helpful widow" (Mrs. Jennings). Each of them is controlled by, or, in some cases, actually controls, money. The men, on the other hand, who ostensibly control the money are often portrayed as weak, subject to the women who control them, whether they be mothers, wives, or fiancées. The fact that major decisions of both men and women are swayed by money indicates Austen's own ambivalence about it: it is not only the marriage market that she is criticizing, it is the marital practices of a certain class that depends upon property to sustain its lifestyle.

Indeed, property and marriage are intricately connected in *Sense and Sensibility*. The plot hinges on the fortunes of the men with whom the Dashwood sisters are involved: Edward Ferrars, whose mother can decide whom he marries (if he wishes to inherit); Willoughby, whose expensive taste makes him marry an heiress whom he does not love; and Colonel Brandon, who steps in and solves both Elinor and Marianne's financial problems.

It is a story in which virtue lies in not needing money. In a highly manipulative dialogue, Elinor and Marianne's sister-in-law, Mrs. John Dashwood, convinces her husband that he need not honor the promise made to his father that he would help his mother and sisters financially. After telling her that he will give them 3,000 pounds, he ends up believing that the 500 pounds a year they already have is enough, without any help from him. His wife says, "Only conceive how comfortable they will be! Five hundred a-year! I am sure I cannot imagine how they will spend half of it; and as to your giving them more, it is quite absurd to think of it. They will be much more able to give *you* something."[58]

Women who are preoccupied with wealth are portrayed as controlling and conniving. Mrs. Ferrars is intent on deciding whom Edward will marry and uses money as a way to get what she wants. Lucy Steele, who is engaged to Edward, leaves him once he has lost his fortune and connives to marry his brother Robert, who has become the heir. Mrs. John Dashwood decides to invite Willoughby, despite his disgrace, to her home because he has married a woman with 50,000 pounds.

Elinor and Marianne, on the other hand, do not allow money to influence their choice of partner. Although one is sensible and the other passionate, both initially choose men regardless of their financial status.

When told that Willoughby has no property of his own, Mrs. Dashwood insists that it does not matter:

> "I do not believe," said Mrs. Dashwood, with a good humoured smile, "that Mr. Willoughby will be incommoded by the attempts of either of *my* daughters towards what you call *catching* him. It is not an employment to which they have been brought up. Men are very safe with us, let them be ever so rich." (29; emphasis in the original)

In the end, Elinor gets her man, but only after he has been rejected by Lucy Steele, to whom he had proposed in a moment of youthful exuberance. Their union is not so much passion as it is companionship; it needs little more than the living at Delaford that Colonel Brandon has given Edward:

> They were brought together by mutual affection, with warmest approbation of their real friends, their intimate knowledge of each other seemed to make their happiness certain—and they only wanted something to live upon. Edward had two thousand pounds, and Elinor one, which, with Delaford living, was all that they could call their own. (252)

Marianne, on the other hand, marries Colonel Brandon by default. Giving up her immature desire for a passionate (but quite possibly fleeting) love, she instead adopts a more mature role as a proper wife:

> Instead of falling a sacrifice to an irresistable passion, as once she had fondly flattered herself with expecting,—instead of remaining even for ever with her mother, and finding her only pleasures in retirement and study, as afterwards in her more calm and sober judgment she had determined on,—she found herself at nineteen, submitting to new attachments, entering on new duties, placed in a new home, a wife, the mistress of a family, and the patroness of a village. (260)

Julie A. Shaffer has called their union "not a reward but more of a punishment."[59] By adopting the "sense" of Elinor, she finds a respectable middle ground, one that is the only possible ending for a woman who has no property of her own and refuses to resort to conniving to find a husband. As Laura Mooneyham White has suggested, the marriages do not enhance the reader's understanding of the central conflicts of the novel.[60] Those conflicts, I would suggest, may be more about money's role in human relationships than about marriage itself. Their unions lack the combination of money and happiness that we would expect from the "happy ending." Marianne has Colonel Brandon's wealth, but not the passion that she once thought she wanted; Elinor is content, but has just enough to live on. In this way, Austen calls attention to the reality that is too often ignored in the marriage plot.

Pride and Prejudice, on the other hand, is a novel about marriage. From the opening maxim, "It is a truth universally acknowledged, that a single man in possession of a good fortune, must be in want of a wife,"[61] Jane Austen challenges contemporary beliefs about marriage. As Karen Newman has pointed out, this sentence poses a disjunction. Neither Darcy nor Bingley, the two men in possession of a fortune, is in obvious want of a wife; it is the young women whose families are in straightened circumstances that are in need of spouses. She notes: "The maxim, then, on which the novel is based does not justify the story; its function is not *vraisemblance* but exposure, for it serves as a continual reminder of the discrepancy or gap between social convention and economic necessity."[62] This discrepancy, I suggest, is highlighted by Elizabeth Bennet's critique of the marriages in *Pride and Prejudice.* That she is the one to make the "best" match at the end only highlights this disjunction. The young woman without property who, like Evelina, does not actively seek marriage, weds a man far above her own station. The most advantageous (and possibly happy) union thus occurs outside of the confines of the marriage market, allowing Austen to criticize the convention but not the institution.

As in marriage novels, the multiple plots revolve around suitability obstacles: the Bennet daughters, although possessing beauty for the most part, have a meddling mother, which only adds to the difficulties arising from their own distressed economic condition. Perceived by the small circle as having neither the social graces seen as admirable nor the financial wherewithal to be appealing, the women face a difficult challenge in the marriage market. These two forces—virtue and property—are central to the plot of *Pride and Prejudice.* The women in the novel use the traditional female virtues of chastity, manners, and beauty as "competitive pieces" in the marriage game, in Nancy Armstrong's words.[63] Austen shows the consequences when these values are transgressed. When Lydia Bennet runs off with Wickham, the fate of her whole family seems to be sealed. The obsequious and moralistic Mr. Collins, in relating his conversation with Lady Catherine and her daughter, exclaims: "They agree with me in apprehending that this false step in one daughter will be injurious to the fortunes of all the others, for who, as lady Catherine herself condescendingly says, will connect themselves with such a family" (225). Indeed, the whole family of women can be tainted by the indiscretions of one of them.

We first see Elizabeth's criticism of the marriage market when she and Charlotte speak about Jane and Mr. Bingley. Charlotte's position suggests that Jane should be speedy in snatching an eligible man; after he has been secured there will be leisure enough for her to fall in love with him. When Charlotte herself decides to marry Mr. Collins, Elizabeth is horrified. Her sister Jane tries to make her see reason: in economic terms, it is a good march for Charlotte. Elizabeth replies:

> For were I persuaded that Charlotte had any regard for him, I should only think worse of her understanding, than I now do of her heart. My dear Jane, Mr. Collins is a conceited, pompous, narrow-minded, silly man; you know he is, as well as I do; and you must feel, as well as I do, that the woman who marries him, cannot have a proper way of thinking. You shall not defend her, though it is Charlotte Lucas. You shall not, for the sake of one individual, change the meaning of principle and integrity, nor endeavour to persuade yourself or me, that selfishness is prudence, and insensibility of danger, security for happiness. (105)

Elizabeth is rejecting more than a hasty marriage for her friend. She is insisting that she simply cannot marry someone as insipid as Mr. Collins for *whatever* reason. One must not marry for the sake of getting married, giving up one's principles in the process.

She also criticizes her parents' marriage. We are told that her father was captivated by her mother's "youth and beauty, and that appearance of good humour, which youth and beauty generally give." Unfortunately he soon realized that "[he] had married a woman whose weak understanding and illiberal mind, had very early in their marriage put an end to all real affection for her. Respect, esteem, and confidence, had vanished for ever; and all his views of domestic happiness were overthrown" (180). By focusing on Mr. Bennet's own mismatch, Austen presents us with the all-too-real results of the marriage market, in which the lure of illusion gives way to the tyranny of reality.

The sole business of Mrs. Bennet's life is to get her daughters married. She settles on the tiresome Mr. Collins for Elizabeth, and when she refuses him, her mother goes on a tirade:

> But I tell you what, Miss Lizzy, if you take it into your head to go on refusing every offer of marriage in this way, you will never get a husband at all—and I am sure I do not know who is to maintain you when your father is dead.—I shall not be able to keep you—and so I warn you—I have done with you from this very day. (87)

By pointing out the economic ramifications of marriage, Austen shows that she clearly understands the cultural expectations of an unwed woman. The sole point of a woman's life is to marry; for Mrs. Bennet, self-respect is wrapped up in snaring a husband. Elizabeth, however, has another definition, one that puts one's own integrity higher than a proposal. This view is voiced by her father: "An unhappy alternative is before you, Elizabeth. From this day you must be a stranger to one of your parents.—Your mother will never see you again if you do *not* marry Mr. Collins, and I will never see you again if you *do*" (85). Mr. Bennet thus takes on an important voice in Austen's critique of the conventions of marriage, a position that is totally the opposite of his wife's. Mrs. Bennet believes that, first and foremost, one must marry for money, an idea that is advocated by most of the characters in the novel. Her father, on the other hand, adopts the one represented by Elizabeth, the idea that she not only has a choice, but that the choice must be based on common interest and affections. Here, he speaks when Elizabeth herself cannot. Again, Austen presents us with a disjunction. Mr. Bennet is hardly the father-mentor of the courtship novel. He is the victim of the marriage market, cannot protect his daughters financially, and although cognizant of Elizabeth's personality is not a good judge of character (he says that his favorite son-in-law is perhaps Wickham, the cad).

Mr. Collins decides that he really doesn't want Elizabeth after all because "if she is really headstrong and foolish, I know not whether she would altogether be a very desirable wife to a man in my situation" (84). Those very traits can be reinterpreted as a sense of independence and integrity and are what attracts Elizabeth to her father; his ideal wife, in fact, probably is actually someone very like her. And, as we discover, these same characteristics are those that attract Darcy.

Throughout the novel, Elizabeth is the one who questions the traditional reasons to marry. A woman does not marry without knowing her spouse. Marrying for money can only lead to unhappiness. Marriage without common interests is disastrous for the family. In choosing Darcy, the dark, brooding counterpart to her own good sense, Elizabeth seems to be the winner among all the women in *Pride and Prejudice*. The woman without economic prospects marries the man with 10,000 pounds a year. In this way, the ending, as Mary Poovey has pointed out, tempts women into believing that the fairy tale will continue even after marriage.[64]

Although Elizabeth and Darcy's marriage might be unrealistic, it certainly appears to be happy well after the ceremony. Her relatives are nearby, and both sides of the family are reconciled. This communal felicity, according to Claudia L. Johnson, is central to *Pride and Prejudice*'s concept of happiness: Elizabeth's marriage to Darcy does not exclude her friendship with her family.[65] The community they create actually valorizes marriage, in the opinion of Julie Shaffer.[66] It is a good marriage precisely because it bypasses the traditional marriage market. The good fortune that comes from rejecting its conventions ties up a family's loose ends. As with Marie de France's *Lanval* and, as we will see, Virginia Woolf's *Orlando*, Austen presents a literary alternative to the debilitative conditions of marriage.

Laura Mooneyham White has speculated that Austen never intended Charlotte Heywood, the heroine of her last and unfinished novel *Sanditon*, to marry. Charlotte does not have, in White's view, a traumatic situation that needs to be reversed.[67] Without the constraints of the marriage plot, Austen could have perhaps envisioned a far different future for Elizabeth, her sisters, and other heroines to come.

Critics of the Marriage Plot III: George Eliot

The marriage plots in *Middlemarch*, written some sixty years after *Pride and Prejudice*, when the call for reform of property laws regarding women was increasing, show both similarities and differences. As in Austen, the novel revolves around couples who overcome obstacles and finally marry. Dorothea Brooke is as headstrong a young woman as Elizabeth Bennet, and, as in *Pride and Prejudice*, the economic circumstances surrounding marriages in the novel are also significant. There are, however, striking differences. Whereas the action in Burney and Austen takes place before marriage, in *Middlemarch* it occurs, for the most part, predominantly after wedlock. The financial obstacles to getting married are replaced by those that arise afterward. Eliot thus focuses more on the plight of the married woman than the woman in search of a husband. Nonetheless, she too questions the social system that governs how and whom young women marry.

Eliot's Prelude sets up Saint Theresa as the model for Dorothea. Theresa's nature is described as "passionate, ideal" and one that "demanded an epic life." But, Eliot explains, this is not a readily obtained goal:

> Many Theresas have been born who found for themselves no epic life wherein there was a constant unfolding of far-resonant action; perhaps only a life of mistakes, the offspring of a certain spiritual grandeur ill-matched with the meanness of opportunity; perhaps a tragic failure which found no sacred poet and sank unwept into oblivion.[68]

She continues:

> These later-born Theresas were helped by no coherent social faith and order which could perform the function of knowledge for the ardently willing soul. Their ardour alternated between a vague ideal and the

> common yearning of womanhood; so that the one was disapproved as extravagance, and the other condemned as a lapse. (1)

In this passage Eliot sets up the novel as the story of a woman with high ideals who is hampered by the circumstances of her own times. This is in radical contrast to Austen's opening, which centers on the want of a marriage. Rather, desire is situated in a lofty ideal that cannot quite be named. Had Eliot not written this Prelude, would we have the same expectations for Dorothea? Once the novel starts, it follows the same marriage plot; it is only with the framing of a desire beyond the ordinary that we see that Eliot has something far different in mind. The characteristics of the perfect woman are not centered in marriage, but rather in service to a higher goal. By using St. Theresa, herself "an emblem of the effective subversion of discourses of femininity," as a model, as Sherry L. Mitchell has noted, Eliot contrasts Dorothea, who is limited in her outlets for accomplishment.[69]

There are three central marriages in *Middlemarch*: Dorothea and Mr. Casaubon, Rosamond Vincy and Mr. Lydgate, and Mary Garth and Fred Vincy.[70] In each, money plays a key role in the dynamics of the relationship. Dorothea is generous where Casaubon is stingy, neither Rosamond nor Lydgate understand what it means to live within their means, and Mary is the reforming angel for Fred's constant state of debt. The different plots of the story revolve around how money both defines and controls.

Dorothea has her own income of 700 pounds a year. Although this makes her highly marriageable, it also presents problems:

> Nothing could hinder it but her love of extremes, and her insistence on regulating life according to notions which might cause a wary man to hesitate before he made her an offer, or even might lead her at last to refuse all offers... Such a wife might awaken you some fine morning with a new scheme for the application of her income which would interfere with political economy and the keeping of saddle-horses: a man would naturally think twice before he risked himself in such fellowship. Women were expected to have weak opinions; but the great safeguard of society and of domestic life was, that opinions were not acted on. (5)

Money makes a woman too independent, which can keep domestic life from functioning smoothly. When Dorothea begins to tell Casaubon in an early conversation her views on agricultural innovation, her uncle is quick to tell him that "young ladies don't understand political economy, you know" (13). For Casaubon, the danger is far greater: he is jealous of the power his cousin Will Ladislaw has over her. In Casaubon's own words:

> In marrying Dorothea Brooke I had to care for her well-being in case of my death. But well-being is not to be secured by ample, independent possession of property; on the contrary, occasions might arise in which such possession might expose her to the more danger. She is ready prey to any man who knows how to play adroitly either on her affectionate ardour or her Quixotic enthusiasm... (401)

Those very traits that Eliot characterizes as the new Theresa are those that Casaubon cites in explaining why independent property is dangerous in Dorothea's hands. In his mistrust of Will, he treats Dorothea as a child who cannot make correct judgments. Because the financial arrangements Casaubon made when he married her "left strong measures open to him" (402), he changes his will to stipulate that she will not inherit any of his property upon his death if she marries Will.

Dorothea, who, it turns out, is actually quite good with property management, sees money as a burden. After Casaubon dies, she is determined to give away her annual income from his estate: "So you see that what I should most rejoice at would be to have something good to do with my money: I should like it to make other people's lives better to them. It makes me very uneasy—coming all to me who don't want it" (728).

When she marries Will, she admits that she doesn't even need all of her own income: "I don't mind about poverty—I hate my wealth" (773). She says to him: "We could live quite well on my own fortune—it is too much—seven hundred a-year—I want so little—no new clothes—and I will learn what everything costs" (774). Even her uncle threatens to cut off her own income if she marries Will: "But I can cut off the entail, you know. It will cost money and be troublesome; but I can do it, you know" (779). Thus was the precarious position of women who had a private income but could not control it themselves. In the end, he does not, but she has nonetheless made a sacrifice perhaps worthy of St. Theresa by renouncing Casaubon's money and sharing what she herself has with Will.

Dorothea married Casaubon because of her yearning for the kind of knowledge that she believed he possessed:

> Those provinces of masculine knowledge seemed to her a standing-ground from which all truth could be seen more truly... And she had not reached that point of renunciation at which she would have been satisfied with having a wise husband; she wished, poor child, to be wise herself. (59)

His work was to compare all of the mythical systems of the world as originally coming from one tradition. Dorothea compares him to Augustine in his attempt to reconcile knowledge and piety (21). When she eventually realizes that he is not the scholar she thought him to be, her doubts come out as a criticism of marriage itself:

> How was it that in the weeks since her marriage, Dorothea had not distinctly observed but felt with a stifling depression, that the large vistas and wide fresh air which she had dreamed of finding in her husband's mind were replaced by ante-rooms and winding passages which seemed to lead nowhither? (186)

Casaubon has tempted Dorothea into thinking she can help him with his masterpiece "The Key to All Mythologies," but he can neither give her a role nor bring the work to completion. The whole project is somehow fraudulent, just as the marriage is. In her naming of Casaubon, Eliot cleverly plays on one of the great exposés of Renaissance philosophy. The Corpus Hermeticum, considered to be the most ancient, primary source of knowledge by the Florentine Neoplatonists, was discovered to have actually been written in the early centuries after Christ. The philologist who exposed this was Isaac Casaubon.[71] The fraud that the original Casaubon exposes becomes the fictional Casaubon's own fraud. The access to knowledge Dorothea had thought would free her instead entraps her. Her marriage, as well as Casaubon's work, is not at all what she had thought it would be. In addition, his intellectual interests situate him in the past: he is an old-fashioned scholar, just as his marriage with Dorothea is old-fashioned.[72]

Eliot demonstrates a different kind of marriage with Rosamond and Lydgate. Rosamond is the opposite of Dorothea. She "had excellent taste in costume," and was held up as an example in Mrs. Lemon's school, which taught "all that was demanded in the accomplished female—even to extras, such as the getting in and out of a carriage" (91). She has the added attraction of possibility coming into rich old Mr. Featherstone's money. Rosamond cares deeply about refinements, but "not about the money that was to pay for them" (112). In short, she is the perfect woman, one "who had just the kind of intelligence one would desire in a woman—polished, refined, docile, lending itself to finish in all the delicacies of life, and enshrined in a body which expressed this with a force of demonstration that excluded the need for other evidence" (152). Her greatest wish was for a husband "whose wealth corresponded to her habits" (158).

Lydgate, however, is just as innocent about money as Rosamond:

> His first impulse was always to be liberal with half-crowns as matters of no importance to a gentleman; it had never occurred to him to devise a plan for getting half-crowns. He had always known in a general way that he

> was not rich, but he had never felt poor, and he had no power of imagining the part which the want of money plays in determining the actions of men. Money had never been a motive to him. (170)

Both Lydgate and Rosamond, then, approached their marriage in a cloud of idealism or even naiveté, thinking that the other was the perfect mate, and totally disregarding how they would finance their tastes for "refinement." Her father's only request when Lydgate asks for Rosamond's hand is that he should insure his life: "This was a delightfully reassuring idea supposing that Lydgate died, but in the meantime not a self-supporting idea. However, it seemed to make everything comfortable about Rosamond's marriage; and the necessary purchases went on with much spirit" (338). Compared to Mr. Bennet's insistence on Elizabeth's happiness, this demand for life insurance seems shallow. Mr. Vincy knows that it will not help one whit in the economics of the marriage. However, it serves the purpose of taking the responsibility for Rosamond off of his shoulders: should Lydgate die, she will have an income of her own.

As one would expect, both Rosamond and Lydate spend without much regard to income and, as a result, are trapped into the very notion of credit and debt that was a source of anxiety to nineteenth-century British writers:

> Eighteen months ago Lydgate was poor, but had never known the eager want of small sums... He was now experiencing something worse than a simple deficit; he was assailed by the vulgar hateful trials of a man who has bought and used a great many things which might have been done without, and which he is unable to pay for, though the demand for payment has become pressing. (559)

As a result, he has to put his furniture up as security for his debts and return both plate and jewelry to the silversmith. Rosamond and Lydgate are saved only by Dorothea's gift to him of an annual income. Again, Eliot connects money and marriage: in this case, the materialistic wife and the man who has no idea how to support her go into debt in order to perpetuate the idea of the perfect marriage.

Eliot sets up the third marriage, that of Fred Vincy and Mary Garth, as the ideal middle-class relationship. Fred, who thought he too might inherit from Mr. Featherstone, "has raised money on his expectations" (100). He, like Lydgate, is innocent about money, always expecting that debt would somehow take care of itself:

> When Fred got into debt, it always seemed to him highly probable that something or other—he did not necessarily conceive what—would come

> to pass enabling him to pay in due time. And now that the providential occurrence was apparently close at hand, it would have been sheer absurdity to think that the supply would be short of the need: as absurd as a faith that believed in half a miracle for want of strength to believe in a whole one. (126)

The whole Vincy family lived in such a way that "the children had no standard of economy, and the elder ones retained some of their infantine notion that their father might pay for anything if he would" (217). Mrs. Vincy looked down on Mary's mother, Mrs. Garth, speaking of her "as a woman had had to work for her bread" (219). Indeed, she is the solid, middle-class housewife, who, having been a teacher, was both frugal in her household habits and stern in her instruction to her children. Mary also has some of these attributes, and refuses to marry Fred because of his debts. He eventually acquits himself with her, and they go on to "achieve a solid mutual happiness": Fred works hard and successfully at farming, Mary writes a children's book, they have three sons, and Middlemarchers attribute Fred's turnaround to Mary. In this marriage, money is carefully managed in a solid, middle-class kind of way.

In a novel in which money controls relationships, Eliot seemingly ties up all of the loose strings at the end. Everyone finds a marriage that is both satisfying yet limiting to some degree. Lydgate dies prematurely and leaves Rosamond with a substantial insurance policy; she later marries an elderly, wealthy man who can fulfill her economic expectations. Mary and Fred have limited economic needs and are happy in their simple life. They succeed, as Margaret Homans has pointed out, because they have such moderate expectations.[73] Dorothea marries Will and bears a son, but perhaps gives up something in return: "Many who knew her, thought it a pity that so substantive and rare a creature should have been absorbed into the life of another, and be only known in a certain circle as a wife and mother" (797). J. Hillis Miller has described her love for Will as much an error as was her marriage to Casaubon; by submitting herself to the will of another she never is shown making her own way in the world. The ending, he argues, leaves us wondering whether it is a good choice.[74] Both Dorothea and Rosamond, Jenni Calder surmises, have husbands who demand absolute authority. As a result, the women find no satisfaction in marriages that put them in a secondary position.[75] Eliot, she concludes, "does not commit herself fully to the energies and aspirations she lets loose in these women."[76]

At the very end, Eliot returns to St. Theresa. Has Dorothea managed to become the new Theresa? The times are gone, she says, when this might have happened: "But we insignificant people with our daily words and acts are preparing the lives of many Dorotheas, some of which may present a far sadder sacrifice than those of the Dorothea whose story we know" (799). What indeed was her sacrifice? Was it Casaubon's money that she forsook for love? Could she have done great things with it? Perhaps, but Eliot reminds us at the end that it is not the epic deeds that change the world:

> But the effect of her being on those around her was incalculably diffusive: for the growing good of the world is partly dependent on unhistoric acts; and that things are not so ill with you and me as they might have been, is half owing to the number who lived faithfully a hidden life, and rest in unvisited tombs.

The "determining acts" of Dorothea's life "were not ideally beautiful. They were the mixed result of young and noble impulse struggling amid the conditions of an imperfect social state, in which great feelings will often take the aspect of error, and great faith the aspect of illusion" (798–799).

By placing Dorothea in a society in which women could not control their own property, Eliot limits the extent to which she can fulfill her aspirations. Had she been able to do what she really wanted—"found a village which should be a school of industry"—perhaps we would have a different ending. But her uncle and Sir James convince her that the risk would be too great, and she gives up her dream. Dorothea's independent income is thus not totally in her own control, nor does she have the benefits of a widow's portion due to her disregard of Casaubon's wishes. Will goes on to advocate reforms in Parliament, and Dorothea "liked nothing better…that she should give him wifely help" (797). Her identity thus is merged with another's through marriage, and she is deprived of any possibility of achievement on her own, except for her own "unhistoric acts."

Burney, Austen, and Eliot each criticized the conditions of marriage prevalent in a society where women could not own property when married, yet often married precisely because they were without property. Without access to money of their own, their female characters do not have any options that are not fraught with danger and insecurity. Nonetheless, they find ways to give their heroines agency within the confines of the marriage plot. Evelina rejects other suitors for Lord Orville, Elizabeth refuses Mr. Collins, Dorothea chooses Will over an inheritance. How does this intervention change after the passage of the Married Women's Property Act? In the next chapter I will focus on the nonfiction and fiction of Virginia Woolf, who, while arguing for women's economic rights, cannot translate that into empowerment for her heroines.

CHAPTER 6

VIRGINIA WOOLF'S WOMEN, TRAPPED AND FREED

"Why are women poor?" asks Virginia Woolf in *A Room of One's Own*.[1] Among the reasons she cites is the fact that "in the first place, to earn money was impossible for them, and in the second, had it been possible, the law denied them the right to possess what money they earned" (23). When Woolf published this book in 1929, the Married Women's Property Act was nearly fifty years old, the professions had been opened to women for ten years, and they had been given the vote nine years previously. As she herself notes, "the excuse of lack of opportunity, training, encouragement, leisure and money no longer holds good" for women's advancement (117).

This chapter examines the disparity in the portrayal of women's poverty between two of Woolf's nonfiction pieces, *A Room of One's Own* and *Three Guineas*, and two of her novels, *Mrs. Dalloway* and *Orlando*. In a sense, it turns her question back to her: Why, Virginia, do your female characters, who have the right to work, vote, and own money in their own name, fail to control their property? Why do you not create strong women who agree with the positions you put forth in your nonfiction works?

As David Dowling has noted, Woolf criticism falls into three distinct categories: stylistic, sociopsychological, and feminist.[2] My own approach, although owing a great debt to feminist literary scholarship over the last twenty-plus years, modifies it by looking at historical and economic questions that Woolf herself raises and the way she appropriates economic metaphors and imagery in her discourses on marriage. As I will show, her nonfiction is both rooted in history and yet subversive in the way it portrays the future as an egalitarian society; her fiction challenges linear notions of time and is yet deeply dependent upon historical events. This interplay, I believe, is the key to understanding why there is such a wide discrepancy in what she believes *should be* and what *actually is.* In regard to women and property, Woolf argues that although things have changed they have actually stayed the same. Thus, in her nonfiction she can argue for women's right to work and own property, while at the same time she can portray her fictional female characters as utterly lacking in the capabilities to carry out this agenda. As Naomi Black has argued, laws do not necessarily change behavior: "entitlement does not mean acquisition."[3] Indeed, it takes many decades to see significant changes, both from a personal and cultural perspective. Clearly, Woolf did not see the full and desired results of legislative action in her own time.

Instead of empowering her women characters, she shows them as outsiders to the masculine world of power and money, a true reflection of their status in early twentieth-century England. As she discusses women in literature in *A Room of One's Own*, she criticizes the way male authors have idealized the female heroine:

> Imaginatively she is of the highest importance. She pervades poetry from cover to cover; she is all but absent from history. She dominates the lives of kings and conquerors in fiction; in fact she was the slave of any boy whose parents placed a ring upon her finger. Some of the most profound thoughts in literature fall from her lips; in real life she could hardly read, could scarcely spell, and was the property of her husband. (45–46)

In order to redress this discrepancy, Woolf uses nonfiction to critique the past and envision the ideal future. Fiction takes on the role of reflecting women's reality.

"A novel," she writes "has this correspondence to real life, its values are to some extent those of real life" (76). Through her portrayal of fictional women, Woolf demonstrates that history still has a tight hold on their economic freedom. In a very deep sense, the legal changes for women and their property have made no discernable difference. It is this gap that Woolf portrays in her novels.

The Curse of the Past, the Vision of the Future

A Room of One's Own was first presented as a series of lectures that Woolf gave at Newnham and Girton Colleges at Cambridge in 1928. At the very beginning, she recounts how she is an outsider at Oxbridge, unable even to tread on the grass at one of the men's colleges, let alone enter the library. As she ruminates on the difference between the endowed men's colleges and the sparsely funded ones for women, she realizes that sociohistorical conditions have precluded women from making the fortunes necessary to support female education. Not only were they not allowed university access until the previous century, childbearing continues to consume women's time. "For, to endow a college," she writes, "would necessitate the suppression of families altogether. Making a fortune and bearing thirteen children—no human could stand it" (22). Although this seems a radical conclusion—as so many of her statements appear to be—it carries with it the force of her argument: women have not only been locked out of institutions and employment, they have also been locked in to family obligations. This metaphor suggests imprisonment, an isolation of the mind as well as an inability to move outside of the confines of history. Woolf uses economic terms to describe this situation:

> I pondered why it was that Mrs. Seton had no money to leave us; and what effect poverty has on the mind; and what effect wealth has on the mind...and I thought how unpleasant it is to be locked out; and I thought how worse perhaps to be locked in; and, thinking of the safety and prosperity of the one sex and of the poverty and insecurity of the other and of the effect of tradition and of the lack of tradition upon the mind of a writer, I thought at last that it was time to roll up the crumpled skin of the day...(24)

Woolf extends the metaphor connecting learning and money to her description of the British Museum. After calling London "a machine," she describes the venerable institution as "another department of the factory" and then lists the steps that must be taken to obtain a book from its Reading Room. She transforms the pursuit of knowledge from a rarified occupation into any other job, full of strict, bureaucratic procedures. And like other professions, it is dominated by men. In looking through the catalogue, Woolf discovers that there are far more books written about women by men than she had originally thought. Her conclusion:

> The most transient visitor to this planet, I thought, who picked up this paper could not fail to be aware, even from this scattered testimony, that England is under the rule of a patriarchy. Nobody in their senses could fail to detect the dominance of the professor. He was the power and the money and the influence. (33–34)

Woolf insists here that economic forces, in the guise of the professor, control even the knowledge we have of women. Furthermore, this knowledge derives from a masculine need to control and to feel superior. She reasons:

> Rich people, for example, are often angry because they suspect that the poor want to seize their wealth. The professors, or patriarchs, as it might be more accurate to call them, might be angry for that reason partly, but partly for one that lies a little less obviously on the surface. (34)

If women become self-confident, she concludes, then a man would lose "his power to believe in himself" (35). The female "looking-glass," which, Woolf contends, allows men to appear twice their size, is so important to the male ego that without it "man may die, like the drug fiend deprived of his cocaine" (36).

Without educational opportunity and financial resources, women writers have been unable to tell their own stories. Woolf therefore firmly believes that having money is more important to women than the vote. Having inherited 500 pounds from her aunt, she recognizes the psychological freedom it gave her: "No force in the world can take from me my five hundred pounds. Food, house and clothing are mine for ever. Therefore not merely do effort and labour cease, but also hatred and bitterness. I need not flatter any man; he has nothing to give me" (38).

She further instructs her readers that it is even better to *earn* five hundred pounds a year. This became possible for women writers because of Aphra Behn, "who earned them the right to speak their minds" (69). But not all women have been smart about their intellectual property. Showing a sophisticated understanding about publishing, she chides Charlotte Bronte because "the foolish woman sold the copyright of her novels outright for fifteen hundred pounds." Although this was a large amount at the time, Woolf is more concerned that Bronte gave up an annual income for a lump sum (73). Woolf declares that "five hundred a year stands for the power to contemplate" (110). She continues:

> Intellectual freedom depends upon material things. Poetry depends upon intellectual freedom. And women have always been poor, not for two hundred years merely, but from the beginning of time. Women have had less intellectual freedom than the sons of Athenian slaves. Women, then, have not had a dog's chance of writing poetry. That is why I have laid so much stress on money and a room of one's own. (112)

At the very end of *A Room of One's Own*, Woolf challenges women to limit the number of children they bear and go out and earn money. There is no longer any excuse, she writes, now that there are female colleges and women can possess their own property, vote, and have access to the professions (116–117). Woolf does not question whether women can *psychologically* do this in *A Room of One's Own*. Except for references to the Married Women's Property Act and having children, the idea of marriage is strangely absent. In this work, as well as in *Three Guineas*, women are plucked from their familial role and given the space to dream about an alternative life. The failure to confront marriage in this text, I believe, is her way of constructing a world in which anything is possible. In *Three Guineas*, written nearly a decade later, this other world is even more powerful and her psychological insight even deeper.

At the very beginning of *Three Guineas* Woolf relates a question that was posed to her, "How in your opinion are we to prevent war?" While attempting to answer this ("even if it is doomed to failure"), she situates her discussion within the larger context of women's rights.[4] She begins by demurring that because she is a woman, her answer may not have any value: "Scarcely a human being in the course of history has fallen to a woman's rifle ... it is difficult to judge what we do not share" (6). Furthermore, the "daughters of educated men" are at a distinct disadvantage in influencing the discussion, since "our class is the weakest of all the classes in the state. We have no weapon with which to enforce our will" (13). Considering how long it took for women to win the vote, she concludes, "influence has to be combined with wealth in order to be effective as a political weapon, and that influence of the kind that can be exerted by the daughters of educated men is very low in power, very slow in action, and very painful in use" (14).

Woolf turns her antiwar argument into a feminist one. While stressing that women do not go to war, at the same time she calls for women to arm—not with rifles, but with political and financial resources. Until recently, women have not had access to the professions, she contends. Instead, there has only been one option, marriage, "the one great profession open to our class since the dawn of time until the year 1919" (6). By gaining the ability to work, women no longer need to depend upon men—husbands or fathers—for money. With this comes a great personal independence:

> She need no longer use her charm to procure money from her father or brother. Since it is beyond the power of her family to punish her financially she can express her own opinions. In place of the admirations and antipathies which were often unconsciously dictated by the need of money she can declare her genuine likes and dislikes. In short, she need not acquiesce; she can criticize. (17)

But history, for Woolf, still influences the status of women. In 1938, when *Three Guineas* was published, women had only been able to attend university for some sixty years. Although the Married Women's Property

Act was passed in 1883, she maintains that women still do not have access to property. She says of men:

> Your class possesses in its own right and not through marriage practically all the capital, all the land, all the valuables, and all the patronage in England. Our class possesses in its own right and not through marriage practically none of the capital, none of the land, none of the valuables, and none of the patronage in England. (18)

This, she concludes, has made the female body, brain, and spirit vastly different from men's: "Though we see the same world, we see it through different eyes" (18).

Even with the professions open to women, Woolf describes how women do not get hired for these jobs. They have not been prepared for university examinations or for the Civil Service Examination. In the end, it all comes down to gender: "At any rate since Miss is a woman, Miss was not educated at Eton or Christchurch. Since Miss is a woman, Miss is not a son or a nephew" (50). Hence "Miss" does not get the same employment opportunities.

Woolf also criticizes how women's work is treated within the home. After determining that in marriage husband and wife are supposedly one flesh and one purse, she argues that the wife is entitled to a half-share of the family income. However, this share is not paid into her hands, but into her husband's (55). Further, once household expenses are paid, she does not have access to half of the surplus fund:

> And yet by far the greater part of this sum is spent upon pleasures which she does not share. She lays out thousands and thousands of pounds upon clubs to which her sex is not admitted; upon racecourses where she may not ride; upon colleges from which her own sex is excluded. She pays a huge bill annually for wine which she does not drink and for cigars which she does not smoke. In short, there are only two conclusions to which we can come about the educated man's wife—the first is that she is the most altruistic of beings who prefers to spend her share of the common fund upon his pleasures and causes; the second, and more probable, if less creditable, is not that she is the most altruistic of beings, but that her spiritual right to a share of half her husband's income peters out in practice to an actual right to board, lodging and a small annual allowance for pocket money and dress. (56)

Woolf concludes that the only way women can have access to money is through working in the professions. If rich women were as common as rich men, she asks, "what could you not do?" (68). This question sets up what Naomi Black has called "a deeply radical sort" of feminism in *Three Guineas*, one that "has a vision of a society completely changed."[5] Woolf not only laments women's position in this work, she sets up an alternative reality that is dictated by the "Outsiders' Society," which consists of *working*, educated men's daughters who have their own methods to achieve "liberty, equality and peace" (106). In this new order, there would be no idea of nationalism and hence no desire to impose a dominant civilization upon another. Women would have a living wage in existing and new professions, and a salary would be paid to wives and mothers, which would assure their emotional independence:

> It is the most effective way in which we can ensure that the large and very honourable class of married women shall have a mind and a will of their own, with which, if his mind and will are good in her eyes, to support her husband, if bad to resist him, in any case to cease to be "his woman" and to be her self. (110)

Woolf thus posits a new society that can only be achieved through the efforts of those who have been enslaved themselves. As outsiders, she believes, women are free from "unreal loyalties" and "interested motives." The ends, however, are the same as those of society at large; the Society of Outsiders wants freedom, peace, and equality, but it differs in that "it seeks to achieve them by the means that a different sex, a different tradition, a different education, and the different values which result from those differences have placed within our reach." As Rachel Bowlby has described this group, there are "more possibilities for forms of activity or reasoning ruled out a priori for those who have to maintain the proprieties of the insider group."[6] Free from any agenda, then, the Society of Outsiders can transform the world order. Even the word "feminist" must be abolished from this new society. It is an old name, Woolf declares, that, along with the "emancipation of women," is "futile and false." They simply do not express "real emotions" (137). This is not, however, a rejection of feminist values; it is, as Naomi Black has noted, an emphasis on larger societal goals instead of individual rights.[7]

In *Three Guineas* Woolf situates the primary male-female relationship in that of father and daughter. Using psychoanalytic language, she names this an "infantile fixation." Citing numerous examples of fathers who would not allow their daughters to marry, she contends that it is because they want to continue to control them: "He wished to keep his daughter in his own power. If she took money from him she remained in his power; if she took it from another man not only was she becoming independent of Mr. Jex-Blake, she was becoming dependent upon another man" (132). The fathers in private, she continues, eventually gave this idea up, but the fathers in public seized upon it even more virulently. The drive to support the family was connected "with manhood itself," and then spread to the scholar protecting his university from the admission of women, the government supporting the policy of giving work only to men, and beyond (138–141). This, Woolf contends, is how private fear has been connected with public fear, "the fear which has led you to ask us to help you to prevent war" (142). By tying war into feminism, Woolf has answered the question: if one wants to transform the bellicose nature of society at large, it must begin with changing women's opportunities.

I also believe that she has answered here her own question: "Why are women poor?" *Three Guineas* is a work that delves so deeply into the reasons why a simple change in laws, important that it may be, cannot immediately transform societal practice. The Society of Outsiders enables a radical change, one in which patriarchy no longer has the upper hand. The fathers are, in effect, emasculated, and have no power over daughters. And yet, for all of its utopian vision, it is a picture that Woolf knew was not the reality of women's lives in early twentieth-century England. It is in her novels that she unequivocally demonstrates their economic entrapment, and that is where we now turn.

The Reality and the Fantasy

Naomi Black, in *Virginia Woolf as Feminist*, contends that Woolf's emphasis on form and medium overpower everything else in her fiction and thus do not truly represent her ideas. "Novels are, in fact," she writes, "the least appropriate source for someone seeking to delineate a writer's belief system."[8] This idea that Woolf's form works to the detriment of ideas is a narrow perspective. Although I agree that Woolf argues forcefully about the history of women's oppression in her nonfiction, I suggest that her novels exhibit her belief that change is not yet possible. After reading *A Room of One's Own* and *Three Guineas*, we expect to see her narratives full of these transformed female characters who, in owning their own property, also have ownership over themselves. It is thus somewhat unnerving to find women whose economic situation is similar to that of a nineteenth-century novel in which marriage controls money. Woolf, I believe, does this deliberately in an effort to show how historical change needs more than legal reform. In *Mrs. Dalloway*, she, like so many other women writers before her, presents marriage as a trap. *Orlando*, on the other hand, is more fairy tale than "fictionalized biography," as it is sometimes called.[9] In both these works of fiction, Woolf expresses her ideas about women's reality every bit as succinctly as in her nonfiction.

Mrs. Dalloway is, quite clearly, a novel about marriage. Woolf presents a continuum of female experience from the yet-to-be married young woman (Elizabeth) to wives (Clarissa, Rezia Warren Smith, Sally Seton), to the widow (Lady Bruton), and, finally, to the unmarried women (Miss Kilman and Ellie Henderson). Woolf drops us into the middle of their lives, and instead of writing a linear marriage plot, we never see the courtships of the married women except in flashbacks that do not so much explain as describe. It is as if she is telling us that women simply find themselves married, married without contemplation or choice. The unmarried women are similarly powerless, swept along by forces that they cannot control

Clarissa is the subject of two parallel marriage plots. *Mrs. Dalloway* begins and ends with Peter Walsh, the man whom Clarissa does not marry. Indeed, her musings on Peter take up more space in the novel than her thoughts on Richard Dalloway, which are remarkably few. She questions whether she made the right choice in marrying the solid Richard instead of the emotional Peter:

> So she would find herself arguing in St. James Park, still making out that she had been right—and she had too—not to marry him. For in marriage a little license, a little independence there must be between people living together day in day out in the same house; which Richard gave her, and she him. (Where was he this morning for instance? Some committee, she never asked what.) But with Peter everything had to be shared; everything gone into. And it was intolerable, and when it came to that scene in the little garden by the fountain, she had to break with him or they would have been destroyed, both of them ruined, she was convinced; though she had borne about with her for years like an arrow sticking in her heart the grief, the anguish; and then the horror of the moment when some one told her at a concert that he had married a woman met on the boat going to India![10]

Here Woolf opposes the emotional distance Clarissa has with Richard, illustrated by an interjection, almost an aside, in parentheses, with a painful, vividly described memory of what she felt over a sustained period about Peter ("an arrow sticking in her heart") and "the horror" when she found out he was married. She is singularly uninterested in Richard's professional life ("some committee, she never asked what"), whereas with Peter everything is shared. Denise Delorey has described how Clarissa is "emotionally unencumbered by intense feelings of identification" with both her husband and daughter and is thus released from the "consumptive passions of marriage and motherhood."[11] True enough, but by allowing Clarissa to continue to muse on Peter throughout the novel, Woolf keeps this alternative relationship alive. As Elizabeth Abel has remarked, Clarissa continues to replay her choice throughout *Mrs. Dalloway*. The romantic plot is thirty years in the past, but it is yet to be resolved.[12] She is by no means sure: one minute she thinks "thank Heaven she had refused to marry him!" and the next, "all in a clap it came over her, If I had married him, this gaiety would have been mine all day" (45–46). She does not actually remember why she did not marry Peter: "Now of course, thought Clarissa, he's enchanting! Perfectly enchanting! Now I remember how impossible it was ever to make up my mind—and why did I make up my mind—not to marry him? She wondered, that awful summer." This sentence, which is grammatically so broken up, makes her decision even more inconclusive. As Lisa Coughlin McGarry has noted, Woolf uses such interruptions to demonstrate how language cannot express human thoughts, and, consequently, human relationships are unfulfilling because they cannot be expressed in words.[13] Yet it is more than that: Clarissa's inability to understand in the present continues her past inability to understand. She really has no idea why she married Richard.

Clarissa is the proper English wife, as Emily Blair has pointed out. She is the powerful woman who, through her parties, indirectly influences the political and moral world of England.[14] She has, in Peter's words "that extraordinary gift, that woman's gift, of making a world of her own wherever she happened to be" (74). She is a role rather than a person, a woman whose job it is to create a harmonious household. Thus it is hard to see her marriage to Richard as a choice. What, really, do we know about Richard and Clarissa's courtship? Very little, as it turns out. He appears for lunch at Bourton, her family's country house, and, for Peter, their marriage becomes a foregone conclusion:

> For of course it was that afternoon, that very afternoon, that Dalloway had come over; and Clarissa called him "Wickham"; that was the beginning of it all. Someone had brought him over; and Clarissa got his name wrong. She introduced him to everybody as Wickham. At last he said "My name is Dalloway!"—that was his first view of Richard—a fair young man, rather awkward, sitting on a deck-chair, and blurting out "My name is Dalloway!" Sally got hold of it; always after that she called him "My name is Dalloway!" He was a prey to revelations at the time. This one—that she would marry Dalloway—was blinding—overwhelming at the moment. There was a sort of—how could he put it?—a sort of ease in her manner to him; something maternal; something gentle. (60)

The very fact that our first view of Richard comes through the mind of Peter—and secondarily of Sally—distances Clarissa from Richard even more. She doesn't quite get his name right, he appears awkward, she takes on a maternal manner with him—all of these describe a marriage that is more arranged than it is emotional. Peter himself gives us an indication of why such a marriage would work for Clarissa. She is, he concludes, self-contained: "That was the devilish part of her—this coldness, this woodenness, something very profound in her, which he had felt again this morning talking to her; an inpenetrability" (59).

Clarissa is not cold, however, with her old friend Sally Seton. With her she is carefree, emotional. She remembers:

> The strange thing, on looking back, was the purity, the integrity, of her feeling for Sally. It was not like one's feeling for a man. It was completely disinterested, and besides, it had a quality which could only exist between women, between women just grown up. It as protective, on her side; sprang from a sense of being in league together, a presentiment of something that was bound to part them (they spoke of marriage always as a catastrophe), which led to this chivalry, this protective feeling which was much more on her side than Sally's. For in those days she was completely reckless; did the most idiotic things out of bravado; bicycled round the parapet on the terrace; smoked cigar. Absurd, she was—very absurd. (33)

The night that Sally kissed her was, for Clarissa, "the most exquisite moment of her whole life":

> Sally stopped; picked a flower; kissed her on the lips. The whole world might have turned upside down! The others disappeared; there she was alone with Sally. And she felt that she had been given a present, wrapped up, and told just to keep it, not to look at it—a diamond, something infinitely precious, wrapped up, which, as they walked (up and down, up and down), she uncovered, or the radiance burnt through, the revelation, the religious feeling! (35)

Although one can easily read in allusions to Woolf's own sexuality here, it is, I believe, more important to contrast the intense feeling she had with a woman to the institution of marriage. This action takes place at the time before she is free to be her own person ("women just grown up") and before her relationship to a man takes center stage in her life. Both Clarissa and Sally understand that marriage ("a catastrophe") will break their emotional tie. Yet, in this moment of innocence, Clarissa experiences a passion that, although fleeting, is retained these many years later. It is a gift, a diamond no less, that provokes a religious experience. She does not feel this for anyone else, not Richard, not Peter, and not even Elizabeth.

Sally, as well, has gone through her transformations. Clarissa is somewhat horrified at her fate. She was always afraid that Sally would meet with some terrible tragedy due to her unbridled vitality. Instead, "she had married, quite unexpectedly, a bald man with a large buttonhole who owned, it was said, cotton mills at Manchester. And she had five boys!" (177). Sally knows that Clarissa is critical of her for marrying down and having so many children. ("'Now all that Clarissa had escaped, unmaternal as she was,' thinks Peter") (186). Sally, in this respect, is the very opposite of her old friend. Clarissa's marriage is sedate, passionless, and proper, whereas Sally's is sudden, fecund, and less than appropriate ("a bald man with a large buttonhole").

In other ways, however, Sally has also capitulated to a supporting role in her marriage. She had always been poor, "without a penny to her name, and a father or a mother gambling at Monte Carlo" (72). Now, with her marriage, she proudly declares that not only does she have an enormous house, but also a substantial income of her own. However, as if the Married Women's Property Act had had no effect, Sally doesn't really control her own money: "'Yes, I have ten thousand a year'—whether before the tax was paid or after, she couldn't remember, for her husband, 'whom you must meet,' she said, 'whom you would like,' she said, did all that for her" (183). We have no idea of Clarissa's personal wealth; all we see is the way she manages the household. This omission is significant: we don't know if she owns property, or if her husband, like Sally's, controls it. More likely, the talk about money is not a part of Clarissa's domestic life.

It is not only Sally who is a counterpoise to Clarissa. David Dowling has noted that Woolf originally intended Clarissa to kill herself, but instead uses Septimus Smith as a double.[15] The Smith's marriage is as chaotic as the Dalloway's is ordered. Whereas Clarissa feels only joy after her romantic encounter with Sally, Septimus has great guilt about his homosexual relationship with Evans. Each marriage, however, feels loveless and is part of a caretaking arrangement. Clarissa takes care of Richard's house and social life, and Rezia is both nurse and babysitter to her psychologically fragile husband. Septimus cannot feel, even in his panic; Clarissa cannot feel in her perfect self-control.

Woolf uses the Smith's marriage to illustrate the catastrophic potential of marriage. Even Rezia understands that it represents loss: "Every one gives up something when they marry. She had given up her home. She had come to live here, in this awful city" (64). Rezia gets precious little in return, she realizes when they cross the street. His arm represents all that she will get from him in the marriage: "She had a right to his arm, though it was without feeling. He would give her, who was so simple, so impulsive, only twenty-four, without friends in England, who had left Italy for his sake, a piece of bone" (16). Rezia is a stranger in a foreign land, and Septimus is a stranger to himself. As much as Clarissa is the perfect hostess who belongs in the thick of London's social and political life, she too is alienated from her spouse. After her illness, Richard insists that she sleep alone so that he will not disturb her. Her attic room, so like a monk's cell with its narrow bed, represents her own alienation from him. She knows that she has failed him: "She could see what she lacked. It was not beauty; it was not mind. It was something central which permeated; something warm which broke up surfaces and rippled the cold contact of man and woman, or of women together" (31). Thus, both Septimus and Clarissa are frigid, impotent in their relationships with those closest to them. His suicide, which intrudes upon the dinner party, at first infuriates her. "What business," she thinks, "had the Bradshaws to talk of death at her party?" (179). This question is followed, however, by her realization that it is a solution to alienation: "Death was defiance. Death was an attempt to communicate; people feeling the impossibility of reaching the centre which, mystically, evaded them; closeness drew apart; rapture faded, one was alone. There was an embrace in death" (180). The single women in *Mrs. Dalloway* are alienated in a different way. On the one hand we have Ellie Henderson, the older cousin whom Clarissa is pressured to invite to her party. She sits on the sidelines at the Dalloway gathering, ignored by all, because, in her eyes, she does not have money:

> though now, past fifty, there was beginning to shine through some mild beam, something purified into distinction by years of self-abnegation but obscured again, perpetually, by her distressing gentility, her panic fear, which arose from three hundred pounds' income, and her weaponless state (she could not earn a penny) and it made her timid, and more and more disqualified year by year to meet well-dressed people who did this sort of thing every night of the season... (165)

Ellie Henderson does not have the "weapons" to work. Miss Kilman, Elizabeth's tutor, on the other hand, does. Although she is a vocal supporter of women's right to employment, Woolf caricatures Miss Kilman. She has a university degree and supports herself. Woolf puts her own words in Miss Kilman's mouth ("all professions are open to women of your generation" she says to Elizabeth), but has extremely harsh things to say about her. She calls her "nauseating" (115) and "one of those spectres with which one battles in the night; one of those spectres who stand astride us and suck up half our life-blood" (12). It is even more troubling that Woolf herself saw Miss Kilman, as well as the widowed Lady Bruton, as "infected with masculinity."[16] Clarissa does not like Lady Bruton who "had the reputation of being more interested in politics than people; of talking like a man… " (103). Miss Kilman is poor, and although Lady Bruton has money, she has none of the self-confidence that goes with it. Rather, she defers to men on important matters:

> Lady Bruton often suspended judgement upon men in deference to the mysterious accord in which they, but no woman, stood to the laws of the universe; knew how to put things; knew what was said; so that if Richard advised her, and Hugh wrote for her, she was sure of being somehow right. (107)

Miss Kilman sees herself as an outsider because of her own financial state and class:

> She was poor, moreover; degradingly poor. Otherwise she would not be taking jobs from people like the Dalloways; from rich people, who liked to be kind. Mr. Dalloway, to do him justice, had been kind. But Mrs. Dalloway had not. She had been merely condescending.She came from the most worthless of all classes—the rich, with a smattering of culture. (120)

The cause of this tension between Clarissa and Miss Kilman is Elizabeth. Woolf sets the distant mother against the loving teacher, the woman who represents marriage and society against the single, working female. Each one is jealous of the other, and the battle between the two alternatives—marriage or work—gets played out through Elizabeth. Clarissa is annoyed when her daughter goes off shopping with Miss Kilman, who in turn feels she has lost when Elizabeth returns home to attend the dinner party ("She had gone. Mrs. Dalloway had triumphed") (130).

Under the influence of Miss Kilman, Elizabeth thinks she perhaps might like to work:

> In short, she would like to have a profession. She would become a doctor, a farmer, possibly go into Parliament…But she was, of course, rather lazy. And it was much better to say nothing about it. It seemed so silly. It was the sort of thing that did sometimes happen, when one was alone…(133–134)

Clearly, Woolf does not allow Elizabeth Dalloway to choose one of the professions. Instead, her vacillation and ultimate realization that she is lazy and the whole idea is rather silly undermines the argument about women's need to work that Woolf later develops in *Three Guineas*. Instead, we are to believe, she will marry. Miss Kilman, and with her, the independent woman, decidedly lose.

But does Clarissa win? Twice in the text Woolf tells us how Elizabeth is poised to follow her mother's footsteps, once from her own perspective and once from Clarissa's. As Elizabeth waits for an omnibus after leaving Miss Gilman, she muses: "And already, even as she stood there, in her very well cut clothes, it was beginning... People were beginning to compare her to poplar trees, early dawn, hyacinths, fawns, running water, and garden lilies... " (131). Her thoughts then run into her mother's:

> Every man fell in love with her, and she was really awfully bored. For it was beginning. Her mother could see that—the compliments were beginning. That she did not care more about it—for instance for her clothes—sometimes worried Clarissa, but perhaps it was as well with all those puppies and guinea pigs about having distemper, and it gave her a charm. (132)

By merging Elizabeth's thoughts into Clarissa's, all of the talk about having a profession disappears. The puppies and guinea pigs that she would have to deal with, if she became a veterinarian, those small animals that belong to well-to-do people, are trivialized. It was indeed beginning; the daughter becomes the mother. At the end of the party, it is Elizabeth, not Clarissa, who stands with Mr. Dalloway as people leave. He is overcome by her beauty and presence:

> For her father had been looking at here, as he stood talking to the Bradshaws, and he had thought to himself, Who is that lovely girl? And suddenly he realised that it was his Elizabeth, and he had not recognized her, she looked so lovely in her pink frock... Richard was proud of his daughter. And he had not meant to tell her, but he could not help telling her. He had looked at her, he said, and he had wondered, Who is that lovely girl? and it was his daughter. That did make her happy. (189)

Just as Elizabeth's thoughts about her future flowed into Clarissa's, so her father's flow into her own. She has effectively rejected being a working woman and chosen marriage.

Woolf does, however, have a final say. Elizabeth's next thought is, "But her poor dog was howling." She cares more for Grizzle than for anything else in the world and would rather be in the country with him than at her mother's dinner party. Grizzle's crying vocalizes Woolf's own feelings about Elizabeth's inevitable end. And just as Elizabeth stands in for her father and thus accepts her future role as wife, Clarissa in the very end is with Peter. Instead of following Sally out when the party is over, he continues to sit. "What is this terror? What is this ecstasy? He thought to himself. What is it that fills me with extraordinary excitement? It is Clarissa, he said. For there she was" (190). Of the two courtship plots in *Mrs. Dalloway*, it is Clarissa and Peter's, the one that does not end in marriage, that triumphs.

Orlando, published in 1928, the same year as *A Room of One's Own*, is a fictionalized biography of an androgynous character who, over the course of three and a half centuries, ages only twenty years. Unlike *Mrs. Dalloway*, whose action takes place in a single day, *Orlando* is epic in scope, traversing not only time but also space.[17] Christy L. Burns has called it both a "parody" (for its emphasis on fashion and cross-dressing) and a "spoof" (by highlighting a man-turned-woman instead of "great men"). This, she notes, displaces truth and is a "negotiation of Victorian mores and modernist experimentation that results in a double mirror, a parodic displacement of any essential and 'true' position."[18] Valid as this argument may be from a structural perspective, I contend that Virginia Woolf had a very important goal in this work: to give a history of women's property rights and to effect an ending in which that property can be reclaimed.

Orlando is dedicated to Vita Sackville-West, Woolf's sometime lover. Nigel Nicolson, Sackville-West's son, reveals that Orlando was modeled after his mother and was intended to show that human nature is androgynous. Woolf had another goal, he contends—to create a history that would give Vita the property she could not rightfully inherit: "Virginia also determined to identify Vita with Knole forever, in compensation for losing it... she could not inherit the house, which she had loved as profoundly as she had loved her father. It passed, with the Sackville title, to her uncle Charles. *Orlando* would be her consolation."[19] The very way that Woolf sets up the book as biography attests to this notion. Throughout, she draws attention to the problems that confront a biographer. (The book even has an index.) Playing on the idea that fiction inserts a creative license into a narrative, she writes: "Happy the mother who bears, happier still the biographer who records the life of such a one! Never need she vex herself, nor he invoke the help of novelist or poet."[20] Furthermore, Woolf discusses the process of collecting historical data and the importance of relating what truly happened:

> The biographer is now faced with a difficulty which it is better perhaps to confess than to gloss over. Up to this point in telling the story of Orlando' life, documents, both private and historical, have made it possible to fulfill the first duty of a biographer, which is to plod, without looking to right or left, in the indelible footprints of truth; unenticed by flowers; regardless of

> shade; on and on methodically till we fall plump into the grave and write *finis* on the tombstone above our heads. But now we come to an episode which lies right across our path, so that there is no ignoring it. Yet it is dark, mysterious, and undocumented; so that there is no explaining it. Volumes might be written in interpretation of it; whole religious systems founded upon the signification of it. Our simple duty is to state the facts as far as they are known, and so let the reader make of them what he may. (46)

Woolf describes the wonderful thing that may happen to a biographer—a sudden gift of evidence that changes historical interpretation. But she insists that it is not her job to show its significance, only to report the facts. Although the facts in this instance may be utterly fantastic ("dark, mysterious and undocumented"), the biographer cannot discount them.

Manuscript damage in another section makes research more difficult. Revolutionary forces set fire to the Record Office and parts of important papers are lost. Nevertheless, Woolf the biographer takes on the task: "We have done our best to piece out a meagre summary from the charred fragments that remain; but often it has been necessary to speculate, to surmise, and even to use the imagination" (84). The scholar must simply plod on, meticulously recording all the days and years of her subject's life. After a full year's chronicling, Woolf admits that it can produce boring results:

> This method of writing biography, though it has its merits, is a little bare, perhaps, and the reader, if we go on with it, may complain that he could recite the calendar for himself and so save his pocket whatever sum the Hogarth Press may think proper to charge for this book. But what can the biographer do when his subject has put him in the predicament which Orlando has now put us? (188)

Tongue-in-cheek? Parody? Yes, perhaps. But it is also Virginia's way of proving to Vita that her loss of the family estate is part of a wider history of women's property rights and that the process of change moves imperceptibly slowly.

The property dispute central to this work is set in motion when Queen Elizabeth I gives Orlando's father a great monastic house. This happens after she has met, kissed, and become enamored with the male Orlando, whom she calls to her side in Whitehall two years later. The childless queen "adopts" him and bequeaths him valuable property:

> For the old woman loved him. And the Queen, who knew a man when she saw one, though not, it is said, in the usual way, plotted for him a splendid ambitious career. Lands were given him, houses assigned him. He

> was to be the son of her old age; the limb of her informity; the oak tree on which she leant her degradation. (18)

Orlando gets the property because he is male: the Queen "knows" a man, he is to be her "son." Armed with land and status, Orlando ponders marriage. Of three possible candidates, the Lady Margaret, whom he calls Euphrosyne, is the most serious contender. She comes from an old Irish family, but possesses other characteristics that "would have made a perfect wife for such a nobleman":

> She was fair, florid, and a triple phlegmatic. She spoke Italian well, had a perfect set of teeth in the upper jaw, though those on the lower were slightly discoloured. She was never without a whippet or spaniel at her knee; fed them with white bread from her own plate; sang sweetly to the virginals; and was never dressed before midday owing to the extreme care she took of her person. (23)

There is nothing in these superficial traits that speak to the heart of the poet Orlando. The marriage has all the markings of a business transaction; indeed, "the lawyers on both sides were busy with covenants, jointures, settlements, messuages, tenements, and whatever is needed before one great fortune can mate with another" (23). Woolf knows her history well: in the Elizabethan era, the function of marriage was to ally great families, not to unite two people in love.

Before this wedding can take place, however, Orlando falls in love with a mysterious Russian princess, who, like many characters in this work, appears at first glance to be androgynous. He sees "a figure, which, whether boy's or woman's, for the loose tunic and trousers of the Russian fashion served to disguise the sex..." He finds this person extraordinarily seductive and surmises that it must be a boy "for alas, a boy it must be—no woman could skate with such speed and vigour." Orlando is vexed because "all embraces were out of the question" with someone of his own sex, but then he realizes that the stranger is a woman (26). With her masculine traits, the Princess Sasha is the exact opposite of the Lady Margaret, a more fitting companion to the passionate Orlando.

Still engaged, Orlando spends all of his time with Sasha, and in the process grows from boy to man: "In one night he had thrown off his boyish clumsiness; he was changed from a sulky stripling, who could not enter a ladies' room without sweeping half the ornaments from the table, to a nobleman, full of grace and manly courtesy" (29). With this transformation, he loses his sense of responsibility to his bloodline: instead of marrying the perfect wife, he decides to run away with the mysterious

Sasha, of whose family he knows nothing. Orlando completely understands the ramifications of this act: "Her kinsmen would abuse him for deserting a great lady; his friends would deride him for ruining the finest career in the world for a Cossack woman... " (35). Woolf here inverts responsibility: as Orlando matures, he becomes less concerned with perpetuating the family name and estate.

Although Sasha suddenly disappears and Orlando is exiled from court for his disgraceful behavior toward Lady Margaret, as a propertied man he is able to withdraw to his country house and write books. After the Sasha debacle, Orlando feels no pressure to marry. He reckons his accounts, promises to pay an obnoxious writer an annual pension of 300 pounds (a nice twist on *A Room of One's Own*), and spends half of his fortune refurbishing his grand manor. When Orlando does marry, Woolf presents it as an act that is totally out of context, but one that changes him forever. We learn about it through his secretaries, who discover a marriage deed between Orlando and a dancer, Rosina Pepita. The only witness to this relationship is a washerwoman who relates that she saw a woman drawn up onto Orlando's balcony the previous night. Woolf thus contrasts the dynastic marriage with Lady Margaret that required ponderous legal arrangements to an inappropriate, spontaneous marriage effected through a deed that is written on the spot. Like Clarissa Dalloway, who does not know why she married Richard, Orlando is similarly in the dark: he sleeps through the entire episode.

As if to highlight that woman's lot changes radically once she marries, Woolf transforms Orlando into a woman once he wakes up. All of a sudden Orlando, the woman, cannot own Orlando's, the man's, property. Woolf is quick to point out that it is only his body, not his identity, that has changed:

> Orlando had become a woman—there is no denying it. But in every other respect, Orlando remained precisely as he had been. The change of sex, though it altered their future, did nothing to alter their identity...It is enough for us to state the simple fact: Orlando was a man till the age of thirty; when he became a woman and has remained so ever since. (97–98)

Why, then, should ownership of property matter when the two sexes (as unified in Orlando) are essentially the same? Woolf pursues this question as Orlando makes the transition from male to female, first living among the gypsies as a female dressed in male clothing and then returning to England dressed as a proper Englishwoman.

Orlando, back upon her native soil and in gender-appropriate attire, suddenly realizes what it is like to be a woman. She sees the situation first from an economic perspective, but quickly chooses to relinquish money and power for love:

> "Better is it," she thought, "to be clothed with poverty and ignorance, which are the dark garments of the female sex; better to leave the rule and discipline of the world to others; better to be quit of martial ambition, the love of power, and all the other manly desires if so one can more fully enjoy the most exalted raptures known to the human spirit, which are," she said aloud, as her habit was when deeply moved, "contemplation, solitude, love." (113)

After this giddy realization, coupled with the knowledge that as a woman she can still love a woman, the economic realities of her change of gender confront her. However, no sooner does she return to London than she is faced with three major law suits. They are:

> (1) that she was dead, and therefore could not hold any property whatsoever;
> (2) that she was a woman, which amount to much the same thing;
> (3) that she was an English Duke who had married one Rosina Pepita, a dancer; and had had by her three sons, which sons now declaring that their father was deceased, claimed that all his property descended to them. (118)

While these suits are being resolved, all of Orlando's property is to be held in abeyance, although she can live at her country house "in a state of incognito or incognita" (119).

Although the female Orlando is the same person as the male Orlando was—indeed, her house staff shows no suspicion that she is any different—in the instant that her gender changes, she is at risk of losing all of her property rights. Woolf uses legal language to convey this situation and links being a woman to being dead. Orlando becomes a nonperson in the eyes of the law until the suits are resolved.

In the years it takes for the property issues to be settled, Orlando plays with her gender identity. She dresses as both male and female, depending on the situation, since "clothes are but a symbol of something hid deep beneath" (133). She even dons a lawyer's gown to go to court to hear how her cases are doing. As Rachel Bowlby has noted, Orlando's strategy is to adopt whichever gender is more advantageous in any given situation.[21] As the nineteenth century begins, women's dress does as well, and Orlando is vexed by the introduction of the crinoline, which to her symbolizes the tenor of the age: "But the spirit of the nineteenth century was antipathetic to her in the extreme, and thus it took her and broke her, and she was aware of her defeat at its hands as she had never been before." She had "submissively adopted" the crinoline, which was "heavier and more drab than any dress she had yet worn." It "impeded her movements" and, as a result, she suffered psychological damage as well:

> She became nervous lest there should be robbers behind the wainscot and afraid, for the first time in her life, of ghosts in the corridors. All these things inclined her, step by step, to submit to the new discovery, whether Queen Victoria's or another's, that each man and each woman has another allotted to it for life, whom it supports, by whom it is supported, till death do them part. It would be a comfort, she felt, to lean; to sit down; yes, to lie down; never, never, never to get up again. (172–173)

In short, as Christy L. Burns has noted, the Victorian Age has forced Orlando into marriage.[22] Just as she is bemoaning her fate, she meets Marmaduke Bonthrop Shelmerdine, Esquire, and falls passionately in love with him. Luckily, both of them are androgynous: they each have the suspicion that the other is the opposite sex. As they investigate this thought, they reach a conclusion: "It was to each such a revelation that a woman could be as tolerant and free-spoken as a man, and a man as strange and subtle as a woman" (182).

With this realization, Woolf tempers the marriage issue for Orlando: Although she and Shelmerdine marry, she is not forced into the terrible dependency that she feared. He is away at sea often, and she muses whether she is indeed really wed:

> She was married, true; but if one's husband was always sailing round Cape Horn, was it marriage? If one liked him, was it marriage? If one liked other people, was it marriage? And finally, if one still wished, more than anything in the whole world, to write poetry, was it marriage? (187)

When Orlando discovers that she can still write, she understands that in spite of marriage, in spite of the spirit of the nineteenth century, she is still herself. "Now, therefore, she could write, and write she did. She wrote. She wrote. She wrote" (188). Writing, not marriage, triumphs.

Orlando's property suits get settled as well. Pepita's children's suit is dismissed, she is pronounced female, and in essence, she gets her property back, although she is now much poorer because of the litigation costs. With this fairy-tale ending, Vita Sackville-West symbolically gets Knole. And fairy tale it is, not biography and not even biographical fiction, for

Woolf gives women economic freedom, the ability to write, the choice of which gender to love, and the stability of marriage without its constraints. It can be argued that both Virginia and Vita, because of their social standing, had all of these in their own lives, but Woolf understood full well that history precluded the vast majority of women from realizing their independence from the patriarchal family and all that it stood for. With all her privilege, however, what Vita could not have was Knole. Woolf recognized that the bonds of history could not be broken simply by a legal change. The vast historical sweep of *Orlando* demonstrates that it takes centuries for women to own what is rightfully theirs. Like Marie de France's wives, freedom can come only in fantasy, for fantasy transcends history. Woolf ends *Orlando* in the present day, thus grounding the fairy tale in a definite date and time: "And the twelfth stroke of midnight sounded; the twelfth stroke of midnight, Thursday, the eleventh of October, Nineteen Hundred and Twenty-eight" (232). In that precise second, the androgynous Orlando is reunited with her androgynous husband and history is ended, thus holding out the possibility for the change Woolf envisioned in the Society of Outsiders.

CHAPTER 7

MID-NINETEENTH-CENTURY RUSSIA: WOMEN WRITERS REJECT THE MARRIAGE PLOT

The Russian critic Maria Tsebrikova, writing in 1884, noted that she was often asked on her travels "how it is that Russia, which by no means occupies the foremost rank in European civilization, is first in this matter of women's emancipation?" "No country in the Old World," she explains, "can vie with Russia in this respect."[1] Tsebrikova contends that because primogeniture never took hold in Russia, women were able to own property in their own right: "We have had no feudal aristocracy which made women slaves and victims to the dynastic interests of the family." Although she concedes that a Russian woman is under the full power of her husband, he does not control her dowry, she contends, "for she is the absolute mistress of her own fortune."[2]

Tsebrikova's observations highlight the differences between the history of women and property in Russia and Western Europe. As I argued in chapter one, the establishment of primogeniture in the eleventh and twelfth centuries played a major role in limiting women's ability to own property. This fact, combined with the church's increasing control of marriage, male misogynistic writings, and the rise of the cult of the Virgin Mary, forced women into both an economic and psychological dependency on their husbands. The two writers I examined in chapter two, Heloise and Marie de France, challenge this marginalization in their critiques of marriage.

In this chapter I test my hypothesis that the ability to own property impacts the way that women write about marriage. The question to which we will consistently return is exactly the same as Tsebrikova's: Why was Russia different? Is the economic reality of women's property rights solely responsible for this? After surveying the history of women's ownership in Russia, I will examine the mid-century debate on the

"Woman Question" and analyze Fedor Dostoevsky's complex depiction of women in order to show how the negative qualities of money become associated with femaleness and create a new Mary/Eve dichotomy that is distinctly Russian. Finally, I look at three mid-nineteenth-century Russian women writers who present decidedly different female heroines, women who are firmly in control of their own fortunes and for whom marriage is not a desired state.

The History of Women's Property Rights

At the same time that women were being excluded from inheritance in medieval Europe, in Russia they were gaining the right to acquire and own land. As Eve Levin has explained, in *Russkaia Pravda*, the concordance of Russian princely law, women could legally own both real and moveable property. It did not distinguish between male and female in property matters. A woman had the same rights as a man would have under similar circumstances, and her property was legally distinct from her husband's. Property was divided into ancestral land (*otchina*), which the clan owned and could not be sold without the agreement of all family members, male and female alike, and newly purchased land (*kuplia*), which could be sold, donated, or bestowed without anyone else's consent. This restriction was also true of movable goods, such as money, clothing, and slaves.[3] In the *chastnye akty* ("private acts") of the fourteenth and fifteenth centuries, women had the same rights as men. They could gain control of property through mortgage and purchase land themselves. Often, however, male relatives played a part, albeit secondary, in land deals.[4] In the inheritance of *otchina*, a wife had no claims and was only guaranteed such property (*chast'*) that her husband settled on her before his death.[5] The Novgorod birchbark documents dating from the eleventh to the fifteenth century that Levin examines show that women took a very active role in the acquisition, disposal, and inheritance of property. In addition, in many cases, widows inherited use of the *otchina*. They could control this property indefinitely, although they could not dispose of it without the permission of all heirs. Unlike the situation later in Muscovy, widows did not receive a fixed portion of his property, but rather were entitled to its entire use.[6]

In Russian law, although the right to dispose of property was strictly limited by the rights of other heirs, this was true for both men and women.[7] As William G. Wagner has shown, the principle of imperial property inheritance law connected immovable property to the kin-group, the *rod*. It could only be bequeathed to direct heirs. Moveable property was considered "acquired property," which the owner could dispose of at will while he or she was alive. If that property became inherited, it became ancestral or patrimonial property unless it was later acquired by nonkin, at which point it would become "acquired" again.[8]

This double tiered categorization of property, ancestral and acquired, was complicated in the fifteenth century by the creation of *pomest'e*, the service estate, which could be held only for the lifetime of the recipient and could not be inherited or sold.[9] Because most of the country's wealth was in land and production was predominantly agricultural, the state used land to support military servitors.[10] In essence, the *pomest'e* curtailed women's right to own property, since women were not in military service. Thus, in 1562 Ivan IV imposed a law prohibiting the passing of hereditary estates to daughters or sisters either by dowry or will. It had the effect of keeping property within the clan so as to support military families. This law, however, was revoked after Ivan's death. Some of women's rights were reinstated in 1627 and then restored almost completely to pre-1562 levels in the *Ulozhenie* of 1649.[11]

In 1714 Peter the Great attempted to impose unigeniture, that is, inheritance by only one child, as a way to prevent estate fragmentation and force younger sons into service. As Michelle Lamarche Marresse has noted, he was not successful: "Russia's devotion to partible inheritance is legendary: inevitably, after centuries of dividing land equally among their sons, bequeathing estates intact to a solitary heir appeared as rank injustice to the service elite."[12] Under Peter's Law of Single Inheritance, daughters could inherit property if there were no sons, but there could be no immovable (real) property in dowries. Women could purchase land with dowry money, however. In addition, a widow received one-fourth of her husband's property as well as the dowry and land she purchased or inherited during her marriage.[13] Nonetheless, this law caused a significant number of disputes involving noblewomen: 57.5 percent of all suits in the Land College involved litigants of both sexes and another 9 percent came from women alone. This began the custom of women appealing to the courts in property disputes.[14]

Empress Anna revoked Peter's law in 1731 as one of her first acts and restored partible inheritance. A widow now received one-seventh of her husband's immovable property, which was less than in the Law of Single Inheritance, but she could freely bequeath, mortgage, or sell it. This presumed, as Marresse has pointed out, "a certain degree of confidence in female administration of property."[15] Daughters received one-fourteenth of landed and one-eighth of movable property, as before the Law of Single Inheritance.[16] This was certainly not an equal share of the estate, but it represented a legal minimum that a woman would receive, a right that her Western counterpart did not have.

Anna's repeal clearly set out the right of all sons to inherit, but was not clear about daughters, especially on the issue of dowries. The ensuing debate involved the question of whether the dowry represented an advance on inheritance or whether daughters who accepted it relinquished their claims on the family fortune. It took decades of debate and legal action before the question was resolved in favor of dowried women's right to inherit.[17] In practice, nobles were often generous to daughters, but there was no legal recourse for women who received less than what their unmarried sisters got for a maintenance portion.[18] The digest of Russian laws (*Svod zakanov*) of 1830 confirmed married women's right to one-fourteenth of the immovable estate: it specified that dowered women could be excluded from inheritance only if they signed away their right to inherit.[19]

In short, as Marresse suggests, during the eighteenth century, through debate, legal action, as well as legislation, Russian noblewomen achieved a significant gain: their inheritance rights became an entitlement (*ukaznaia chast'*), a share of their parents' estates, which was fixed by law. Previously, they had only received a maintenance portion (*prozhitok*), which was often used solely to support their husbands' military service.[20] This entitlement, of course, was in addition to whatever property women themselves owned. By the second half of the eighteenth century, women were established landholders: they owned as much as a third of the estates held in private hands, as well as substantial numbers of serfs and holdings of urban real estate.[21]

Religious and Social Concepts of Marriage

The control that women had over property, however, was paradoxical, since within the family, women were expected to show complete subservience to their husbands. In Imperial Russia, both the state and the church believed that the family was a metaphor for political authority and social organization.[22] The Digest of Laws divided gender roles into the public and socioeconomic (male) and the domestic (female) spheres.[23] Without permission from her husband, a wife could not work, study, trade, or travel.[24] The *Domostroi*, rules for households written in the sixteenth century, had as its precept, "a place for everything, and everything in its place... Everyday details became symbols of one's moral state, bringing concomitant rewards or punishments."[25] In the *Domostroi*, women were generally seen as good. Feminine virtues were industry, competence, firmness, fairness, and initiative. Woman's sins were gossip, secrecy, and tolerance of sorcery.[26] In reading its chapters, one is struck by its moderate tone in discussing women. Chapter 29, for example, has this instruction:

> A wife should ask her husband every day about matters of piety, so she will know how to save her soul, please her husband, and structure her house well. She must obey her husband in everything. Whatever her husband orders, she must accept with love; she must fulfill his every command. Above all, she must fear God and keep her chastity as decreed above.[27]

It is interesting that three things (saving her soul, pleasing her husband, and structuring her household well) are connected. All are based on ideas of hierarchy, in reverse order of importance: if she runs a competent household this will please her husband and assure her a place in heaven. Furthermore, in the *Domostroi* her relationship with her children is not emotional or spiritual, but material: she must provide a well-run home and accumulate a dowry for her daughters.[28] The dowry, at least in part, was therefore the mother's responsibility.

As in Western Europe, clerical writers identified women with sin, especially sexual temptation. In the "Parable of Feminine Evil," John Chrysostom called them "insinuating, cunning, stealthy, slanderers, ensnarers, heretics, wolverines, serpents, scorpions, vipers."[29] Because women were thought to have no natural intelligence, it was believed that they resorted to supernatural intelligence, that is, witchcraft.[30] An eighteenth-century sermon asked the question, "What is a woman like on earth?" Answer: "A slanderer of saints, a serpent's resting place, the Devil's consolation, an incurable sickness, a treasure that inflames, a temptation for the saved, an incalculable evil, a whore by day, an inn where one cannot rest, the Devil's accomplice."[31]

Dorothy Atkinson has posited that the Russian male's fear of women may have come from the pagan Slavs' worship of the goddess Lada, the source of the female power of sexual attraction.[32] Although in primitive societies the fire that the goddess gave to women was associated with sunshine, by the Middle Ages it became connected to hellfire. "The only good woman," she explains, "was the desexualized female: the elderly saint, or the virgin." This resulted in the institution of the terem in the thirteenth century.[33] The terem, according to Stites, was a separate quarter whose purpose was not only to protect women, but also to contain the filth that came from their sexual organs. The belief that sexuality was evil was so profound, he notes, that during intercourse, icons had to be covered.[34]

In some ways, this physical exclusion of women, enclosing them in their own space, would seem to be a worse fate than the experience of

Western European women in the same time period. On the one hand, Russian women were able to own property and thus were part of the economic mainstream. On the other, they were marginalized by both religious and social norms. This situation changed with Peter the Great's reforms. In the attempt to Europeanize Russia, he invited women and men together to social functions. This began the "de-isolation" of women as they took on French customs and the free thinking and flirtation of the salon.[35] Women became, as Engel calls them, the "arbiters of taste." Literary language, she claims, became femininized and the measure of cultural superiority. With the rise of Sentimentalism in the late eighteenth and early nineteenth centuries, women became seen as "vessels of emotion" and models of virtue and moral education.[36]

During the 1850s, critics of imperial family law began to argue that patriarchal authority was incompatible with the idea of mutual affection between family members. Sentimentalism and Romanticism had revised legal attitudes about women. They became viewed as equally worthy rather than as the source of sin and temptation.[37] In actuality, the law in Russia had always been seen as a means to order society and secondary to its intended end. As a result, laws were disregarded when necessary.[38] This conflict was complicated in family law because ecclesiastical authorities often interfered with the rule of law.[39] Ecclesiastical courts had jurisdiction over marriage. Women of all classes had access to official divorce, for example, but they rarely initiated actions in the ecclesiastical courts. For the peasantry, especially, marriages were seen as private contracts; divorce and bigamy were often resolved with church knowledge and interference.[40] This was simply another example of how theory and practice diverged in Russian legal history.

The debate on the affective nature of marriage had a religious history as well as a legal one. Orthodox writers had a contradictory position on marriage. The husband was seen as the preeminent authority in the relationship in order to keep the family order, but husband and wife were seen as "voluntary partners who comforted one another, who helped each other control base passions and strive for moral perfection, and who played equally worthy and important family roles."[41] This affective ideal predominated after the 1870s, rather than the patriarchal view. It argued that women should share in equal inheritance in order to keep them from marrying for convenience and hence possible abusive treatment by their husbands.[42] The Civil Cassation Department, which heard legal complaints, began to stress the ideal of the affective family. It strictly enforced the statutory right of a married woman to own property, defended a wife's interests against a husband's creditors, and affirmed the power of a wife to dispose of her own property.[43]

As Marresse has argued, women's property rights during this period were part of a larger trend toward the privileging of individual over family interests. Gender, she argues, was not the concern in terms of property ownership; it was the right of the individual. In Western Europe, unlike Russia, legislators believed that "property relations should mirror the hierarchical relationship of husband and wife and . . . separate property violated the very essence of marriage."[44] Why, again, did this not become the norm in Russia? Certainly, the religious and political assumptions were the same: women were inferior to men. Marriage was expected of women, as exemplified in the Russian saying "*Ne zhenat, ne chelovek*" ("not married, not human").[45] As in the West, it was an economic arrangement, in which husbands were chosen for daughters, who, after their weddings, went to live in the houses of their husbands' families. Emotional intimacy between a husband and a wife was not the norm; rather, mothers and daughters were the closest emotional ties.[46]

Engel argues that one of the reasons for Russia's uniqueness is that it did not develop a middle class, as in most of Western Europe. Therefore, unlike the early stages of Western capitalism in which husband and wife worked side by side, there was no partnership between spouses. Because women could own property, marriage did not automatically establish community property. Motherhood, as well, was different. In noble families, others took care of the children. The mother's responsibility was to marry off her daughter, and it was at this stage that mothers and daughters became close.[47]

Joanna Hubbs offers another explanation. In her book, *Mother Russia: The Feminine Myth in Russia Culture*, she explains how ancient female divinity worship in Russia was kept alive both by peasant as well as noble women. Alongside the patriarchal culture of woman as Eve the temptress, Russians believed in Eve as the omnipotent goddess fallen from her once high status, as evidenced in such popular spiritual verses as "Dukovnye stikhi."[48] Even in Orthodoxy, Mary was not seen as the opposite to Eve (as in Western Europe): the church did not accept the idea of the Immaculate Conception, but rather believed in the full humanity of Christ, with which it was difficult to reconcile Mary's virginity. The Greek "Theotokos," literally, "god-bearer," was the designation of the Virgin Mary as the Mother of God. The Nestorians, who stressed the independence of the divine and human natures in Christ, opposed its use on the grounds that it compromised the human nature of Christ. They believed "Christotokos" ("Christ-bearer") was the more proper term. The Council of Ephesus in 431 concluded, however, that Mary truly was the Mother of God.[49] As Hubbs explains that in the Russian version, "Bogoroditsa," the connection of Mary with God was stressed: "More weight was placed upon Mary than on her son, the God-Child. In fact, the Russian Mother of God is not merely the vessel for the Lord; she is the universal mother and mistress of all things."[50]

This belief in a strong feminine figure, whose humanity comes from her own capabilities rather than those of her son and whose positive qualities are emphasized, is another difference from the way Mary was viewed in Western Europe. Along with other factors, such as the rejection of unigeniture, it helps explain why women never lost their property rights in Russia.

The "Woman Question"

The "Woman Question" was first posed by Nikolai Pirogov (1810–1881), the surgeon who initiated the idea of sending nurses to the front in the Crimean War. His essay "Questions of Life," written in 1856, while pointing out women's talents for raising a family, stressed the need for improvements in their education.[51] The first serious discussion of the issue was by M. L. Mikhailov, who wrote a series of articles between 1859 and 1865. Mikhailov refuted the antifeminist arguments of the Frenchmen Proudhon and Michelet, who believed that women's physiological characteristics make them inferior. Mikhailov argued that women's socialization and lack of education were the problem. Marriage, he continued, should be based on equal education and status. In all of his writings, however, there was no mention of political rights for women.[52]

The emphasis of the "Woman Question" was, at first, on education. Between 1764 and 1858, there were only a few secondary schools for gentry girls. In places such as the Smolny Institute, run by both the government and private individuals, female students learned to read and write, but their education, on the whole, was not intellectual.[53] As Tsebrikova writes of her own time, the 1880s: "The instruction is superficial, and the scholars go forth entirely unprepared for real life."[54] In the 1850s Alexander II approved of secondary schools for girls of all classes, the *gimnaziia* and the *progimnaziia*. Tsebrikova calls these intermediate girls' schools "far from perfect," since the curriculum (Russian, French, German, arithmetic, rudimentary science) "falls far short of what is needed for entrance into the university."[55]

The "Woman Question" was not, however, limited to education, and, in fact, took many different paths after its initial discourse. Barbara Alpern Engel delineates three different approaches to the topic in mid-nineteenth-century Russia. The first group wanted to liberalize the family and expand women's public role, but within politically acceptable limits. The second group was comprised of more radical women, the nihilists, who believed that women needed to liberate themselves from "family despotism." Some of these argued that the family itself should be abolished. The third group focused on political and social change rather than individual transformation. The more radical of these views eventually triumphed. Ultimately, the "Woman Question" was set aside in order to pursue revolution.[56] Even the educational component of the movement was challenged. Conservatives saw this as a threat to the social order and succeeded in banning women from universities in 1863 and excluding them from state service in 1871. By the late 1870s, however, these laws were reversed.[57]

Richard Stites has argued that the debate about women's emancipation was carried out almost exclusively by men in the 1860s.[58] The sentimental ideal of woman was challenged by an emphasis on equality between the sexes. Arja Rosenholm has noted that the three books of that period presenting women in the context of the questions of the time, Turgenev's *Fathers and Sons* and *On the Eve*, as well as Chernyshevsky's *What Is To Be Done?*, show women's emancipation through male eyes.[59] Although these three reflect a changing attitude toward women, I contend that their prime goal is still seen as marriage, liberated though their ideas may be.

What Is To Be Done?, in particular, was seen as the rallying cry around women's oppression. The main female character, Vera Pavlovna, seeks economic independence for all women, as well as sexual freedom for herself. All of the characters inevitably move toward a more rational approach to marriage. When Vera Pavlovna falls in love with her husband's friend, Kirsanov, we are led to believe that the husband kills himself so that she can be with the one she truly loves. After hearing arguments from various sources on why the suicide was a logical act, Vera Pavlovna comes to the conclusion that her love for Lopukov, her husband, was not the love of a mature woman. His feeling for her "было соединением очень сильной привязанности ко мне как другу с минутными порывами страсти ко мне как женщине" ("was a combination of very strong attachment to me as a friend, with fleeting bursts of passion towards me as a woman").[60] Her husband's suicide thus is rationalized and justified as a selfless act, allowing Vera Pavlovna to be fulfilled through a passionate love.[61]

The idealistic view that love among equals is a never-ending honeymoon is based, paradoxically, on a rational approach to the relationship. Both Vera Pavlovna and her new husband have a strict privacy policy and division of rooms in their residence. She proclaims, "пока женщины не станут стараться о том, чтоб разойтись на много дорог, они не будут иметь самостоятельности" ("until women strive to branch out in different ways, they'll never enjoy independence") (632,347). She is a financial equal; she starts a sewing collective, in which she selflessly shares the profits with her workers. In the end, however, *What Is To Be Done?* is based on the marriage plot. Although it is a new kind of marriage, one based on equality, the novel essentially is about women finding love through the right marriage. In a subplot, another young woman, Katerina Vasilyevna, rejects an unequal suitor and marries the ideal man for her, who happens to be Vera Pavlovna's "dead" husband. The two couples, in an idyllic ending, begin to live communally.

A similar idealistic view of woman occurs in Turgenev's *On the Eve*. Elena, a young woman, falls in love with Insarov, a Bulgarian patriot, marries him secretly, and sets out with him to his embattled homeland. He dies along the way, and she takes him back to Bulgaria for burial. She writes to her parents that they will never see her again; she has decided to stay and carry on his work. Although Elena is a "new woman" who chooses her husband and her future for herself, she is, at heart, a romantic sentimentalist whose entire existence is determined by Insarov's decisions. It has an ambiguous ending—we never know what happens to her—but it is still a story with the marriage plot as its prime focus.

As Arja Rosenholm has noted, Elena and other women enable men to tell *their* stories. Elena herself has no history, homeland, or ending. She is simply an example of "mythical womanhood" created by a male writer.[62] Barbara Heldt has called this idealization of the Russian heroine, the "terrible perfection," which she describes as "frightening to men, who could not match it in 'manly' action and inhibiting to women who were supposed to incarnate it, or else."[63] For Heldt, women characters created by men are used solely for their authors' ends, "a discourse of male self-definition."[64]

This description sounds remarkably like the position of women in medieval literature, as we saw earlier. In Heldt's analysis, Russian heroines that are created by male authors are liminal to men; in other words, they have no stories of their own. In some cases, they do not even speak to the reader directly, but are rather a "mere episode in a longer story concerning the male."[65] Women, as dangerous creatures, she argues, are neutralized in literature by bringing them under the subjection of men. Although I do not agree categorically with Heldt's thesis, it cannot be denied that women characters occupy a unique position in Russian literature. As owners of property, they have the means to control the lives of the men with whom they are involved. Writers such as Fedor Dostoevsky, as we will see, give them extraordinary power because of this ability. If women characters are indeed "neutralized," I would argue that male authors achieve this by placing them within the traditional family by means of the marriage plot.

In *Fathers and Sons*, for example, women have their own property. Bazarov's parents live on his mother's estate. Anna Sergeevna Odintsova also owns a large estate. Nonetheless, the marriage plot figures prominently in this novel. The parents of both Arkadii and Bazarov had happy marriages, and Arkadii's father, after his wife dies, finds love again with a young servant girl, Fenechka. Aside from all of the intergenerational differences, the sons, like their fathers, are preoccupied with questions of marriage. Arkadii marries Katia, Odintsova's sister, who does not have property of her own. Bazarov, rejected by Odintsova, dies of typhus, but only after she rushes to his bedside. As in *What Is To Be Done?*, marriage becomes a way of enclosing the woman within the family structure, where she seemingly leads a happy existence, content to be both an equal and subservient at the same time. A conversation between Katia and Arkadii illustrates this paradoxical situation:

> - Например, ведь вы, - извините мой вопрос,
> - вы бы не пошли замуж за богатого человека?
> - Если б я его очень любила... Нет, кажется, и тогда бы не пошла.
> - А! вот видите! - воскликнул Аркадий и, погодя немного, прибавил:- А отчего бы вы за него не пошли?
> - Оттого, что и в песне про неровнюшку поется.
> - Вы, может быть, хотите властвовать или...
> - О нет! к чему это? Напротив, я готова покоряться, только неравенство тяжело. А уважать себя и покоряться - это я понимаю; это счастье; но подчиненное существование... Нет, довольно и так.
>
> ["For instance, you—please forgive the question—wouldn't marry a rich man, would you?"
> "If I loved him very much... no, I think that I wouldn't marry him even then."
> "There, you see!" Arkadii cried. And after a short pause, he added, "And why wouldn't you marry him?"
> "Because of what's said in ballads about unequal matches."
> "Maybe you want to have control, or..."
> "Oh, no! Why would I? On the contrary, I'm ready to obey someone. But inequality is oppressive. To respect oneself and obey someone else—that I can understand, that's happiness. But a subordinate existence... No, I've had enough of that as it is."][66]

Katia, who has no property of her own, believes that she cannot marry a man who is wealthy because it would put her in a subservient position. She is ready to obey a husband, but only if he is equal financially. Katia, in essence, is the paradigm of the propertied Russian woman who will be subservient in marriage.

She has experienced an unequal relationship already. "Enough of that as it is" refers to her life with her sister, Odintsova, who is financially independent but also cold and reserved. Jane Costlow has called her the most important female character in the novel. She is, according to Costlow, "a solitary, regimented woman...a nihilist of passion; a motherless child; a daughter—like the goddess Athena—of men, of her father and of a husband old enough to claim paternity; a woman who is *odin* (one, alone; masculine form) not *odna* (one, alone; feminine form)." Odintsova is an outsider: the other women in the novel are "creatures of context, of relationship, of imitation; women who are representative or emblematic of larger social and symbolic groups."[67] She is caught in the historical paradox of the Russian woman: she is able to own property, but at the same time she is supposed to be subservient. After her wealthy, much older husband dies, she does not remarry. Indeed, she is afraid of the emotional ramifications of loving Bazarov. This rejection of what a woman is supposed to feel determines her marginality; she is—as her name suggests, alone.

The women in these novels that were influenced by the "Woman Question" are strong, decisive women, and, at the same time, dangerous. Why are there such female characters in Russian literature? The strong symbolism of Mother Russia is relevant to literary depictions of women. Rosalind Marsh has pointed to the particularly Russian version of the Mary/Eve dichotomy. Woman is the object, immanent, the symbol of nature and death, as opposed to man the subject, transcendent, active, and symbolic of life.[68] The heroine is either a whore, a "demonic woman," or a strong woman who "acts as mentor or muse to the weak 'superfluous man.'"[69]

Central to this argument, however, is the idea of *Matushka-Rus'*, the image of Mother Russia whose suffering is the source of strength.[70] In Imperial Russia, this was the symbol of "the suffering motherland crushed by autocracy," in the words of Joanna Hubbs.[71] Because women held the values and heart of Russia, she argues, in nineteenth- and twentieth-century Russian literature, there is

> a constant adulation of the ethical struggles of the good woman and the refusal to consider the virtues of male heroism. Male identity is perceived as precarious, contingent, existing only in the ethereal world of ideas rather than rooted in the "real" world.[72] Woman, on the other hand, is regarded as the essence of stability, of life, of growth...

In addition, the Orthodox values of humility, suffering, and self-sacrifice gave women a genuine moral authority, and consequently, the

Russian heroine, in the view of Barbara Alpern Engel, has a "special strength of character." She is more strong-willed, emotional, and multifaceted than Western heroines.[73]

Dostoevsky's Women and Their Money

These arguments for the unique character of women in Russian history are persuasive. However, no one has suggested that an additional source for both the strength of and fear of Russian heroines lies in their ability to own property. My argument is that because women could control both land and money, male authors used these issues as a way to portray their propertied heroines as dangerous and controlling. This theme can be seen clearly in the writings of Fedor Dostoevsky. Informed by the conflicting views of women in mid-nineteenth-century Russia, he constructs a financial morality in which women embody the potential dangers of money. As S. K. Somerwil-Ayrton has pointed out, Dostoevsky was preoccupied with the psychological effects of the power hierarchy related to both the possession and lack of money in Russian society.[74] A gendered reading of these texts allows us to see how he filtered archetypes from the past as well as stereotypes of the "New Woman" through the subject of money in order to present the larger issues of evil and redemption.

Dostoevsky manipulates the dichotomy that we saw earlier between women as owners of property and women as subservient to their husbands by dividing his women characters into those who have money and use it to control others and those who are poor. This becomes his own adaptation of the Mary/Eve archetype. For example, in three of his novels, *Crime and Punishment*, *Demons*, and *The Brothers Karamazov*, women either own the property in the family or have more money than their husbands; they use this power as a means of control. In *Demons*, Yulia Mikailovna certainly has more property and influence than her husband, van Lembke. She not only owns two hundred souls "by the old reckoning," but she also has important connections. Because she has financial power over him, she decides what he will do with his life. She wants to "pour her ambition into him" and herself wants to "rule the province."[75] When he finally has enough, he delivers an angry tirade, accusing her of belittling him to the point that he no longer believes in himself. He blames her control on the Woman Question, saying that he would "что душок этот выкурит" ("smoke out that little spirit") (339,440).

Likewise, Varvara Petrovna is richer than her husband. They lived separately before his death, and she provided him with a living allowance.

The only child of a very rich tax farmer, she owns all the wealth of Skvoreshniki, whereas he has only his salary and 150 souls. She is a very good money manager: her estate prospers in spite of the reforms, and she is able to increase her income almost to its former level in just a few years. Her money also supports her acquaintance, Stepan Trofimovich, whom she controls both financially and psychologically. He is referred to as a fifty-year-old infant, who becomes her creation, but in return for her financial support, must give in to her demands. He is powerless to refuse Varvara's demand that he marry Dasha, because she promises him a pension in return. Their relationship is the result of an economically unbalanced partnership, or as Pyotr Stepanovich calls it, their mutual profit: "она капиталистшкой, а ты при ней сентиментальным шутом" ("she as a capitalist, and you as her sentimental fool") (239,305).

In *Crime and Punishment*, Dostoevsky presents us with another couple for whom the power relationship is reversed: Svidrigaylov comes into money through his wife, Marfa Petrovna. She buys off his debt for 30,000 rubles and never lets him forget it:

> И заметьте, всю-то жизнь документ против меня, на чужое имя в этих тридцати тысячах держала, так что задумай я в чемнибудь взбунтоваться, - тотчас же в капкан! И сделала бы! У женщин ведь это все вместе уживается.
>
> [All her life she held that document (made out to someone else) over my head, that note for thirty thousand roubles, so that if I had ever had any thought of rebellion, it would have been straight into the trap with me! And she would have done it! Women, you know, see nothing incongruous in all that.] (218,241)[76]

In *The Brothers Karamazov*, both Grushenka and Katerina Ivanovna have money that they use to control the men in their lives. As Nina Pelikan Straus has remarked, they "attempt to use money to achieve power and independence, either through their understanding of the way money seduces (Grushenka) or the way money creates guilt (Katerina)."[77] Dostoevsky, I would suggest, uses these two figures because they both were once poor and dependent upon men. With money, they become independent and controlling. He pits them against one another to show their "fallen" status. When Grushenka's visit to Katerina Ivanovna erupts into a verbal battle, each calls the other some version of a slut. Grushenka wins by refusing to kiss Katerina's hand after she had kissed Grushenka's. In this way, Dostoevsky strikingly emphasizes the connection between money and power. These two do not possess the innocence and humility of two women we see in *Crime and Punishment*: Sonya, the prostitute who becomes Raskolnikov's spiritual guide, and his sister Dunya, who volunteers to marry someone who will save the family financially. Instead, possessing money and hence the ability to control, Grushenka and Katerina are vipers turned on one another.

The women who do not have money or property, on the other hand, are seen in a saintly light. This is clearly the case in his portrayal of poor women who must resort to prostitution to support themselves and their families. Through the speech of Marmelodov when he first meets Raskolnikov, Dostoevsky makes the connection between the good intentions of the prostitute and the forgiven sinner singled out for her goodness. In fact, both Sonya and Dunya, in trading themselves for money, do so only for the good of their families, not for themselves. This selflessness cancels out any sin they might be committing; in fact, they are portrayed in saintly terms.

In this way, Dostoevsky takes the traditional stereotypes of Mary and Eve and inverts them. The wife is not necessarily "good" and the prostitute is not "evil." These women are neither the madonna nor the whore of Orthodoxy, but the strong woman, who, again in Rosalind Marsh's words, "acts as mentor or muse to the weak 'superfluous man.'"[78] The poor, selfless woman is honored, and the rich, controlling woman takes the form of the devouring mother of folklore, who, in Heldt's words, must somehow be neutralized.[79]

In the end, Dostoevsky's women, if not "neutralized," are at least touched by compassion. Varvara Petrovna rushes to the bedside of the dying Stepan Trofimovich and tends him alone until he dies. After the fire, Yulia Mikhailovna cries out for her husband. Marfa Petrovna gives the note back to Svidrigaylov, along with a considerable amount of money. Grushenka and Katerina Ivanova are redeemed as well. Katerina gave Dmitri Karamazov money, knowing that he would spend it on Grushenka. The revenge that she seeks at his trial backfires when she realizes that in betraying him, she has betrayed herself. Grushenka also is transformed: once reunited with Dmitri at Mokroe, he confesses that he has stolen money from Katerina. She tells him that her money is his. Although they retain their ability to control, there is a hint that love has the power to redeem them.

By using women in powerful roles in these novels and often relying on old religious stereotypes or the new ones of the "Woman Question," Dostoevsky confronts the contradiction in women's lives of owning property and yet being subjugated to their husbands' authority. These women use their money to get the upper hand in their personal relationships. In the end, however, that control is taken away from them, voluntarily or by circumstance. In this way, he in fact neutralizes the woman of property, subjugating their wealth to spiritual redemption. Women are pivotal in these novels, as they are the vehicles through which Dostoevsky conveys his larger message about the evils of money. Indeed, as Gary Rosenshield has argued, his portrayals of women cannot be neatly categorized; he neither victimizes them nor empowers them. "To him gender and victimization are not modes of characterization but themes for development and exploration. To read him otherwise is to finalize that which cannot be finalized."[80]

The fact that Dostoevsky assigns the negative qualities of money to women, however, shows that culturally, the propertied woman was not only an accepted part of life, but also someone who had significant control over others. The question, then, becomes: How do women portray themselves in relation to property in mid-nineteenth-century Russian literature? Do they see a contradiction between their ability to own property and the subservience to their husbands that is expected of them? If the "Woman Question" was indeed a male invention, do women writers refer to it? And, more importantly, how do they view marriage? Does their right to own property affect their ability to accept or reject suitors or even the idea of marriage itself?

Russian Women Reject the Marriage Plot

The Russian critic Vissarion Belinskii, reviewing the works of Maria Zhukova and Elena Gan in the 1840s, argued that women could not be good Russian Realist writers since they imitated reality only superficially.[81] Because they copied only from life experience, he postulated, they lacked originality. Furthermore, the way women wrote about feelings showed their inability to do abstract thinking.[82] This gendering of writing in many ways defined the period between the 1840s and 1870s in Russian literature. As Joe Andrew writes, this was a time "in which issues of gender, of male and female roles were discussed much more keenly than in perhaps any other period in Russian literature of the nineteenth century (and perhaps of any period)."[83] The three women whose work I discuss in this chapter, Karolina Pavlova, Nadezhda Khvoshchinskaya, and Sofia Soboleva, all suffered from this critical reaction. Their own formulations of the "Woman Question" and the debates about marriage, work, and social revolution display a vastly different female heroine than those we see in male authors in the same time period.

It is perhaps this identification of women with sentimentalism that accounts for the absence of Russian women writers in the literary canon. As Catriona Kelly has observed, the terms "*zhenskoe tvorchestvo*" ("women's creativity") and "*zhenskaya proza/poeziya*" ("women's prose and poetry") have negative connotations and imply a lack of intellectual power. They are the "counter-image" of "*muzhskoe*" ("manly writing"), "the huge, passionate, sprawling 'baggy monsters' of prose on the one hand, the intellectual depths of the 'philosophical lyric' on the other."[84]

Kelly explains that women's writing in Russia can only be traced back to the late eighteenth century. With increased educational opportunities beginning with Catherine the Great, both the number of female readers and writers increased.[85] Russian women began writing lyric poetry, which, in the eighteenth century, placed its emphasis on style not on feeling. This, Kelly believes, was a fertile environment for women since there were "no gender-based restrictions in an artistic sense." With the rise of Romanticism in the 1820s and its emphasis on creativity, the question arose whether women were capable of writing poetry, intellectually, spiritually, and physiologically.[86] The breakdown of Romanticism after 1840 and the rise of political verse in Russia marked the decline of poetry viewed as marginal, "a genre which could more readily be appropriated by those whose gender automatically made them marginal to literary life."[87]

Jehanne M. Gheith has a somewhat different answer to the question of why women writers were not part of the literary establishment. In the 1830s, she explains, there began an effort to define a Russian national literary tradition. Describing women's writing as "bad" provided the negative pole by which the standards for "good" writing could be established.[88] Women's writing was thought to focus on love and the family as opposed to issues of social importance. Because these subjects were considered trivial, their works were not recognized.[89] Olga Demidova argues that the women writing in the 1830s and 1840s, such as Katerina Pavlova, emphasized their gender by the use of female pseudonyms. By the 1860s, however, women "aspired to be just writers" and began using male pseudonyms.[90] As Mary F. Zirin points out, the identity of these women writers were an "open secret"; nevertheless, the pseudonyms "gave them an official male viewpoint from which to treat the broader society without being accused of infringing on a sphere beyond their ken."[91]

Nadezhda Khvoshchinskaya, for example, uses the pseudonym V. Krestovskii to write prose fiction and criticism, but not poetry. Every July 15, her family held a name-day party for "V. Krestovskii" as well as for some of the heroes and heroines of her novels.[92] In this way, she not only makes herself into one of her fictionalized characters, she also constructs an identity for herself as author that is distinct from herself as an individual living in the world. Her authority as a writer thus is derived from her role as author. It is through her production of words that she derives her importance. Just as the thirteenth-century Silence is able to transcend her gender through cross-dressing, Khvoshchinskaya, some 550 years later, needed to find a way to get outside of her female identity to be taken seriously.

The subject matter of women's writing shifted during this period of the mid-nineteenth century, as well. As Catriona Kelly describes it, the earlier years saw the "Society Tale," usually a novella of upper-class life in the city. The exterior and public world of the social event was juxtaposed with the interior world of the boudoir. This, she explains, contrasted the "pretense of outward existence" with the "reality of inner feeling." From 1840 through 1880, two other forms take prominence. One, the "Provincial Tale" emphasizes external action from the point of view of the third-person omniscient writer. Its plots concerned escape both through marriage and later from marriage.[93] "The "Escape Plot," on the other hand, shows the influence of the Russian feminist movement. The action is hindered only by external obstacles; there is, no doubt, confusion, or shifting perceptions on the part of the heroines.[94]

Unlike the emphasis on marriage in the works of Turgenev and Chernyshevsky, the women writers whose work I use here criticize marriage and, like twelfth-century Heloise, see it essentially as a restrictive institution. Rather than finding happiness through a new definition of marriage, they either perceive it as the end of imagination and creativity (Pavlova), forcefully reject it in favor of the independent life (Khvoshchinskaya) or invert marriage roles entirely (Soboleva). These three are also examples of Kelly's three types of plots in mid-nineteenth-century Russian women's literature, subtle perhaps in their differences, but forceful in their criticism of marriage as a satisfying experience for women.

Karolina Pavlova's Double Life

Karolina Pavlova, born Karolina Karlovna Jaenisch in 1807, was both criticized and praised because she did not write like a woman. Her critics attacked her for being an "insufficiently feminine woman" at the same time her work was praised by Belinsky for its "manly energy."[95] Barbara Heldt describes her "as much as any woman of her time could in Russia... [she] lived in a man's world." Her father, a professor of physics and chemistry in Moscow, made certain that Karolina received a first-class education at home. Adam Mickiewicz, the great Polish poet, was her first love and was impressed by her literary talents. She spoke Russian, French, German, Spanish, Italian, Swedish, Dutch, and Polish, and in her early twenties she was already translating and writing her own poetry.[96] Her literary salon in the late 1830s and 1840s drew members of the Russian intellectual elite, among them, Turgenev, Plonsky, Hertzen, and Ogarev.[97] In addition to discussing important topics of the time, such as the Slavophile-Westerner debate, the Pavlovs' salon was where Karolina read her own poetry.[98] She wrote continuously until her death in 1893.

Why has this prolific writer not been remembered in the corpus of nineteenth-century Russian literature? After a youth spent as part of the Russian literary establishment, Pavlova died alone, poor, and in a foreign country. There were no obituaries in Russian newspapers.[99] The centenary of her death in 1993 passed without any kind of commemoration. It has only been in the United States and Germany that she has received critical interest. As Alexander Lehrman has noted, although she was privileged in wealth and education, she was not pretty, was considered "cold," and had a disastrous marriage. These factors, along with her decision to leave Russia, contributed to her literary obscurity.[100] Although she was rediscovered at the turn of the century by the Russian symbolists and women poets of the time such as Tsvetaeva and Akhmatova dedicated poems to her, she was shunned after the Revolution because of her unprogressive political views.[101]

Donald Loewen has remarked that because Pavlova "aggressively" moved into the literary sphere that had been traditionally inhabited by men, her "otherness" is not the same as women who willingly took secondary roles in that world. "Instead," he writes, "she found herself in an ambivalent social zone somewhere between the roles associated with women and those associated with men, and she was judged accordingly." Her passion for poetry was the culprit; it was traditionally a male genre.[102]

In her personal life, as well, she acted in a typically unfeminine way. She married Nikolai Pavlov, an unremarkable minor literary figure, who confessed that he had wed her for her money. It was, his friend Chicherin wrote, "a social misdemeanor that is quite usual and looked upon with indulgence." He gambled away her estate, and after he secretly mortgaged her property, she began divorce proceedings and had him arrested.[103] This did not endear her to the literary establishment, some of whom were Pavlov's friends. Although she claimed to have spent fourteen years "dans un lit virginal [*sic*]," she was accused of treating her husband inhumanly. During his arrest, the police found censored books in his home, and he was exiled to Perm. Pavlova and her poetry were uniformly criticized after this time.[104] Nekrasov, Dobrolyubov, and Schedrin, in particular, remarked on her archaic language and structure.[105] She left Russia in 1856 and settled in Dresden in 1858, where she remained for the rest of her life.

Although Pavlova herself was an influential participant on the literary scene, she does not give a corresponding personal power to her heroines.

Ginger B. Lazarus has noted that she does not allow them to rise above societal pressures, as she herself did.[106] She actually shows her women as more complex creatures than the stereotypical heroine or even more than her own life suggests. For instance, Stephanie Sandler and Judith Vowles have analyzed the poems in which Pavlova treats the issue of abandonment. Her own biography hints that this comes from personal experience, especially in her relationships with Mickiewicz and Boris Utin, a law student with whom she became involved in the 1850s. Nonetheless, they argue, "She took on one of the canonical roles for women poets, that of the abandoned woman, with great complexity. She refused to embrace its pathos entirely, but she ever blinded herself to its painful appropriateness in her own biography."[107]

Pavlova's ability to see women's position—social, economic, emotional—both in light of and in spite of her own experience can be seen most prominently in her one novel titled *A Double Life* (*Dvoinaia Zhizn*). Its publication "was the great literary event of 1848," according to Munir Sendich.[108] This was at the height of her literary career, and reviews were mostly favorable, although after this there was no more mention of the novel until Briusov's publication of her works in 1915.[109] This exclusion is ironic, since Pavlova, according to Diana Greene, used two different genres in *A Double Life* so that she could be accepted by the male literary establishment. The *svetskaia povest'* (society tale) was written by both men and women, whereas the *ocherk* (sketch) told women's stories from a female perspective.[110] By writing society tales, Greene suggests, women writers could "protest against their constricted lives."[111]

A Double Life is the story of a young woman of means, Cecily, whose mother, Vera Vladimirovna, has made it her duty to find her a husband. Olga, Cecily's best friend, and her mother, Madame Valitsky, successfully plot to have Cecily marry Dmitry Ivachinsky, a relatively impoverished young man, so that Olga will have a chance to snare the wealthy Prince Victor. Pavlova transforms this rather mundane narrative into something quite different by giving Cecily a parallel "life" in her nightly dreams. There she meets a mysterious stranger who encourages her to develop her poetic self, a self that is alive compared to the deadliness of her existence. Pavlova also enlivens the society tale by providing biting criticism throughout the novel about a culture that forces women into artificial roles for the primary purpose of making a "good" marriage.

She opens *A Double Life* by using a quotation from Byron, which explains the title:

> Our life is twofold: Sleep has
> its own world,
> A boundary between the things
> misnamed Death and existence.[112]

Pavlova uses sleep as the state in which Cecily can experience a vision of the world beyond her experience. It is not the boundary between death and existence, because once she marries, in Pavlova's formulation, they become one and the same. Rather, it is where Cecily can see her own poetic potential, which might enable her to separate existence from death, the boundary between a deadly marriage and a life devoted to her inner soul. Her dream life is expressed through poetry, while the narrative unfolds to her inevitable fate as wife.

Beneath these lines by Byron, Pavlova offers a dedication:

Вам этой мысли приношение,
Моей поэзий привет,
Вам этот труд уединения,
Рабыни шума и сует,
Вас всех, не встреченных Цецилий,
Мой грустный вздох назвал в тиши,
Вас всех, Психей, лишенных крылей,
Немых сестер моей души!
Дай Бог и вам, семье безвестной,
Сред грешной лжи хоть сон святой,
И неволи жизни этой тесной
Хоть взрыв мгновенный жизни той.
[To you the offering of this thought,
The greeting of my poetry,
To you this work of solitude.
Slaves of din and vanity.
In silence did my sad breath name
You Cecilys unmet by me.
All of you Psyches without wings,
Mute sisters of my soul!
May God grant you too, unknown family,
Just one bright dream mid sinful lies,
In the prison of this narrow life
Just one brief burst of that other life.]

Although this dedicatory poem shows Pavlova's sense of sisterhood with other Russian women, it also stresses her separateness: the "you too" implies that she has this other life, and she sets herself up as an objective narrator, a commentator, not a participant in the social situation of Cecily and others like her. Although Pavlova's own history of a husband who misspent her money may suggest that she is a victim, this was a role she did not embrace. She was by all accounts a woman who believed passionately in her poetic talents and put their pursuit above all else. The attainment of this vision is the "one bright dream" that Pavlova wishes for the "mute sisters of my soul."

Although most scholarly commentary on *A Double Life* has been about Pavlova's keen criticism of the marriage practices of the day and its resulting entrapment of women, there is, I suggest, an important related theme: the connection of women as owners of property with their status as property. The novel opens with a discussion of Cecily's family's wealth. The very first line is: "А богати?" ("But are they rich?"). After an affirmative answer, one of the young men asks, "А дочь какова?" ("What's the daughter like?"). The other replies, "Ничего нет особеннаго; довольно хороша собой и, говорять, не глупа . . . " ("Nothing special; good looking enough and not stupid . . . "). The interrogator asks a third question, "A good match?" "No," is the answer. "There's a younger brother" ("Партия хорошая?" "Нет! Есть меньшой брат") (5,3).

This conversation clearly judges Cecily's worth by her ability to inherit a sizeable estate. The fact that there is a son makes her less desirable than if she were an only child. Her beauty is only secondary; "nothing special" indicates that her looks are tolerable. Her friend Olga's mother, however, makes her far more enticing to Dmitry Ivachinsky. In an elaborate plot to get him to propose before Prince Victor does, she reveals that Cecily is the only heir of an old aunt's estate. Furthermore, the aunt is gravely ill, as is Cecily's brother. Dmitry is suddenly very interested:

> Дмитрий Ивачинский быль добрый человек, даже благородный человек, в обыкновенном значений этого слова; но почему доброму и благородному человеку не желать вдобавок быть и богатым. Как дла большей части нашего поколения, деньги, и даже много денег, были дла него нужнейшей стихией жизни. Он сам имел изрядное состояние, но к чему служит в наш век изрядное состояние, как разв к тому, чтобы безпрестанно органичивать свои желания, и живие и болезненние чувствовать всю необходимость богатства?

[Dmitry Ivachinsky was a good man, even a noble man in the ordinary sense of the word, but why should a good and noble man not wish to be a rich man as well? As with the greater part of our generation, money, and even a lot of money, was the most essential element of life for him. He himself had a fine fortune, but what does a fine fortune serve for in our age if it only incessantly limits one's desires and makes one feel the need for wealth even more keenly and morbidly.] (51,35)

Because his own income barely covers his expenses, Dmitry knows that he will have to marry a woman with property in order to keep up his lifestyle. He suddenly sees Cecily in a new light and decides "she could make a husband very happy" ("девушка, которая могла сделать мужа пречастливим") (52,36). As Dmitry sets out to make her fall in love with him (with a great deal of help from Olga's mother), both he and Cecily become participants in the marriage market. He has eloquently described his consumptive need for even more wealth, money feeding on itself in a greedy vicious cycle. It is not Cecily that he desires, but her fortune. If she becomes his property, he believes, he will have access to her property. And rather than marriage having a tempering effect on him, he declares to all of his friends the night before the wedding that he will continue to carouse afterward. It is not a fair trade: he refuses to give up any of his behaviors in return for Cecily's money, whereas she enters into the marriage expecting his love and faithfulness.

If this were the entire story in *A Double Life*, it would not be different from other society tales. Pavlova, however, gives Cecily the chance to opt out of the marriage market, the marriage mystique. Each chapter ends in the evening with Cecily receiving a kind of inspiration in verse as she tries to sleep. In the first such visitation, the mysterious stranger "looks into her eyes with his eyes, / Looks into her soul with his soul" ("Он ей глядит очами в очи, / Глядит он в душу ей душой"). She is beckoned to a place outside of the boundaries of her existence:

Она идет—идет невольно
Через немеющий простор,
Туда, где властный и унылый
Тот взгляд сияет, как призыв,
И стала пред безвестной силой,
Главу покорную склонив.
[She walks—walks against her will
Across distances ever more silent
To where, powerful and despondent
That glance shines, like a summons.
And she stood before the unknown force,
Bowing from a submissive head.] (15,10)

Emotionally, Cecily is having a liminal experience, crossing into an unknown area. The dream lover is not identified, nor are we led to believe that he is there for any kind of selfish reason. Instead, he is her guide into another world of feeling. Unlike Marie de France's unhappily married women, Cecily is not secondary to a male hero. She *is* the hero of *A Double Life*. She is not marginal to the story, for it *is* her story.

In fact, men play only secondary roles in Pavlova's novel. Vera Vladimirovna's husband is unnamed. His identity comes from her:

> Муж Веры Владимировны (упоминая о нем, его обыкновенно называли мужем Веры Владимировны, и он сам, раз как незнакомец спросил его, с кем он имеет честь говорить, представился ему под этим названием...
>
> [he was generally referred to as the husband of Vera Vladimirovna, and once when a stranger asked him with whom he had the pleasure of speaking he introduced himself thus...] (26,17)

The two young men in *A Double Life*, Prince Victor and Dmitry, are, as Anthony D. Briggs has noted, "pasteboard creations moved on and off stage according to the tiresome needs of the plot which called for the presence of two potential husbands-to-be."[113] Despite Briggs's obvious criticism of the novel (he calls it "that strange study in metempsychosis"),[114] there is some truth to his characterization. But rather than see this as a shortcoming of the novel, I would suggest that Pavlova does this intentionally. She insists on keeping the focus on Cecily as the center of her own tale. The role of the mystery man is, as he himself puts it, to help her through dreams to "understand inspiration's secret" and "live the soul's life fully" ("Поймешь ты тайну вдохновений/Жизнь духа проживешь вполне") (28–29,19). He is, in essence, her muse, another male figure about whom we know nothing.

One day Olga and Cecily are out riding and venture far ahead of the men "with that violent female daring which is so far from manly valor" ("с той безумной женской смелостью, которая так далека от храбрости") (46,32). Cecily is comfortable outside the restrictions of her family's home, and finds this episode freeing: she "suddenly wanted to gallop away from life's imprisonment, from all dependencies, from all obligations, all necessities" ("ей вдруг захотелось ускакать от всей жизненной неволи, от всех зависимостей, от всех необходимостей") (47–48,33). In a physical sense she is crossing the boundaries of propriety and not behaving like a marriageable girl should. It is far different from the young women in Marie de France's *lais*, who cannot freely go beyond their imprisoned environment. Later that evening, her dream poem describes a young woman who urges her love to use her as a hostage to buy a horse for his military duty. After he does this, he leaves her for another woman. Cecily's mysterious visitor cautions her about pairing love with selflessness, saying it leads to unhappiness. She must close her heart to passion: "You are a woman! Learn to control yourself, / Close your lips and chain your soul"

("Ты, женщина! Умей владеть собою, / Сомкни уста, и душу ты закуй!") (58,40). Instead, she is urged to "preserve the sacred visions" ("ты храни священные химеры") by closing herself off from men's "pagan passions" ("язычеслих страстей") (59,41).

These words of advice are particularly pertinent to Cecily. She is described as a "perfected" daughter, one who recognizes that marriage is the goal and has been kept innocent of all else:

> Ее душа была так обделана, ея понятия так перепутаны, ее способности так переобразованы и изувечены неутомимым воспитанием, что всякий жизненный вопрос затруднял и страшал ее.
>
> [Her soul was so highly polished, her understanding so confused, her natural talents so overorganized and mutated by the unsparing way she had been brought up that every problem of life embarrassed and terrified her.] (61–62, 43)

As a way to enlighten her about the dangers of an unequal, economic marriage, her poem that night is about a woman, Madame Stentsova, who died at the age of thirty-two, and whose husband already knows whom he will marry. It describes Stentsova's empty life:

> Любила горестно и страстно,
> В чужия вермла сердца,
> И до конца ждала напрасно,
> И уповала до конца.
> [She loved sorrowfully and passionately,
> Believing in another's love,
> And waited to the end in vain,
> And hoped until the end.] (74,52)

Here the dream man is cautioning her again about loving too much, for it surely ends in pain. The theme continues the following night, the night when she becomes aware of her feelings for Dmitry, in a poem that forecasts sorrow:

> Учись, жена, жены страданьям,
> Знай, что, покорная, она
> К своим мечтаньям, к своим желаньям
> Искать дороги не должна;
> Что роптат сердце в ней напрасно,
> Что долг ее неумолим,
> Что вся душа ему подвластна,

Что скованы и мысли им.
[Learn, as a wife, the suffering of a wife,
Know that, submissive, she
Must not seek the path
To her own dreams, her own desires;
That her heart protests in vain,
That her duty is implacable,
That all her soul is in his power,
That even her thoughts are fettered.] (92–93, 65)

This is perhaps Pavlova's strongest indictment against marriage. In a passage strongly reminiscent of Heloise's connection of marriage with chains, Cecily is warned about what her life will become. And indeed, throughout the novel, there are metaphors of woman's imprisonment. Descriptions of being encased in expensive clothing and corsets abound; beauty becomes a commodity worth paying for with discomfort. Marta Laura Wilkinson has called this "gender as performance": women accept the restrictions society puts upon them in "complete submission to the ideals of femininity."[115] Cecily, Wilkinson writes, is finally buried by marriage.[116]

On the night of her engagement, the mysterious stranger tells her there is something within her stronger than the suffering that is ahead of her. In another discourse on the uneven "trade" that Cecily is making, the voice uses economic metaphors to advise her:

Пойми, что тщетны все желанья
Что бытие чреда утрат;
Что жертвы в нем без воздаянья,
Что в нем страданья без наград.
И чувствуй, что и тебе есть что-то,
Неизъяснимое теперь,
Что выше всякаго расчета,
И всех блаженств, и всех потерь!
[Understand that all desires are in vain,
That life is a series of losses,
That its sacrifices have no recompense,
That its sufferings have no reward.
And feel that within you there is something
Inexplicable at present,
Higher than any estimate,
And any blessings, any losses.] (116,82)

As a prefigurement of her future, the weather on the day before the wedding turns cold and gray. Summer has disappeared and with it, Cecily's optimism. That evening she realizes her fate:

> Больнее и больнее стесняла душу безсмысленная боязнь загадочное горе. Нервы ее напрягались тягостно. В ней не было силы сбросить с сердца подавляющую думу, она сидела с поникшей головой, вся немая под бременем неизъяснимаго чувства.
>
> [More and more a senseless fear, a perplexing sadness made her soul timid. Her nerves were painfully strained. She didn't have the strength to throw off the oppressive thought from her heart. She sat with bowed head, mute under the weight of this inexplicable feeling.] (142,101)

Again, Pavlova uses words that are synonymous with imprisonment and chains. In her dream that night, the stranger says goodbye in a final verse that ties the economic reality of her state to her emotions:

> Бытие поймешь земное
> Созревающей душой:
> Купишь благо дорогое
> Дорогою ты ценой.
> [You will understand earthly reality
> With a maturing soul:
> You will buy dear wealth
> At a dear price.] (146,104)

He holds out no hope for her future:

> Не тревожь преступно неба,
> Загдуши свои мечты;
> И насущного лишь хлеба
> Смей просить у Бога ты.
> [Don't disturb the heavens, transgressing,
> Silence your own dreams.
> And dare to ask of God
> Only for your daily bread.] (146,105)

The night of the wedding is rainy with "heavy, menacing clouds." Cecily remembers a phrase from the one of her nightly poems, even though the mysterious man told her the first night she would remember nothing. This vague memory—Cecily cannot place it—perhaps holds out hope for her.

The novel ends with a poem, this one from a woman, as evidenced by the feminine endings in Russian. Is it Pavlova or Cecily herself? It is somewhat ambiguous in its ending, leaving the reader to wonder, along with the narrator, if "this is, perhaps, the final song." The last verse gives us hope:

Пусть брошу я, средь жизненного моря,
За кладом клад на бурной глуби дно:
Блажен и тот, кто мог, с грозою споря
Себ сласти сокровище одно.
[Let me throw treasure after treasure
Into the stormy depths of the sea of life:
Blessed is he who, arguing with the story,
Can salvage something precious for himself.] (152, 111)

Does Cecily, then, have any real options? She has been raised to be a "perfected" daughter, ready for the marriage market, innocent, uncomplicated. As a woman who will come into property, this defines her worth rather than her internal value. The entreaties by the man in her dreams to hold onto her own poetic soul appear to have had no influence. Will she end up like her mother, Vera Vladimirovna, suddenly a mature, conniving woman after her marriage, perpetuating the tradition through her own daughters? By ending the novel on Cecily's wedding night, I believe that Pavlova gives her a choice, a choice that we do not get to see made. Although she is not supposed to remember her poetic dreams, she begins to do just that. And in this, there is a glimmer that she can overcome the chains of marriage and develop her artistic soul.

Khvoshchinskaya's Lelenka: A New Model for Women?

Nadezhda Khvoshchinskaya has been the center of substantial scholarly interest over the last decade. Arja Rosenholm devotes a section to her in *Gendering Awakening: Femininity and the Russian Woman Question of the 1860's*,[117] and she is one of the central figures in Jehanne M. Gheith's *Finding the Middle Ground: Krestovskii, Tur, and the Power of Ambivalence in Nineteenth-Century Russian Women's Prose*. In addition, she has become a mainstay in any discussion of Russian women's writing during this period.[118] Khvoshchinskaya's novella *Pansionerka* (*The Boarding School Girl*) is, according to Catriona Kelly, an example of the "provincial tale," in which there is an emphasis on external action and country settings, all told from the point of view of the third-person omniscient writer.[119] The plots of such tales, she continues, emphasize both escape *through* marriage and later, escape *from* marriage. *Pansionerka*, clearly, belongs to this latter category.[120]

Khvoshchinskaya, as I noted earlier, took the pen name of V. Krestovskii. The most common explanation for this is that she chose it at random after meeting a man by the same name. In the late 1850s a male author starting publishing under the name of Vsevolod Krestovskii, and so she simply added "*psevdomin*" to her name. This, as Gheith suggests, expressed her sense of *being* a pseudonym.[121] Besides being an "act of self-creation," it allowed Khvoshchinskaya the status of a man and the ability to "play with attractions across gender."[122]

Born in 1824 into a gentry family, she was an avid reader whom young men found to be too intelligent. On the day of her debut, she was reading Victor Hugo's *Le dernier jour d'un condamné*.[123] The fact that she remembers this fact later is evidence that even at an early age she connected marriage with a fate worse than mere imprisonment. She did not marry until she was forty. It was not a happy marriage, and she bore no children. Gheith observes that "marriage and writing did not go together" for Khvoshchinskaya; her literary output was greater before she was married and after her separation.[124] She wrote both fiction and criticism, using a different pseudonym, "V. Porechnikov," in the journal *Otechestvennye zapiski* (*Notes of the Fatherland*).[125] Her most enthusiastic readers were mostly provincial women, but also progressive youth. By the 1870s she was one of the highest paid authors in terms of honoraria, third only to Turgenev and Tolstoy.[126]

Pansionerka was published in 1861. It is the story of a fifteen-year-old girl, Lelenka, who, when the story opens, is in her garden memorizing vast quantities of information for her upcoming examinations. Over the garden fence, she strikes up an acquaintance with her neighbor, Veretitsyn, a man who has been exiled to her small provincial city because, we are told, of something he wrote. Influenced by his diatribes about the worthlessness of rote learning, Lelenka fails her examinations, and her family arranges a marriage for her. She adamantly refuses to marry. The novella then skips ahead eight years. She and Veretitsyn meet again in a museum in Petersburg, where she lives with an aunt and supports herself by copying paintings. She has not married.

As Nancy Folbre and Heidi Hartmann argue in their article "The Rhetoric of Self-Interest: Ideology and Gender in Economic Theory," economics have assumed separate spheres for men and women. Men live outside in the public world; women reside inside in the domestic space.[127] This concept is central to *Pansionerka*. The action of the first part of the novella takes place outside, in the fenced-in garden of the family home. It is where Lelenka prefers to be and is where she makes decisions and suffers through what can conceivably be described as adolescent angst. Although the garden is an extension of the family space, it represents to Lelenka an escape from the claustrophobic atmosphere of the house. In this sense, "outside" is where she can try out boundaries without actually having to cross them. She must always reenter the home and carry with her whatever knowledge she has gained from the outside. When Lelenka moves to St. Petersburg and becomes economically and psychologically self-sufficient, however, the action of the novella shifts to inside—the museum or her apartment. She is independent and self-confident enough to be comfortable in the domestic sphere, no longer the scene of constraint. She has become the master of both the inside and the outside.

Arja Rosenholm has described the garden as the site of the awakening of her desire, which is transformative only for her, not Veretitsyn.[128] She has complicated feelings for Veretitsyn—attraction, jealousy, curiosity, a schoolgirl "crush." But he is in no way the kind of romantic figure we find in the marriage plot. The desire he has fueled is for independence. Joe Andrew has described him as her double, "a model of what she might become, or indeed, surpass."[129] He too is an outsider, and, like Lelenka, socially alienated. His role is to give voice to her own unhappiness. The frustrated marriage plot is actually Veretitsyn's—he is in love with Sofya Aleksandrovna, who he believes to be perfect:

> Такие существа, как она, посылаются на свет в редкие, особенно щедрые минуты. Красивица, мила, как ребенок, думает, чувствует за всех, кроткая, с ответом на всякую мысль, с слезами на всякое страдание…
>
> [Such a being is bestowed on the world at rare, particularly charitable moments. Beautiful, kind as a child, she thinks and feels for everyone; gentle, she responds to any idea, sheds a tear for any suffering…] (104,20)[130]

This is not the description of Lelenka.

Indeed, throughout the novella, Lelenka resists being the ideal marriageable girl. Her mother accuses her of putting on airs and being sophisticated. She is also a disobedient daughter. When a friend of the family, Pelageya Semyonovna, suggests that she needs better clothes to bring attention to her beauty, Lelenka replies that she doesn't want new clothes. Her mother exclaims, "How dare you not want what your father and mother want!" ("Да как же ты смеешь не хотеть, когда отец твой с матерью хотят?") (127,51). In fact, she is horrified at the thought that she might become like her parents. "Will I really have children someday?" she worries. "Will I really live like this?" ("Неужели у меня будут когда-нибудь дети? неужели я буду жить так же?") (155,92). A friend of the family, Pelageya Semyonovna scolds her about upsetting her mother and advises: "You'd better break that habit, my angel, break it—tone yourself down! You'll have to live with your husband and his family…Just submit, you have to submit" ("Отвыкайте вы, мой ангел, отвыкайте, сократите себя! Как в семье да с мужем жить придется...Только покорятбся, покоряться надо") (172,115).

When Lelenka discovers that her parents have found a suitor for her, she begins to cry. Her mother extols her fiance's virtues:

> И человек прекраснейший, с достатком; поди барыней жить будешь. Это надо господа бога ьлагодарить, что такого сожителя посылает...А ты хоть кричи не кричи, а я все-таки отдам.
>
> [And the finest man, with money. I daresay you'll be living like a lady. You have God to thank for sending you such a mate...But whether you carry on about it or not, I'm still marrying you off.] (174,118)

Lelenka retorts, "Mama, you can kill me right where I stand, but I won't marry Farforov!" ("Вы, маменька, можете меня убить на месте, но я не пойду за Фарфорова!") (175,119).

And indeed she does not. When she meets Veretitsyn again in St. Petersburg, he asks her if life is easy. Lelenka answers: "Of course! I'm free...I'm not obligated to anyone for anything" ("Еще бы! Я свободна! Я никому ничем не обязана") (181,128). She asks Veretitsyn about Sofya, the woman whom he believed to be perfect. He replies that she is married and living in the country. Lelenka retorts that she is a woman who "sold her will, plunged into a void" ("продала свою волю, бросилась в пустоту") (184,131). She goes on to criticize not only marriage, but the family:

> Рабство, семья!.. Женщина высшая подчинена какому-то доброму малому, пожертвовала собой дла прихоти матери- эгоистки, примирила, то есть свела опять, двух друных людей, чтоб они вдвоем больше зла наделали! Как-нибудь, среди стеснений, из-под насмешек передает что-нибудь человекеское детям...Но человеское ли, здравое ли? Она передает им те же нечастные заповеди самоотвержения, от которых погибает сама! Заповеди покорности произволу!...Она виновата, ваша Софья! Она служит злу, учит злу, она готовит страдалиц!
>
> [Slavery, the family!...A more elevated woman is subjugated to some nice fellow; she sacrificed herself at the whim of her egotistical mother; she reconciled—that is, reunited again—two bad people so they could cause even more harm together! Somehow, amid the constraints, despite the derision, she passes something humane on to the children...But is it really humane, is it healthy? She passes on to them the same unfortunate precepts of selflessness that are destroying her! Precepts of submission to tyranny!...She's guilty, your Sofya! She serves evil, teaches evil. She's training victims!] (185,133)

Describing falling in love as "foolish," Lelenka vows that she will never again give anyone power over her again. Jehanne M. Gheith believes that such a bold rejection of love is rare in nineteenth-century fiction and notes that critics thought her a dangerous role model. She cites a letter that Khvoshchinskaya wrote to a friend suggesting that Lelenka's life (as well as Sofya's) was only half a life. The ending, Gheith believes, is ambiguous.[131]

It was, perhaps, only "half a life," but, I believe, it was a good life for Lelenka. At the very end of *Pansionerka*, Lelenka shows Veretitsyn out and returns to her room:

> не останавливаясь ни минуты, придвинула кресло к столу, достала тетради и диксионер, и скоро в комнате слышались только стук часов, падание догоравшего угля в камине и шорох пера по бумаге...
>
> [and without hesitating even for a moment, she moved an armchair up to the desk and got out a notebook and dictionary, and soon only the ticking of the clock, the sound of a smoldering coal falling in the fireplace, and the scratching of a pen on paper could be heard in the room...] (188,137)

We are left with the picture of an independent woman, fulfilled by work and study rather than by a family. By rejecting Veretitsyn's idea of a perfect woman, Lelenka is, in fact, closing the circle that began in the garden. She no longer needs him to be the only model of an alternative life. Her physical and psychological journey into the outside world has enabled her to feel free in what was once the claustrophobic world of the home. In rejecting the marriage plot, Lelenka has, instead, adopted one that is much more satisfying.

Concepts of Value in Sofia Soboleva's "I pro, i contra"

We see a strikingly different situation in Sofia Soboleva's story "I pro, i contra," published in 1863. She, too, wrote under a male pseudonym, V. Samoilovich. Born in 1840 in the small town of Schlüsselburg, where her father was an engineer, she was educated at Madame Kamerat's pension in St. Petersburg. Soboleva supported herself for much of her life. She was an assistant in the editorial offices of *Otechestvennye zapiski*, where "I pro i contra: Mechty i dumy nadvornoi sovetnitsy Lisitsynoi" was published, and after a short marriage to a middle-ranking civil servant, worked as a private teacher. In 1867 she turned her writing to children's fiction, perhaps due to the large number of poor children she had adopted. In this endeavor, Soboleva was critically quite successful. When she died in 1884, however, she was nearly penniless, due to the costs of caring for these children.[132]

Catriona Kelly has noted that most post-1840s fiction by Russian women writers follows a formula: an exceptional heroine, making her way in a world in which everyone is hostile to her progress, is often juxtaposed with a female relation who conforms to societal expectations. "I pro, i contra," she contends, is an exception. Although it deals with the same subject of women's progress, it is "rich in irony, ambiguity, and in various types of literary self-consciousness."[133]

This story is also nonformulaic in that it shows a woman who self-confidently uses her money to insure her independence. There is none of the insecurity of the young Lelenka here; rather, we see a mature heroine who understands the role of economics in marriage. Madame Lisitsyna, a woman of means, consents to marry the man her parents present to her; she is, after all, twenty-seven years old. Marriage is important to her parents, but not to her. She is not afraid to remain single:

> Родители мои приходили в отчаяние, что я останусь старой девой, хотя, по правде сказать, приходить в отчаяние было не от чего. Как бы ни смеялись над старыми девами, но всё-таки остаться старой девой добросовестнее, чем выйти замуж не любя. Дайте женщине другое направление, тогда и старые девы не будут существами бесполезными и смешными.
>
> [My parents were in desperation; they were persuaded that I should remain an old maid. In truth, of course, there was no cause for desperation in that: for surely it is far better to remain an old maid, no matter what the ridicule one may attract by doing so, than to enter a loveless marriage? And in any case, if you once allow women to change their way of life, then old maids will no longer seem so useless and ridiculous.] (83)[134]

In fact, she makes fun of the traditional marriage plot:

> процветали Владимир и Ольга, два прекрасных существа, страстно любящие друг друга. Встречались различные препятствия для их соединения, и четвёртая часть оканчивалась или их законным браком, или один из героев где-нибудь погибал, оставляя другого на всю жизнь в неутешных слезах.
>
> [Vladimir and Olga, two delightful young people living somewhere or other, are madly in love with each other. But for some reason or other, there are obstacles to their marriage, and the fourth part concludes with their

> joyous nuptials, or else with one of the partners perishes somewhere, and the other left in consolable tears for the rest of his (or her) life.] (296,72)

Once married, her husband quits his position to live off the income from her property. She is not surprised that he retires, since the money earned was "too insignificant a sum to support us" (84). Lisitsyn expects to take charge of her property, but much to his dismay, she insists on administering the estates herself. She explains: "I was a patient, attentive, and obedient wife in all things save one: I had very firm and strong-minded notions concerning my own property rights" ("Я была терпеливой, внимательной и послушной женой, кроме одного пункта: я имела прямые, здравые понятия о праве собственности") (85). He tries to convince her that a married couple should share all they have: if, he says, she entrusts him with her heart, then why doesn't she entrust him with her money?

> —Как же- прибавил он в заключение,- ты ведь отдала мне сердце и руку, а не хочешь разделить со мной труда управления имением. Такое логическое рассуждение нисколько меня не убедило. Неужели ты ценишь деньги выше твоей руки и сердце,—Я отдала тебе, мой друг- отвечала я - мою руку и сердце.Но деньги—совсем другое дело. Деньги с моего имения созданы именно дла того, чтобы быть моими и не доставаться никому, пока я жива.
>
> ["How can it be," he said in conclusion of his argument, "that you could be prepared to entrust me with your hand in marriage, and with your heart, and yet do not wish to share the work of managing your estate with me? Can you really value money more than your hands and heart? "Yes, my dear, I did entrust you with my hand and heart. But that is not at all the same thing as sharing my money with you. The income from my estate is meant for me; it was made over to me so that it should support me in my own lifetime, and not so that I might cede it to anyone else whatsoever."] (85)

Soboleva reverses gender roles by putting him in the position of the supported spouse. Lisitsyna tells him:

> Ведь ты создан, право, не для труда, а для того, чтобы наслаждаться жизнью.Я хочу, чтобы ты был совершенно счастлив. При том же, неужели ты женился на мне из-за моего состояния?
>
> [You are a man whose life should be devoted to pleasure, not to hard labor. I want you to enjoy perfect happiness...am I to suppose that you only married me for my money?"]

He, of course, has done just that. He values her money more than he values her. There ensues an exchange on whether a woman can love a man who marries her for her income. He argues that it is not wrong to choose a wife based to some extent on a consideration of her income. She replies that this is worse than criminal, it is base, which is more offensive than anything else. It is more honorable, she continues, for a man to have a trade than to live on his wife's income. Only then can a wife value her husband.

> Э, мой друг, мало ли найдётся на свете занятий, которые приносят действительную пользу и вполне вознаграждают труды. Торгуйте, изобретайте машины, стройте их, разводите огороды, наконец, это всё-таки лучше, чем рассчитывать на женины деньги.
>
> [My dear, are there so few kinds of employment which are really useful and which are profitable at the same time? You could go into trade; you could invent different kinds of machinery or build them; you could plant market gardens. All those things would be more honorable than living on your wife's income.]

In English there are many definitions of "value": it is the quality that renders something desirable; the amount of goods, money, or services that is considered to be a fair equivalent for something else; it can mean to prize or hold dear, or to judge the worth of something. The Russian verb that Soboleva uses, *цетить*, also has a few meanings: to value, but also to appreciate. In "I pro, i contra," "value" has two main meanings: the ability to produce money and to hold dear, or prize. The first depends on the production of income, the second says, "I value you" in a non-monetary way.

But in this story, the two are irrevocably intertwined. He values her *for* her money, which is precisely why she will not give him control of it. She sees that a woman cannot *be* valued if she is perceived as *having* value. The sole way to change the situation is to ensure that the husband *has value* in and of himself; this is the only way she *can value* him. In other words, he has to have a value based on production in order to have a value based on worthiness. Lisitsyna tells her husband:

> Если же мужчина женится для того, чтобы посредством своей жены приобрести удобства и роскошь жизни, то и самая ограниченная поймёт наконей, что она --нуль, как в отношении к мужу, так и в отношении к обществу.
>
> [If a man marries in order to exploit his wife's funds, and to ensure himself a comfortable or a luxurious existence, then even the most limited

> woman will eventually realize that she is worth nothing in her husband's eyes, and nothing in the eyes of society at large.] (86)

If a poor man marries a rich woman, she states, he must accept that he has no right to her money. She is willing to share it with him, but it is at her discretion, not his:

> Но только в таком случае он не должен никогда посягать на ее имение. Он должен смотреть на него, как на достояние своей жены, а не как на свое собственное. Если она любит мужа, то сама поделится с ним земными благами. А любовь и уважение жены он должен заслужить. Я понимала очень хорошо, что деньги—единственная гарантия моих прав против надворного советника Лисицына.
>
> ["But if he does marry her, then he should not make any attempt to lay hands on her fortune. He must regard his wife's money as her own, and accept that he has no right to it. If she loves her husband, then she will share with him all the things that money can buy. But he should still make every effort to earn her love and respect." I said this knowing very well that, so far as Monsieur Court Counsellor Lisitsyn was concerned, the only guarantee of my rights was my money.]

Soboleva's story is all the more extraordinary in the heroine's refusal to allow her husband to control her land and in her declaration that husbands should earn their own keep. The lesson in this story is that to be valued, you must have value, which is as true for men as it is for women.

Soboleva understands that Madame Lisitsyna's situation is not universal. There is a parallel narrative in the story about an educated, poor young man who rejects a financially appropriate girl, Lyuba, for the vivacious and propertied Zina. Just as Katya in *Fathers and Sons* cannot marry a man who had money, Lyuba believes that she cannot marry a man who is educated. Although Zina is hardly a paragon of virtue in this story, she has power because she has both wealth and intelligence. In this way, Soboleva, like Khvoshchinskaya and Pavlova, sees the life of the mind as having worth in its own right.

Unlike their Western counterparts, Russian women writers did not make the marriage plot the center of their stories. Rather, they imbued their heroines with the emotional independence to find alternatives to the restrictions of marriage. Although Pavlova uses the traditional framework of the courtship plot to tell her story, she gives Cecily the possibility of release from the restrictions of marriage. Writing some twenty years later, Khvoshchinskaya and Soboleva construct women who deliberately subvert the device, creating instead strong, independent heroines. In literature, certainly, Tsebrikova's assertion that Russia led the way in women's emancipation rings true.

CONCLUSION: WHY ARE WOMEN POOR?

This book began with the story of Silence, the girl who was forced to dress and act male in order to inherit her family's property. Chapter six ends with Orlando, who, like Silence, owns property when she is a man, but faces the loss of it when she becomes a woman. In medieval Europe, as well as through 700 years of British history, women's inability to own and control their own property was reflected in their writings on wedlock. The medieval writers I have analyzed articulate the boundaries and limitations imposed on them once they are married. For the British women, the problem starts earlier. Once a young woman enters marriageable age, she has one goal: to find a husband. Nonetheless, all of these authors strive to gain some supremacy over their plight, whether it be Heloise's privileging of the word "whore," Marie's fantasy story resolutions, or Woolf's creation of the Society of Outsiders. They refuse to be silenced, but instead find ways to give their women characters agency.

The Russian case demonstrates that when women can own property, their narratives differ remarkably from these other cultures. The female protagonists can reject marriage as easily as they can choose it; even when they seem to be pressed into wedlock, as in *A Double Life*, an imaginative world lies open to them: the body may be imprisoned, but the mind is not. This message is wholly absent in the medieval and non-Russian modern authors (Burney, Austen, and Eliot) we have examined.

Certainly, all three periods share similarities. The influence of religious and moral beliefs was strong. Characterizations of women as either Mary or Eve for medieval writers, conduct book ladies or women of the streets for the British writers, or Dostoevsky's righteous prostitutes versus wealthy, controlling wives—these images impede women's self-sufficiency. The Russians, however, had a millennium of female property rights to balance the inherent misogyny in the Orthodox Church; the Western Europeans had none.

While Western European writers, both male and female, draw heavily on the marriage plot in their narratives, nineteenth-century Russian women do not. Their heroines are the center of their own action, making independent decisions; husbands are secondary to the plotlines. In this way, women are not on the margins, but rather in the center. The narrative tensions revolve less on relationships than on their own coming-of-age as individuals.

The medieval women writers lived in a time when, at least in some areas, their rights to own property had been recently diminished. Their narratives show women who are not afraid to be angry, to try to change the stultifying effects of marriage. In contrast, by the eighteenth century in England, there was no memory of married women owning property. Over the next century, women would be shaped into the image of domestic helpmate to the husband and the family. It is easy to see why the passage of the Married Women's Property Act did not immediately change their perceptions. Even Virginia Woolf understood women's psychological dependence on men. We see Elizabeth Dalloway, a modern woman, seemingly with the world open to her, choosing (we imagine, we fear) the same path as her mother.

So, why are women poor? I would suggest that history has indeed trapped women into conflating being property with owning property: being owned, it is impossible to own. If women do not have the memory that goes back millennia to the time Engels described, then the social and legal institutions that have "encoded" us since the Middle Ages lie deep within our psyches. Woolf delineated the psychological tyranny of the patriarchal family in *Three Guineas*, which in some ways is the key to understanding *Mrs. Dalloway*. Her triumph, however, in this author's mind, is *Orlando*, where she ends the history of male economic power. Orlando the woman becomes the center of her own story. It is in her breaking of the sound barrier that the beginnings were made to ensure that Silence no longer needs to become male.

The history of women and property, however, is broader than the three examples used here. Two directions for future investigation come immediately to mind. The first is geographical: Did non-European cultures neighboring Russia, such as the Ottoman Empire, Persia, or Georgia, share its rejection of primogeniture and acceptance of female property rights? Have other parts of the world produced women writers who connect marriage and property? The second is temporal: Have the laws providing equal opportunity to women in the United States and Britain allowed contemporary female writers to take possession of their own money? Do they accept marriage as the central event in their heroines' lives?

The women I have investigated use authorship to establish their authority. Their texts negotiate the line between being property and owning property and, in doing so, question marriage as the marker of female identity. These narratives, however, are more than merely descriptive: when viewed historically, they have a deeply transformative effect. Even in the worst of times, they tell us, words have power, a power to see where we have been and where we might go.

NOTES

Introduction: Silence and Women's Authority

1. The Old French text of *Le Roman de Silence*, along with an English translation, can be found in Heldris de Cornuälle, *Silence: A Thirteenth-Century French Romance*, ed. and trans. Sarah Roche-Mahdi (East Lansing: Michigan State University Press, 1999).
2. It has been suggested that the author of *Le Roman de Silence,* Heldris de Cornuälle, was actually female, writing pseudonymously as a man. This opinion has been expounded by Lorraine Kochanske Stock, "The Importance of Being Gender 'Stable': Masculinity and Feminine Empowerment in *Le Roman de Silence*," *Arthuriana* 7.2 (1997), 7–34; Kathleen J. Brahney, "When *Silence* was Golden: Female Personae in the *Roman de Silence*," in *The Spirit of the Court: Selected Proceedings of the Fourth Congress of the International Courtly Literature Society*, ed. Glyn S. Burgess and Robert A. Taylor (Dover, NH: D.S. Brewer, 1985), pp. 52–61; Barbara Newman, *God and the Goddesses: Vision, Poetry, and Belief in the Middle Ages* (Philadelphia: University of Pennsylvania Press, 2003); and Erin F. Labbie, "The Specular Image of the Gender-Neutral Name: Naming Silence in *Le Roman de Silence*," *Arthuriana* 7.2 (1997), 63–77.
3. Even the word "wedlock" implies restriction. As Evelyn J. Hinz has remarked, "wed" suggests optimism, whereas "lock" means suffering and entrapment. See her article, "Hierogamy versus Wedlock: Types of Marriage Plots and Their Relationship to Genres of Prose Fiction," PMLA 91.5 (1976), 902–903. *The Concise Oxford Dictionary of English Entymology*, ed. T. F. Hoad (Oxford: Oxford University Press, 1993), p. 537, however, shows its origin in the Old English *wedlāc*, "wed pledge."
4. I am not alone in seeing a connection between the loss of property rights in the Middle Ages and the strict roles for women of the nineteenth century. See Linda Mitchell, *Portraits of Medieval Women: Family, Marriage, and Politics in England 1225–1350* (New York: Palgrave Macmillan, 2003), pp. 135–136; and JoAnn McNamara, "Women and Power Through the Family Revisited," in *Gendering the Master Narrative: Women and Power in the Middle Ages*, ed. Mary C. Erler and Maryanne Kowaleski (Ithaca: Cornell University Press, 2003), pp. 25–30.

5. Frederich Engels, *The Origin of the Family, Private Property, and the State* (New York: Pathfinder Press, 1972), pp. 64–67.
6. Engels, *The Origin of the Family*, p. 68.
7. Gayle Rubin, "The Traffic in Women: Notes on the 'Political Economy' of Sex," in *Toward an Anthropology of Women*, ed. Rayna R. Reiter (New York: Monthly Review Press, 1975), pp. 173–174.
8. Ibid., p. 183.
9. Gayatri Chakravorty Spivak, *A Critique of Postcolonial Reason: Toward a History of the Vanishing Present* (Cambridge: Harvard University Press, 1999), p. 310.
10. Ibid., p. 173.
11. Caroline Walker Bynum, "Women's Stories, Women's Symbols: A Critique of Victor Turner's Theory of Liminality," in *Fragmentation and Redemption: Essays on Gender and the Human Body in Medieval Religion* (New York: Zone Books, 1992), p. 32.
12. For a discussion of the economic role of women, see Nancy Folbre and Heidi Hartmann, "The Rhetoric of Self-Interest: Ideology and Gender in Economic Theory," in *The Consequences of Economic Rhetoric,* ed. Arjo Klamer, Donald N. McCloskey, and Robert M. Solow (Cambridge: Cambridge University Press, 1988), pp. 184–203.
13. Michael Camille, *Image on the Edge: The Margins of Medieval Art* (London: Reaktion Books, 1992), p. 10. Paula R. Backscheider has also commented on the function of the marginalized voice: "Every text has a space within it for the Other, for opposition, for obstacle, for whatever occupies the position that is not expressive of the dominant." See "The Novel's Gendered Space," in *Revising Women: Eighteenth-Century "Women's Fiction" and Social Engagement,* ed. Paula R. Backscheider (Baltimore: John Hopkins University Press, 2000), p. 6.
14. Mary Carruthers, *The Book of Memory: A Study of Memory in Medieval Culture* (Cambridge: Cambridge University Press, 1992), pp. 192–193. It is fitting that the remembrance of the past is delegated to women in these romances. As Elizabeth van Houts has noted in *Memory and Gender in Medieval Europe, 900–1200* (Toronto: University of Toronto Press, 1999), p. 67, medieval memory is kin-centered, and women were the transmitters of family knowledge.
15. Patrick Geary has described how suppressed elements of the past "continued to live in the discordances, inconsistencies, and lacunae of the created past as well as in the dreams, visions, and anxieties of those who suppressed it." See his *Phantoms of Remembrance: Memory and Oblivion at the End of the First Millennium* (Princeton: Princeton University Press, 1996), pp. 7–8.

1 Property's History, Property's Literature

1. Certainly, the loss of property due to primogeniture was not specifically a gendered problem. Younger sons also bore the consequences of a solution

meant to resolve the land situation. Judith Kellogg has demonstrated that medieval romance lays bare the anxieties of the time, a belief echoed by Geraldine Heng, who calls it "the will of a collective culture." Gabrielle M. Spiegel has observed that thirteenth-century prose has a social function, responding to cultural needs. Helen Cooper has noted that there were two social changes that contributed to the emergence of romance: primogeniture and consent as the determining factor of the validity of marriage. It is not surprising, she believes, that "history and romance can sometimes chime very closely." See Judith Kellogg, *Medieval Artistry and Exchange: Economic Institutions, Society, and Literary Form in Old French Narrative* (New York: Peter Lang, 1989); Geraldine Heng, *Empire of Magic: Medieval Romance and the Politics of Cultural Fantasy* (New York: Columbia University Press, 2003), p. 8; Gabrielle M. Spiegel, *Romancing the Past: The Rise of Vernacular Prose Historiography in Thirteenth-century France* (Berkeley: University of California Press, 1993), p. 2; and Helen Cooper, "When Romance Comes True," in *Boundaries in Medieval Romance*, ed. Neil Cartlidge (Rochester, NY: D.S. Brewer, 2008), pp. 16–17.

2. It must be noted, however, that the amount of surviving evidence from the early Middle Ages is far less than that of the period after 1200, making a true comparison difficult.
3. Steven Weinburger, "Women, Property and Poetry in Eleventh Century Provence," *Proceedings of the Annual Meeting of the Western Society for French History* 8 (1980), 25. Suzanne Fonay Wemple has traced the fusion of Roman and Germanic law in Merovingian and Carolingian society in her *Women in Frankish Society: Marriage and the Cloister 500 to 900* (Philadelphia: University of Pennsylvania Press, 1981). On the right of daughters to inherit equally with sons, see Antii Arjava, *Women and Law in Late Antiquity* (Oxford: Clarendon Press, 1996), pp. 70–73 and 154–156. Although women could pass on their property, they needed support to ensure that their wishes were carried out. See Janet L. Nelson, "The Wary Widow," in *Property and Power in the Early Middle Ages*, ed. Wendy Davies and Paul Fouracre (Cambridge: Cambridge University Press, 1995), p. 94.
4. Susan Stuard, "The Dominion of Gender: Women's Fortunes in the High Middle Ages," in *Becoming Visible: Women in European History*, ed. Renate Bridenthal, Claudia Koonz, and Susan Stuard (Boston: Houghton Mifflin Company, 1987), pp. 155–156.
5. David Herlihy, "The Making of the Medieval Family: Symmetry, Structure, and Sentiment," *Journal of Family History* 8.2 (1983), 122.
6. David Herlihy, "Land, Family, and Women in Continental Europe," *Traditio* XVIII (1962), 92–100.
7. Herlihy, "The Making of the Medieval Family," 124.
8. Georges Duby, *La Société aux XIe et XIIe Siècles Dans La Région Mâconnaise* (Paris: Librairie Armand Colin, 1953), pp. 53–54.
9. Janet Martindale traces notions of primogeniture back to the Old Testament (Genesis, 27, Exodus, 12); Christ can also been viewed as *primogenitus*

(Luke, 2 vii, Colossians, 1xv). Janet Martindale, "Succession Politics in the Romance-Speaking World, c. 1000–1140," in *England and Her Neighbours, 1066–1453: Essays in Honour of Pierre Chaplais*, ed. Michael C. E. Jones and Malcolm Vale (London: The Hambledon Press, 1989), p. 26.

10. Jo Ann McNamara, "The *Herrenfrage*: The Restructuring of the Gender System, 1050–1150," in *Medieval Masculinities: Regarding Men in the Middle Ages*, ed. Clare Lees (Minneapolis: University of Minnesota Press, 1994), p. 4. Among many other analyses of the societal implications of primogeniture, two in particular stand out: Mary Frances Wack's *Lovesickness in the Middle Ages: The Viaticum and its Commentaries* (Philadelphia: University of Pennsylvania Press, 1990), in which she argues that younger sons, torn from their mothers, sought to replace them by romantic alliances with the lords' wives; and Kellogg, *Medieval Artistry and Exchange*, in which she shows how anxiety over changing economic models influenced romance literature.
11. Weinburger, "Women, Property and Poetry in Eleventh Century Provence," 29.
12. Stuard, "The Dominion of Gender," p. 161.
13. Diane Owen Hughes, "From Bridepiece to Dowry in Mediterranean Europe," *Journal of Family History* 3 (1978), 266.
14. Hughes, "From Bridepiece to Dowry," 23.
15. David Herlihy, *Medieval Households* (Cambridge: Cambridge University Press, 1985), pp. 50–51.
16. Herlihy, *Medieval Households*, p. 90.
17. Hughes, "From Bridepiece to Dowry," 34–35. Hughes's thesis has recently been challenged by Cynthia Johnson, who argues that cash contributions did not replace gifts of land, but, rather, augmented them. Cash, she contends, was actually preferred to land because it was easily portable, easily investible, and easily divided among heirs. See her "Marriage Agreements from Twelfth-Century Southern France," in *To Have and To Hold: Marrying and Its Documentation in Western Christendom, 400–1600*, ed. Philip L. Reynolds (Cambridge: Cambridge University Press, 2007), pp. 224–225.
18. Mark Angelos, "Urban Women, Investment, and the Commercial Revolution of the Middle Ages," in *Women in Medieval Western European Culture*, ed. Linda A. Mitchell (New York: Garland Publishing, Inc., 1999), p. 259.
19. Jack Goody, "Inheritance, Property and Women: Some Comparative Considerations," in *Family and Inheritance: Rural Society in Western Europe 1200–1800*, ed. Jack Goody, Joan Thirsk, and E. P. Thompson (Cambridge: Cambridge University Press, 1976), pp. 10–36.
20. McNamara, "The *Herrenfrage*," p. 8.
21. Weinburger, "Women, Property and Poetry in Eleventh Century Provence," 29.
22. Penny Shine Gold, *The Lady and the Virgin: Image, Attitude, and Experience in Twelfth-century France* (Chicago: University of Chicago Press, 1985), pp. 121–132.
23. Gold, *The Lady and the Virgin*, p. 141.

24. Birgit Sawyer, "Women as Landholders and Alienators of Property in Early Medieval Scandinavia," in *Female Power in the Middle Ages: Proceedings from the 2. St. Gertrud Symposium*, ed. Karen Glente and Lise Winther-Jensen (Copenhagen: C.A. Reitzel, 1989), pp. 165–166.
25. Claire deTrafford, "Share and Share Alike? The Marriage Portion, Inheritance, and Family Politics," in *Studies in Medieval and Early Modern Women: Pawns of Players?* ed. Christine Meek and Catherine Lawless (Dublin: Four Courts Press, 2003), pp. 37–41. By the fifteenth century in England, the power of rich widows to even keep their property was severely challenged. See Rhoda Lange Friedrichs, "Rich Old Ladies Made Poor: The Vulnerability of Women's Property in Late Medieval England," *Medieval Prosopography: History and Collective Biography* 21 (2000), 211–219.
26. Jo Ann McNamara, writing in 2003, upheld the conclusion that she and Suzanne Wemple came to in 1973 ["The Power of Woman Through the Family in Medieval Europe: 500–1100," *Feminist Studies* 1.3/4 (1973), 126–141] that aristocratic women's power to control their property declined. See Jo Ann McNamara, "Women and Power Through the Family Revisited," in *Gendering the Master Narrative: Women and Power in the Middle Ages*, ed. Mary C. Erler and Maryanne Kowaleski (Ithaca: Cornell University Press, 2003), pp. 21–22.
27. Theodore Evergates, ed., *Aristocratic Women in Medieval France* (Philadelphia: University of Pennsylvania Press, 1999), pp. 1–2.
28. Amy Livingstone, "Aristocratic Women in the Chartrain," in Evergates, *Aristocratic Women in Medieval France*, pp. 44–73.
29. Amy Livingstone, "Noblewomen's Control of Property in Early Twelfth-Century Blois-Chartres," *Medieval Prosopography: History and Collective Biography* 18 (1997), 55–71. Rebecca Lynn Winer, in *Women, Wealth, and Community in Peripignan, c. 1250–1300: Christians, Jews, and Enslaved Muslims* (Aldershot: Ashgate, 2006), analyses women's property rights in the context of three different religious communities. The variations within these settings argue for significant variations in the actual practice of Roman dowry in Western Europe.
30. Amy Livingstone, *Out of Love For My Kin: Aristocratic Family Life in the Lands of the Loire, 1000–1200* (Ithaca: Cornell University Press, 2010), p. 112. Michelle Armstrong-Partida contends that not only could women inherit in the Blois-Chartres region, they could also assume all of the responsibilities associated with ownership. "Mothers and Daughters as Lords: The Countesses of Blois and Chartres," *Medieval Prosopography* 26 (2005), 77–107.
31. Theodore Evergates, "Aristocratic Women in the County of Champagne," in Evergates, *Aristocratic Women in Medieval France*, p. 89.
32. Evergates, "Aristocratic Women in the County of Champagne," in Evergates, *Aristocratic Women in Medieval France*, pp. 162–163.
33. Martha C. Howell, *The Marriage Exchange: Property, Social Place, and Gender in the Cities of the Low Countries, 1300–1550* (Chicago: University of Chicago Press, 1998), p. 3. In an earlier work, Howell shows how women

were restricted from membership in craft and guild positions that carried prestige and power during the same time period, mainly because the patriarchal order required it. See her *Women, Production, and Patriarchy in Late Medieval Cities* (Chicago: University of Chicago Press, 1986).

34. Howell, *The Marriage Exchange,* pp. 8–9.
35. Howell, *The Marriage Exchange,* p. 168. Howell describes the marriage contract as "less like a pact between partners in life than an exhaustive list of bargaining points among hostile participants."
36. Howell, *The Marriage Exchange,* p. 153.
37. Howell, *The Marriage Exchange,* p. 164.
38. Shennan Hutton, *Women and Economic Activities in Late Medieval Ghent* (New York: Palgrave Macmillan, 2011), p. 2.
39. Hutton, *Women and Economic Activities,* pp. 3–5.
40. Hutton, *Women and Economic Activities,* p. 150. In this, Hutton follows Judith Bennett, whom I discuss in chapter five, who found the same results in England.
41. An interesting example of women gaining patrimonies is given by Joëlle Rollo-Koster. In late medieval Avignon the plague caused a scarcity of patrilineal heirs allowing dowered daughters to inherit. Joëlle Rollo-Koster, "The Boundaries of Affection: Women and Property in Late Medieval Avignon," in *Across the Religious Divide: Women, Property, and Law in the Wider Mediterranean (ca. 1300–1800),* ed. Jutta Gisela Sperling and Shona Kelly Wray (New York: Routledge, 2010), p. 39.
42. Linda Mitchell, *Portraits of Medieval Women: Family, Marriage, and Politics in England 1225–1350* (New York: Palgrave Macmillan, 2003), pp. 6–7.
43. Craig Berry believes this is the case, calling *Le Roman de Silence* "a romance of property rights." Craig R. Berry, "What Silence Desires: Female Inheritance and the Romance of Property in the *Roman de Silence,*" in *Translating Desire in Medieval and Early Modern Literature,* ed. Craig R. Berry and Heather Richardson Hayton (Tempe: Arizona Center for Medieval and Renaissance Studies, 2005), p. 193.
44. For example, see the following representative articles: (1) *Le Roman de Silence,* Lorraine Kochanske Stock, "The Importance of Being Gender 'Stable': Masculinity and Feminine Empowerment in *Le Roman de Silence,*" *Arthuriana* 7.2 (1994), 7–34; Peggy McCracken, "The Boy Who Was a Girl,: Reading Gender in the *Roman de* Silence," *Romanic Review* 85 (1995), 517–536; and Kate Mason Cooper, "Elle and *L*: Sexualized Textuality in *Le Roman de Silence,*" *Romance Notes* XXV.3 (1985), 341–360. (2) *La Manekine,* the work of Carol Harvey, in particular, "Incest, Identity and Uncourtly Conduct in *La Manekine,*" in *The Court Reconvenes: Courtly Literatures Across the Disciplines,* ed. Barbara K. Altmann and Carleton W. Carroll (Rochester, NY: D.S. Brewer, 2003), pp. 161–168. (3) *Havelok,* Michael Faletra, "The Ends of Romance: Dreaming the Nation in the Middle English Havelok," *Exemplaria: A Journal of Theory in Medieval and Renaissance Studies* 17.2 (2005), 347–380; and Judith Weiss, "Structure and

Characterization in Havelok the Dane," *Speculum* 44.2 (1969), 247–257. In addition to Craig A. Berry, three other scholars have raised the inheritance issue in *Le Roman de Silence*: Christopher Callahan, "Canon Law, Primogeniture, and the Marriage of Ebain and Silence, " *Romance Quarterly* 49.1 (2002), 12–20; Sharon Kinoshita, "Mail-Order Brides: Marriage, Patriarchy, and Monarchy in the *Roman de Silence*," *Arthuriana* 12.1 (2002), 64–75; and Erika E. Hess, "Inheritance Law and Gender Identity in the *Roman de Silence*," in *Law and Sovereignty in the Middle Ages*, ed. Robert S. Sturges (Brepols, 2011), Arizona Studies in the Middle Ages and the Renaissance, volume 28, pp. 215–235.

45. Text and translation from Sarah Roche-Mahdi, *Silence: A Thirteenth Century French Romance* (East Lansing: Michigan State University Press, 1999).
46. Berry argues that elder daughters were expected to share their inheritance with their sisters, which often gave rise to the kind of conflict seen in *Le Roman de Silence*, pp. 199–201.
47. Loren Ringer has analyzed the name "Malduit" and contends that it has multiple meanings, the most interesting of which is "mal conduit" in modern French: "One cannot help but notice that the difference between 'Malduit' and 'ma*con*duit' (i.e. "con" or the female sex) is exactly what Silence is being forced to hide." Loren Ringer, "Exchange, Identity, and Transvestism in *Le roman de Silence*," *Dalhousie French Studies* 28 (1994), 8.
48. Barbara N. Sargent-Baur, "Dating the Romances of Phillipe de Remi: Between an Improbable Source and a Dubious Adaptation," in *Essays on the Poetic and Legal Writings of Philippe de Remy and His Son Philippe de Beaumanoir of Thirteenth-Century France*, ed. Sarah-Grace Heller and Michelle Reichert (Lewiston: The Edwin Mellen Press, 2001), p. 22. I use the text and translation of Irene Gnarra, *Philippe de Remi's "La Manekine": Text, Translation, Commentary* (New York: Garland Publishing, Inc. 1988).
49. Nancy B. Black, *Medieval Narratives of Accused Queens* (Gainesville: University of Florida Press, 2003), p. 36.
50. Harvey, "Incest, Identity and Uncourtly Conduct in *La Manekine*," p. 166.
51. Margaret Schlauch, *Chaucer's Constance and Accused Queens* (New York: New York University Press, 1927), p. 45.
52. Judith Weiss, "Structure and Characterisation in Havelok the Dane," 247.
53. Richard J. Moll, "'Nest pas autentik, mais apocrophum': Haveloks and Their Reception in Medieval England," *Studies in Philology* 105.2 (2008), 179.
54. G. Smithers, ed., *Havelok* (Oxford: Clarendon Press, 1987), p. lvii. I use Smithers's edition as the text for *Havelok*.
55. Smithers, *Havelok, p.* lvii.
56. Judith Weiss, "The Power and Weakness of Women in Anglo-Norman Romance," in *Women and Literature in Britain, 1150–1500*, ed. Carol M. Neale (Cambridge: Cambridge University Press, 1996), pp. 7–8.
57. K. S. Whetter, "*Gest* and *Vita*, Folktale and Romance in *Havelok*," *Parergon* 20.2 (2003), 25.

2 Silence, Language, Sexuality

1. R. Howard Bloch, *Medieval Misogyny and the Invention of Western Romantic Love* (Chicago: University of Chicago Press, 1991), pp. 15–20.
2. Jack Goody, *Production and Reproduction: A Comparative Study of the Domestic Domain* (Cambridge: Cambridge University Press, 1976), p. 13.
3. Georges Duby, *Medieval Marriage: Two Models from Twelfth-Century France* (Baltimore: Johns Hopkins University Press, 1978), p. 4.
4. Duby, *Medieval Marriage*, pp. 105–116. The decrease in growth, according to Goody, is due to peace: "The coming of peace threatened the Church because nobles who had lived on a war-footing for so long now had to be enfeoffed out of ecclesiastical estates. Many had provided so many fiefs to their vassals that they had now to extort land from other sources" (p. 116).
5. Augustine, *Confessiones*, ed. Gillian Clark (Cambridge: Cambridge University Press, 1995), Book IV.2, pp. 68–69. English translation by P. S. Pine-Coffin, *Saint Augustine: Confessions* (London: Penguin Books, 1961), p. 72.
6. Augustine, *De bono coniugali, De sancta virginitate*, ed. and trans. P. G. Walsh (Oxford: Clarendon Press, 2001), p. 10. English translation for this passage only from Ray Kearney, St. Augustine, *The Excellence of Marriage, Holy Virginity, The Excellence of Widowhood, Adulterous Marriage, Continence* (New York: New City Press, 1999), p. 36.
7. Dyan Elliott, *Spiritual Marriage: Sexual Abstinence in Medieval Wedlock* (Princeton: Princeton University Press, 1993), p. 22.
8. Elliott, *Spiritual Marriage*, p. 31.
9. Augustine, *De bono coniugali*, p. 14.
10. Augustine, *De bono coniugali*, pp. 6–8.
11. Augustine, *De bono coniugali*, p. 12.
12. Augustine, *De bono coniugali*, p. 8.
13. Georges Duby, *Love and Marriage in the Middle Ages* (Chicago: University of Chicago Press, 1994), pp. 8–9.
14. Duby, *Love and Marriage in the Middle Ages*, p. 8.
15. James A. Brundage, *Law, Sex, and Christian Society in Medieval Europe* (Chicago: University of Chicago Press, 1987), p. 137.
16. James A. Brundage, "Implied Consent to Intercourse," in *Consent and Coercion to Sex and Marriage in Ancient and Medieval Societies*, ed. Angeliki E. Laiou (Washington: Dunbarton Oaks Research Library and Collection, 1993), pp. 246–248. Charles Donahue, Jr. clarifies this decretal. Marriage was made by consent of the parties; however, in the case of consent to a future marriage, intercourse was needed in addition to consent. Charles Donahue, Jr., *Law, Marriage, and Society in the Later Middle Ages* (Cambridge: Cambridge University Press, 2008), p. 32.
17. Charles J. Reid, Jr., *Power Over the Body, Equality in the Family: Rights and Domestic Relations in Medieval Canon Law* (Grand Rapids: William B. Eerdmans Publishing Company, 2004), p. 52.
18. Audrey B. Davidson and Robert B. Ekelund, Jr., "The Medieval Church and Rents from Marriage Market Regulations," *Journal of Economic Behavior and Organization* 32 (1997), 215–245.

19. Brundage, *Law, Sex, and Christian* Society, pp. 220-221. See also Anne Llewellyn Barstow, *Married Priests and the Reforming Papacy: The Eleventh-Century Debates* (New York: The Edwin Mellen Press, 1982), p. 1.
20. Jack Goody, *The Development of the Family and Marriage in Europe* (Cambridge: Cambridge University Press, 1983), pp. 77–80. See also Irven M. Resnick, "Marriage in Medieval Culture: Consent Theory and the Case of Joseph and Mary," *Church History* 69.2 (2000), 350.
21. Neil Cartlidge, *Medieval Marriage: Literary Approaches, 1100–1300* (Cambridge: D.S. Brewer, 1997), p. 14.
22. Elliott, *Spiritual Marriage,* p. 141.
23. Jo Ann McNamara, "The Herrenfrage: The Restructuring of the Gender System, 1050–1150," in *Medieval Masculinities: Regarding Men in the Middle Ages*, ed. Clare A. Lees (Minneapolis: University of Minnesota Press, 1994), p. 11.
24. Alcuin Blamires, ed., *Woman Defamed and Woman Defended: An Anthology of Medieval Texts* (Oxford: Clarendon Press, 1992), pp. 2–5.
25. Prudence Allen, *The Concept of Woman: The Aristotelian Revolution 750 BC–AD 1250* (Montreal: Eden Press, 1985), p. 247.
26. E. Ann Matter, "The Undebated Debate: Gender and the Image of God in Medieval Theology," in *Gender and Debate from the Early Middle Ages to the Renaissance,* ed. Thelma S. Fenster and Clare A. Lees (New York: Palgrave, 2002), p. 41.
27. Sharon Farmer, "Persuasive Voices: Clerical Images of Medieval Wives," *Speculum* 61.3 (1986), 520.
28. Bloch, *Medieval Misogyny,* p. 69.
29. Shulamith Shahar, *The Fourth Estate: A History of Women in the Middle Ages* (London: Routledge, 1983), pp. 77–78.
30. Walter Map, *De Nugis Curialium: Courtiers' Trifles*, ed. and trans. M. R. James (Oxford: Clarendon Press, 1983), p. 292. Translation mine.
31. Map, *De Nugis Curialium*, p. 290.
32. Map, *De Nugis Curialium*, p. 292.
33. John Toland, *Petrus Alfonsi and His Medieval Readers* (Gainesville: University Press of Florida, 1993), p. 74.
34. Toland, *Petrus Alfonsi*, pp. 132–138.
35. Petrus Alfonsi, *Disciplina clericalis,* ed. María Jesús Lacarra (Zaragoza: Guara Editorial, S.A., 1980), pp. 125–126. Translation mine. "The Well" was adapted by Boccaccio, Toland notes, to promote sympathy for the cuckolded husband. Toland, *Petrus Alfonsi,* p. 156.
36. Alfonsi, *Disciplina clericalis*, p. 124.
37. Map, *De Nugis Curialium*, p. 292.
38. *De Nugis Curialium*, p. 306.
39. *De Nugis Curialium*, p. 300. Jerome, in his *Adversus Jovinianum*, includes the example of Cicero, as well as many others, to argue that marriage and philosophy are mutually exclusive. The best known of these was that of Theophrastus, who declared, "Non est ergo uxor ducenda sapienti. Primum enim impediri studia philosophiae, nec posse quemquam libris

et uxori pariter inservire" ("The philosopher should therefore avoid taking a wife, for to begin with this hinders the study of philosophy, and no one can minister to books and a wife at the same time"). Quoted in P. G. Walsh, "Antifeminism in the High Middle Ages," in *Satiric Advice on Women and Marriage: From Plautus to Chaucer*, ed. Warren S. Smith (Ann Arbor: University of Michigan Press, 2005), p. 225.

40. *De Nugis Curicalium*, p. 300.
41. Katharina M. Wilson and Elizabeth M. Makowski, *Wykked Wyves and the Woes of Marriage: Misogamous Literature from Juvenal to Chaucer* (Albany: State University of New York Press, 1990), p. 7.
42. Wilson and Makowski, *Wykked Wyves*, p. 164. Barbara Feichtinger argues, without any supporting data, that the period in which medieval misogynistic writings were popular were times of improving financial circumstances for women, due to "the increasing freedom, power, influence, education, and financial independence of wives." This, she concludes, "threatened to destabilize the patriarchal system." It is likely that these comments apply to a later period of her study when she discusses popular misogynistic literature. Barbara Feichtinger, "Change and Continuity in Pagan and Christian (Invective) Thought on Women and Marriage from Antiquity to the Middle Ages," in Smith, *Satiric Advice on Women and Marriage*, p. 185.
43. Farmer, "Persuasive Voices," 520–521.
44. P. H. Cullum, "Gendering Charity in Medieval Hagiography," in *Gender and Holiness: Men, Women and Saints in Late Medieval Europe*, ed. Samantha J. E. Riches and Sarah Salih (London: Routledge, 2002), p. 144.
45. Farmer, "Persuasive Voices," 534–535.
46. Alcuin Blamires, *The Case for Women in Medieval Culture* (Oxford: Clarendon Press, 1997), p. 17.
47. Blamires, *The Case for Women in Medieval Culture*, pp. 134–136.
48. Blamires, *The Case for Women in Medieval Culture*, p. 237.
49. Marbod of Rennes, *Liber decem capitulorum* (Roma: Herder Editrice e Libreria, 1984), p. 125.
50. Ambrose, *De virginibus*, Corpus Scriptorum Latinorum Paravianum, ed. Egnatius Cazzaniga (Torino: G.B. Paravia, n.d.), I, 21, p. 11. Translation mine.
51. Ambrose, *De virginibus,* I, 19, p. 10.
52. Ambrose, *De virginibus.*
53. Jocelyn Wogan-Browne, "Saints' Lives and the Female Reader," *Forum for Modern Language Studies* 27 (1991), 15.
54. An excellent analysis of the married woman saint appears in Marc Glasser's "Marriage in Medieval Hagiography," *Studies in Medieval and Renaissance History* 4 (1981), 3–34.
55. Glasser's "Marriage in Medieval Hagiography," 20.
56. John W. Baldwin, "Five Discourses on Desire: Sexuality and Gender in Northern France around 1200," *Speculum* 66.4 (1991), 797.
57. Resnick, "Marriage in Medieval Culture," 355.
58. Resnick, "Marriage in Medieval Culture," 364.

59. Matter, "The Undebated Debate," p. 49.
60. Barbara Newman, *Sister of Wisdom: St. Hildegard's Theology of the Feminine* (Berkeley: University of California Press, 1987), p. 35.
61. John Van Engen, "Letters and the Public *Persona* of Hildegard," in *Hildegard von Bingen in ihrem historischen Umfeld*, ed. Alfred Haverkamp (Mainz: Verlag Philipp von Zabern, 2000), p. 415. As Van Engen points out, this persona of a "Spirit-filled" writer rather than one trained in the Schools was Hildegard's own creation. "Indocta" did not mean that Hildegard was illiterate, but rather that she did not attend a cathedral school, follow a wandering teacher, or study at a convent with a good library. A vita of Jutta of Sponheim, her teacher, discovered in 1992 shows that Jutta was very capable intellectually and knew Latin. Newman, however, characterizes Hildegard's Latin grammar as "always shaky." See Barbara Newman, "Sibyl of the Rhine: Hildegard's Life and Times," in *Voice of the Living Light: Hildegard of Bingen and Her World*, ed. Barbara Newman (Berkeley: University of California Press, 1998), pp. 6–7.
62. *Hildegardis Bingensis Epistolarium*, ed. Lieven Van Acker (Turnholt: Brepols, 1991), Corpus Christianorum 91, Ep. 31R, 83. Translation mine.
63. Barbara Newman, "Hildegard and Her Hagiographers: The Remaking of Female Sainthood," in *Gendered Voices: Medieval Saints and Their Interpreters*, ed. Catherine M. Mooney (Philadelphia: University of Pennsylvania Press, 1999), pp. 26–27.
64. *Epistolarum*, Ep. 39, 100.
65. *Epistolarum*, Ep. 39R, 101.
66. *Epistolarum*, Ep. 40, 102.
67. *Epistolarum*, Ep. 40R, 105.
68. Ann W. Astell, *The Song of Songs in the Middle Ages* (Ithaca: Cornell University Press, 1990), pp. 3–4.
69. Stephen D. Moore, "The Song of Songs in the History of Sexuality," *Church History* 69.2 (2000), 332. Moore goes beyond the traditional interpretation of the text as a sexual relationship between male and female to one between two males.
70. Moore, "The Song of Songs in the History of Sexuality," 336.
71. E. Ann Matter, *The Voice of My Beloved: The Song of Songs in Western Medieval Christendom* (Philadelphia: University of Pennsylvania Press, 1990), p. 6.
72. Matter, *The Voice of My Beloved*, p. 122.
73. Matter, *The Voice of My Beloved*, p. 133.
74. Astell, *The Song of Songs in the Middle Ages*, p. 96.
75. Bernard of Clairvaux, *Sermones Super Cantica Canticorum* I.1 (Rome: Editiones Cistercienses, 1957–1958), p. 3. Translation mine.
76. Bernard of Clairvaux, *Sermones Super Cantica Canticorum*, p. 4.
77. Bernard of Clairvaux, *Sermones Super Cantica Canticorum*, I.2, p. 4.
78. Bernard of Clairvaux, *Sermones Super Cantica Canticorum*, I.11, p. 7.
79. Bernard of Clairvaux, *Sermones Super Cantica Canticorum*, VII.2, p. 31.
80. Bernard of Clairvaux, *Sermones Super Cantica Canticorum*, p. 32.
81. Bernard of Clairvaux, *Sermones Super Cantica Canticorum*, VIII.1, p. 36.

82. Bernard of Clairvaux, *Sermones Super Cantica Canticorum*, IX.7, p. 46.
83. Bernard of Clairvaux, *Sermones Super Cantica Canticorum*, IX, 10, p. 47.
84. Bernard of Clairvaux, *Sermones Super Cantica Canticorum*, p. 48.
85. Astell, *The Song of Songs in the Middle Ages*, p. 98.
86. Astell, *The Song of Songs in the Middle Ages*, p. 11.
87. Matter, *Voice*, p. 151.
88. Matter, *Voice*, p. 158.
89. Jaroslav Pelikan, *Mary through the Centuries: Her Place in the History of Culture* (New Haven: Yale University Press, 1996), p. 8.
90. Pelikan, *Mary through the Centuries*, pp. 11–14.
91. Peter Brown, *The Body and Society: Men, Women, ad Sexual Renunciation in Early Christianity* (New York: Columbia University Press, 1998), pp. 273–274.
92. Rachel Fulton, *From Judgment to Passion: Devotion to Christ and the Virgin Mary, 800–1200* (New York: Columbia University Press, 2002), pp. 303–306.
93. Fulton, *From Judgment to Passion*, p. 199.

3 Medieval Women Reject Marriage: Heloise and Marie de France

1. Betty Radice, trans., revised by M. T. Clanchy, *The Letters of Abelard and Heloise* (London: Penguin Books, 2003), p. 51.
2. Peter Dronke, *Abelard and Heloise in Medieval Testimonies* (Glasgow: University of Glasgow Press, 1976), pp. 16–22.
3. M. T. Clanchy, "The Letters of Abelard and Heloise in Today's Scholarship," in Radice, *The Letters of Abelard and Heloise*, pp. lviii–lix.
4. Radice, *The Letters of Abelard and Heloise*, p. ix.
5. "In your mother superior you have guidance which can be adequate for you to all purposes, namely, to exemplify virtues as well as to learn scholarship. Grounded not only in Latin but also in Hebrew as well as in Greek texts, she alone in this age seems to have acquired expertise in the three sacred languages." Jan M. Ziolkowski, ed. and trans., *Letters of Peter Abelard, beyond the Personal* (Washington, D.C.: The Catholic University of America Press, 2008), p. 28.
6. For a philological analysis that disputes Mews's claims, see Jan M. Ziolkowski, "Lost and Not Yet Found: Heloise, Abelard, and the Epistolae Duorum Amantium," *Journal of Medieval Latin* 4 (2004), 171–202.
7. It is not unusual that such a letter would reach Heloise. During the Middle Ages, letters were, as John Van Engen points out, public or semipublic communications, often read out loud and used to compile the thought and "even the self-consciousness or inner spirit" of a person. See John Van Engen, "Letters, Schools, and Written Culture in the Eleventh and Twelfth Centuries," in *Dialektik und Rhetorik im früheren und hohen Mittelalter*, ed. Johannes Fried (München: R. Oldenbourg Verlag, 1997), p. 104.

8. Glenda McLeod, "'Wholly Guilty, Wholly Innocent': Self-Definition in Héloïse's Letters to Abélard," in *Dear Sister: Medieval Women and the Epistolary Genre*, ed. Karen Cherewatuk and Ulrike Wiethaus (Philadelphia: University of Pennsylvania Press, 1993), p. 66. Robert R. Edwards notes that the word "debitum" is also from the parable of the unforgiving servant (Matt 18:23–35): the servant is forgiven an enormous debt by his master, but then demands a smaller debt repayment from another servant. Robert R. Edwards, *The Flight from Desire: Augustine and Ovid to Chaucer* (New York: Palgrave Macmillan, 2006), p. 75.
9. Peter Dronke, *Women Writers of the Middle Ages: A Critical Study of Texts from Perpetua (†203) to Marguerite Porete (†1310)* (Cambridge: Cambridge University Press, 1984), p. 137.
10. John W. Baldwin, "Consent and the Marital Debt: Five Discourses in Northern France around 1200," in *Consent and Coercion to Sex and Marriage in Ancient and Medieval Societies*, ed. Angeliki E. Laiou (Washington: Dunbarton Oaks Research Library and Collection, 1993), p. 251.
11. Charles J. Reid, Jr., *Power over the Body, Equality in the Family: Rights and Domestic Relations in Medieval Canon Law* (Grand Rapids: William B. Eerdmans Publishing Company, 2004), p. 103. For a fuller discussion of the medieval debate on the marital debt, see John W. Baldwin, "Five Discourses on Desire: Sexuality and Gender in Northern France around 1200," *Speculum* 66.4 (1991), 797–819.
12. Philip Lyndon Reynolds, *Marriage in the Western Church: The Christianization of Marriage during the Patristic and Early Medieval Periods* (Leiden: E.J. Brill, 1994), p. 255.
13. Reid, *Power over the Body,* p. 202.
14. James A. Brundage, "Sexual Equality in Medieval Canon Law," in *Medieval Women and the Sources of Medieval History,* ed. Joel T. Rosenthal (Athens, GA: University of Georgia Press, 1990), pp. 67–69.
15. McLeod, "'Wholly Guilty, Wholly Innocent,'" p. 66.
16. The Latin text is from J. T. Muckle, "The Personal Letters between Abelard and Heloise," *Mediaeval Studies* 15 (1953), 47–94. All translations are mine. The letters are hereafter referred to using M. T. Clanchy's system, beginning with the *Historia calamitatum* as Letter 1.
17. Muckle, "The Personal Letters between Abelard and Heloise," p. 65. Nancy A. Jones has argued, quite accurately, I believe, that "these shifts between the first person singular and first person plural pronouns reveal the intensification of her private feelings about Abelard and their mutual past." See her "By Woman's Tears Redeemed: Female Lament in St. Augustine's *Confessions* and the Correspondence of Abelard and Heloise," in *Sex and Gender in Medieval and Renaissance Texts: The Latin Tradition*, ed. Barbara K. Gold, Paul Allen Miller, and Charles Platter (Albany: State University of New York Press, 1977), p. 28.
18. Claire Nouvet, "The Discourse of the 'Whore': An Economy of Sacrifice," *MLN* 105 (1990), 758.

19. Ruth Mazzo Karras, *Sexuality in Medieval Europe: Doing unto Others* (New York: Routledge, 2005), p. 104.
20. Peggy Kamuf, *Fictions of Feminine Desire: Disclosures of Heloise* (Lincoln: University of Nebraska Press, 1982), pp. 20–21.
21. Martin Irvine, "Heloise and the Gendering of the Literate Subject," in *Criticism and Dissent in the Middle Ages*, ed. Rita Copeland (Cambridge: Cambridge University Press, 1996), p. 102.
22. Catherine Brown, "Muliebriter: Doing Gender in the Letters of Heloise," in *Gender and Text in the Later Middle Ages*, ed. Jane Chance (Gainesville: University Press of Florida, 1996), p. 27.
23. Dronke, *Women Writers*, p. 121.
24. McLeod has described it in this way: "For Abélard, Hélöise's past has been obliterated and Hélöise's present absorbed into the love of Christ, but Hélöise's private love for Abélard continues to impinge on her public role as bride of Christ." McLeod, "'Wholly Guilty, Wholly Innocent,'" p. 73.
25. Ann W. Astell, *The Song of Songs in the Middle Ages* (Ithaca: Cornell University Press, 1990), p. 1.
26. Lewis and Short, *A Latin Dictionary* (Oxford: Clarendon Press, 2002), p. 378. It is interesting that Radice translates it as "transfer" (*Letters*, 138). One may speculate on other words Abelard could have used to describe the change in Heloise's status. For example, had he wanted to stress the spiritual change in her stature, could he have used "translatio"?
27. Peter Abelard, *Opera theologia: Corpus Christianorum Continuato Mediaevalis XIII* (Turnholt: Brepols, 1987), p. 402.
28. Heloise's response to this letter has generated considerable scholarly debate. Although its tone is so different from the first two, Glenda McLeod rejects the idea that she has undergone some kind of conversion ("'Wholly Guilty, Wholly Innocent,'" p. 77). As Peter Dronke has explained, there is, in fact, significant continuity in her letters: her desire for a monastic rule reflects her "ceaseless quest for complete and honest understanding" (Dronke, *Woman Writers of the Middle Ages*, pp. 138–139). Linda Georgianna suggests that it is an "institutionally-centered version of what she has asked of Abelard all along: consolation and guidance for an unruly heart." See Linda Georgianna, "Any Corner of Heaven: Heloise's Critique of Monasticism," *Mediaeval Studies* 49 (1987), 247. For Peggy McCracken, Heloise's third letter continues McCracken's interest in the representation of the female body. See her chapter titled "The Curse of Eve: Female Bodies and Christian Bodies in Heloise's Third Letter," in *Listening to Heloise: The Voice of a Twelfth-Century Woman*, ed. Bonnie Wheeler (New York: St. Martin's Press, 2000), p. 227. Others, however, argue for a conversion—Abelard's, not Heloise's. Katharine Wilson and Glenda McLeod claim that she has won their rhetorical debate. See their "Textual Strategies I the Abelard/Heloise Correspondence" in Wheeler, *Listening to Heloise,* p. 122. Barbara Newman views Heloise's last letter as the silencing of her desire as well as her feminine voice. See her chapter, "Authority, Authenticity, and the Repression of Heloise," in *From Virile Woman to WomanChrist: Studies*

in Medieval Religion and Literature (Philadelphia: University of Pensylvania Press, 1995), p. 74. Jane Chance also contends that Heloise is the "magistra" in her "Classical Myth and Gender in the Letters of 'Abelard' and 'Heloise': Gloss, Glossed, Glossator," in Wheeler, *Listening to Heloise,* p. 177. Joan Ferrante has argued in a similar vein: Heloise has directed Abelard's thought from the beginning of the correspondence, which continues on an intellectual rather than emotional level in her third letter. See her *To the Glory of her Sex: Women's Roles in the Composition of Medieval Texts* (Bloomington: Indiana University Press, 1997), p. 59.

29. The Latin text of this letter is from J. T. Muckle, "The Letter of Heloise on Religious Life and Abelard's First Reply, *Mediaeval Studies* 17 (1955), 240–281.
30. In addition, other words of Abelard, including the *Hymnarius Paraclitensis,* the dedicatory letter to the *Expositio in Hexaemeron,* and the prologue to the book of sermons have dedications to Heloise. See Jan M. Ziolkowski, *Letters of Peter Abelard, beyond the Personal,* p. xlii.
31. Clanchy refers to Heloise's entrance into religious life as the "silencing of Heloise," which he calls a "prelude to the silencing of academic women as a class for the next eight centuries." This statement is somewhat misleading, since she went on to pursue her intellectual interests after she had become a nun. M. T. Clanchy, *Abelard: A Medieval Life* (Oxford: Blackwell, 1997), p. 46.
32. R. Howard Bloch, *The Anonymous Marie de France* (Chicago: University of Chicago Press, 2003), pp. 2–6. Bloch gives a full accounting of the conflicting scholarly positions on Marie's identity in these pages.
33. Bloch, *The Anonymous Marie de France,* p. 6.
34. See, e.g., Roberta L. Krueger, "Beyond Debate: Gender at Play in Old French Courtly Fiction," in *Gender in Debate from the Early Middle Ages to the Renaissance,* ed. Thelma S. Fenster and Clare A. Lees (London: Palgrave, 2002), pp. 79–95; Laurie A. Finke and Martin B. Shichtman, "Magical Mistress Tour: Patronage, Intellectual Property, and the Dissemination of Wealth in the *Lais* of Marie de France," *SIGNS* 25 (2000), 479–503; and Dolliann Margaret Hurtig, "'I Do, I Do': Medieval Models of Marriage and Choice of Partners in Marie de France's 'Le Fraisne,'" *Romanic Review* 92, 4 (2001), 363–379.
35. Bloch, *The Anonymous Marie de France,* p. 20.
36. Hurtig, "'I Do, I Do,'" 365.
37. Caroline Walker Bynum, "Women's Stories, Women's Symbols: A Critique of Victor Turner's Theory of Liminality," in Caroline Walker Bynum, *Fragmentation and Redemption: Essays on Gender and the Human Body in Medieval Religion* (New York: Zone Books, 1992), pp. 29–30. The connection of this essay to Marie de France has been raised by Elizabeth Archibald, "The Female Foundling and the Problem of Romance Genre," in *The Spirit of Medieval Popular Romance,* ed. Ad Putter and Jane Gilbert (Harlow, Essex: Longman, 2000), p. 48.
38. Bynum, *Fragmentation and Redemption,* p. 37.

39. Bloch, *The Anonymous Marie de France*, pp. 28-29.
40. Sarah Kay, *Courtly Contradictions: The Emergence of the Literary Object in the Twelfth Century* (Stanford: Stanford University Press, 2001), pp. 2–3.
41. Kay, *Courtly Contradictions,* p. 23.
42. Michelle A. Freeman, "Marie de France's Poetics of Silence: The Implications for a Feminine *Translatio*," PMLA 99 (1984), 865.
43. Kay, *Courtly Contradictions,* p. 19.
44. All textual references are from Alexandre Micha, trans., *Lais de Marie de France* (Paris: GF Flammarion, 1994). Only abbreviated forms of *lai* title and line numbers will be given for future references. English translations are from *The Lais of Marie de France*, ed. and trans. Robert Hanning and Joan Ferrante (Grand Rapids: Baker Books, 1978), modified when appropriate.
45. Frederick Hodgson, "Alienation and the Otherworld in *Lanval, Yonec,* and *Guigemar,*" *Comitatus: A Journal of Medieval and Renaissance Studies* 5 (1974), 27.
46. R. Howard Bloch, "The Medieval Text—'Guigemar'—as a Provocation to the Discipline of Medieval Studies," *Romanic Review* 79 (1988), 70.
47. Bloch, *The Anonymous Marie de France Question: Where are you deleting Anonymous? It is in the title of the book.*, pp. 45–47.
48. Bloch, *The Anonymous Marie de France*, p. 64.
49. Miléna Mikhaïlova, "L'espace dans les *Lais* de Marie de France: lieux, structure, rhétorique," *Cahiers de civilization médiévale* 40 (1997), 147.
50. H. Marshall Leicester, Jr., "The Voice of the Hind: The Emergence of Feminine Discontent in the *Lais* of Marie de France," in *Reading Medieval Culture: Essays in Honor of Robert W. Hanning*, ed. Robert M. Stein and Sandra Pierson Prior (Notre Dame: University of Notre Dame Press, 2005), p. 137.
51. Kay, *Courtly Contradictions,* pp. 343–344.
52. Heather Arden, "The *Lais* of Marie de France and Carol Gilligan's Theory of the Psychology of Women," in *In Quest of Marie de France, a Twelfth-Century Woman*, ed. Chantal E. Marechal (Lewiston: Edwin Mellen Press, 1992), p. 214.
53. Mikhaïlova, "L'espace dans les *Lais* de Marie de France," p. 148.
54. R. Howard Bloch, *Medieval Misogyny and the Invention of Western Love* (Chicago: University of Chicago Press, 1991), p. 123.
55. Miranda Griffin, "Gender and Authority in the Medieval French Lai," *Forum for Modern Language Studies* 35 (1999), 51.
56. K. Sarah-Jane Murray, "The Ring and the Sword: Marie de France's *Yonec* in Light of the *Vie de Saint Alexis,*" *Romance Quarterly* 53.1 (2006), 29.
57. Robert W. Hanning, "The Talking Wounded: Desire, Truth Telling, and Pain in the *Lais* of Marie de France," in *Desiring Discourse: The Literature of Love, Ovid Through Chaucer,* ed. James J. Paxson and Cynthia A. Gravlee (Selinsgrove: Susquehanna University Press, 1998), p. 142.
58. Robert M. Stein, *Reality Fictions: Romance, History, and Governmental Authority, 1025–1180* (Notre Dame: University of Notre Dame Press, 2006), p. 156.

59. Finke and Shichtman, "Magical Mistress Tour," p. 489. Jane Chance has noted that Lanval is a foreign knight, and Arthur may not want to give his wealth to an outsider. Jane Chance, *The Literary Subversions of Medieval Women* (New York: Palgrave Macmillan, 2007), p. 58.
60. Leicester, "The Voice of the Hind," p. 150.
61. Although we are not told that Lanval is not a firstborn son, the fact that he has spent all his wealth suggests that his property was not in land (which was more often passed through primogeniture), but rather in moveable goods or cash.
62. Leicester, "The Voice of the Hind," p. 152.

4 Sexual Purity as Property: *Vie Seinte Audree* and *The Book of Margery Kempe*

1. Erotic love in twelfth-century monasticism, as Ruth Mazo Karras argues, was not sexual, but rather an extension of a passionate spiritual love that went beyond friendship. Ruth Mazo Karras, "Friendship and Love in the Lives of Two Twelfth-Century English Saints," *Journal of Medieval History* 14 (1998), 305–320.
2. Claire deTrafford, "Share and Share Alike? The Marriage Portion, Inheritance, and Family Politics," in *Studies in Medieval and Early Modern Women: Pawns or Players?*, ed. Christine Meek and Catherine Lawless (Dublin: Four Courts Press, 2003), p. 37.
3. Ann J. Kettle, "'My Wife Shall Have It': Marriage and Property in the Wills and Testaments of later Mediaeval England," in *Marriage and Property*, ed. Elizabeth M. Craik (Aberdeen: Aberdeen University Press, 1984), p. 90.
4. Kettle, "'My Wife Shall Have It,'" p. 91.
5. Janet S. Loengard, "Common Law for Margery: Separate But Not Equal," in *Women in Medieval Western Culture*, ed. Linda E. Mitchell (New York: Garland Publishing, Inc., 1999), p. 123.
6. Loengard, "Common Law for Margery," p. 92.
7. Loengard, "Common Law for Margery," p. 94.
8. Janet Senderowicz Leongard, "*Rationabilis Dos*: Magna Carta and the Widow's 'Fair Share' in the Earlier Thirteenth Century," in *Wife and Widow in Medieval England*, ed. Sue Sheridan Walker (Ann Arbor: University of Michigan Press, 1993), p. 60.
9. Barbara A. Hanawalt, *The Wealth of Wives: Women, Law, and Economy in Late Medieval London* (Oxford: Oxford University Press, 2007), pp. 4–7. Kathryn Staples argues that although real property in London was distributed to both sons and daughters, parents placed more conditions on daughters' bequests, specifically on whom they could or could not marry and at what age. Kathryn Staples, *Daughters of London: Inheritance Practice in Late Medieval London* (PhD Dissertation, University of Minnesota, 2006), p. 58.
10. Hanawalt, *The Wealth of Wives*, p. 9.
11. Barbara J. Harris, *English Aristocratic Women, 1450–1550: Marriage and Family, Property and Careers* (Oxford: Oxford University Press, 2002),

pp. 18–19. Before the enactment of the Statue of Treason in 1352, there were no legal grounds for the killing of an adulterous wife. See, e.g., Frederik Pederson's article, "Marriage Contracts and the Church Courts of Fourteenth-Century England," in *To Have and to Hold: Marrying and Its Documentation in Western Christendom*, ed. Philip L. Reynolds and John Witte, Jr. (Cambridge: Cambridge University Press, 2007), pp. 291–293, 315–318. Pederson gives the example of Baron John Cameys, who released his adulterous wife Margaret from their marriage vows.

12. S. A. M. Gavigan, "Petit Treason in Eighteenth-Century England: Woman's Inequality before the Law," *Canadian Journal of Women and the Law* 3.2 (1989–1990), 335–374. Abstract: www.ncjrs:gov/App/Publications/abstract.aspx?ID=123740.
13. Hanawalt, *The Wealth of Wives,* p. 104.
14. Rhoda Lange Friedrichs, "Rich Old Ladies Made Poor: The Vulnerability of Women's Property in Late Medieval England," *Medieval Prosopography: History and Collective Biography* 21 (2000), 211–229.
15. Barbara A. Hanawalt, "Women and the Household Economy: An Assessment of *Women, Work, and Family,*" *Journal of Women's History* 11.3 (1999), 10–16.
16. Judith M. Bennett, *History Matters: Patriarchy and the Challenge of Feminism* (Philadelphia: University of Pennsylvania Press, 2006), pp. 86–89. For a discussion of the traditional view of historians such as Joan Kelly, Margaret King, Eileen Power, Marjorie McIntosh, and Martha Howell, to cite only a few examples, see pp. 82–86.
17. Bennett, *History Matters*, pp. 92–103.
18. Bennett, *History Matters*, p. 104; emphasis in the original.
19. Bennett, *History Matters*, pp. 72–73.
20. Margaret R. Hunt, *The Middling Sort: Commerce, Gender, and the Family in England, 1680–1780* (Berkeley: University of California Press, 1996), p. 136.
21. Hunt, *The Middling Sort,* pp. 138–139.
22. Jennifer Summit, "Women and Authorship," in *The Cambridge Companion to Medieval Women's Writing,* ed. Carolyn Dinshaw and David Wallace (Cambridge: Cambridge University Press, 2003), pp. 93–95.
23. Laurie A. Finke, *Women's Writing in English: Medieval England* (London: Longman, 1999), p. 81.
24. Jocelyn Wogan-Browne believes that Marie is probably one of the female religious living at Chatteris. See her "Rerouting the Dower: The Anglo-Norman Life of St. Audrey by Marie (of Chatteris?)," in *Power of the Weak: Studies on Medieval Women*, ed. Jennifer Carpenter and Sally-Beth MacLean (Urbana: University of Chicago Press, 1995), p. 31. June Hall McCash and Judith Clark Barban, in their translation *The Life of Saint Audrey: A Text by Marie de France* (Jefferson, NC: McFarland & Company, Inc., 2006), pp. 5–8, make the case that she is the better-known twelfth-century Marie.
25. Wogan-Browne, "Rerouting the Dower," p. 31.
26. Wogan-Browne, "Rerouting the Dower," pp. 5–8.

27. Wogan-Browne, "Rerouting the Dower," p. 4. The manuscript appears in B.L. Additional 70513, a collection of thirteen metrical saints' lives, and once belonged to an Augustinian nunnery in Suffolk.
28. Virginia Blanton, *Signs of Devotion: The Cult of St. Aethelthryth in Medieval England, 695–1615* (University Park: The Pennsylvania State University Press, 2007), p. 174.
29. Blanton, *Signs of Devotion*, p. 183.
30. *The Book of Margery Kempe*, ed. Lynn Staley (Kalamazoo: Western Michigan University, 1996), p. 20. The modern English translation is taken from *The Book of Margery Kempe*, trans. B. A. Windeatt (Harmondsworth, Middlesex: Penguin Books, 1985), pp. 36–37.
31. John C. Hirsch, "Author and Scribe in *The Book of Margery Kempe*," *Medium Aevum* 44 (1975), 146.
32. Lynn Staley, *Margery Kempe's Dissenting Fictions* (University Park: The Pennsylvania State University Press, 1884), p. 3.
33. Nicholas Watson, "The Making of *The Book of Margery Kempe*," in *Voices in Dialogue: Reading Women in the Middle Ages*, ed. Linda Olson and Kathryn Kerby-Fulton (Notre Dame: University of Notre Dame Press, 2005), p. 397.
34. Felicity Riddy, "Text and Self in *The Book of Margery Kempe*" in Olson and Kerby-Fulton, *Voices in Dialogue*, pp. 435–453, and more specifically in "Afterwords," written jointly with Watson, "The Making of *The Book of Margery Kempe*," p. 457.
35. Jocelyn Wogan-Browne, "Rerouting the Dower: The Anglo-Norman Life of St. Audrey by Marie (of Chatteris?)" in Carpenter and MacLean, *Power of the Weak*, p. 28.
36. Friedrichs, "Rich Old Ladies Made Poor," pp. 211–219. By Elizabeth I's time, English common law refused to enforce women's wills regarding the distribution of their property. Upon a wife's death, the husband did not have to follow her wishes and could dispose of her property as he wished. See Michael M. Sheehan, "The Influence of Canon Law on the Property Rights of Married Women in England," *Mediaeval Studies* 23 (1961), 370–371.
37. Virginia Blanton forcefully argues that Marie highlights Audrée's struggles with sexual desire as a model for her reading audience—aristocratic widows entering religious life. Virginia Blanton, "Chaste Marriage, Sexual Desire, and Christian Martyrdom in *La vie seinte Audrée*," *Journal of the History of Sexuality* 19.1 (2010), 94–114.
38. Sheila Delany, "Sexual Economics, Chaucer's Wife of Bath and *The Book of Margery Kempe*" in *Feminist Readings in Middle English Literature: The Wife of Bath and All Her Sect*, ed. Ruth Evans and Lesley Johnson (London: Routledge, 1994), p. 79. Kathleen Ashley also proposes an economic reading of Margery, stating the she "symbolically enacts a solution to the cultural dilemma of how to achieve spiritual validation while remaining an active member of mercantile society." Kathleen Ashley, "Historicizing

Margery: *The Book of Margery Kempe* as Social Text," *Journal of Medieval and Early Modern Studies* 28.2 (1998), 374.

39. Delany, "Sexual Economics," p. 76.
40. Delany, "Sexual Economics," pp. 83–84.
41. Delany, "Sexual Economics," p. 81.
42. David Aers, *Community, Gender, and Individual Identity: English Writing 1360–1430* (London: Routledge, 1988), p. 76.
43. Aers, *Community, Gender, and Individual Identity*, pp. 78–79.
44. Aers, *Community, Gender, and Individual Identity*, p. 87.
45. Aers, *Community, Gender, and Individual Identity*, p. 95.
46. Nona Fienberg, "Thematics of Value in *The Book of Margery Kempe*," *Modern Philology* 87 (1989), 135.

5 Property and Propriety in Eighteenth- and Nineteenth-century England: Burney, Austen, Eliot

1. For a full discussion of jointure, see Susan Staves, *Married Women's Separate Property in England, 1660–1833* (Cambridge: Harvard University Press, 1990), pp. 95–118.
2. Lee Holcombe, *Wives and Property: Reform of the Married Women's Property Law in Nineteenth-century England* (Toronto: University of Toronto Press, 1983), pp. 38–39. Although originally intended to avoid paying feudal dues, this type of trust was viewed by the early lord chancellors as a possible cause for trustee abuse since the beneficiaries were not named. The Statute of Uses of 1535 barred the courts of equity from enforcing trusts of this type.
3. A lively debate ensued after the publication of Lawrence Stone's book *The Family, Sex, and Marriage in England, 1500–1800* (New York: Harper & Row, 1977), which concluded that these separate estates showed that women had increased value. He posited that the family underwent an emotional change in the eighteenth century: the patriarchal family was replaced by the "affective" family held together by love. For a rebuttal to this argument, see Eileen Spring, *Law, Land, and Family: Aristocratic Inheritance in England, 1300 to 1800* (Chapel Hill: University of North Carolina Press, 1993), pp. 150–183. In fact, Spring argues, female inheritance declined during this period.
4. Susan Moller Okin, "Patriarchy and Married Women's Property in England: Questions on Some Current Views," *Eighteenth-century Studies* 17(2) (1983–1984), 133.
5. Staves, *Married Women's Separate Property*, pp. 135–136.
6. Virginia M. Duff, "Woman and Property, Woman as Property: Woman, Property, and Law as Imagined by British Female Novelists, 1680–1740" (PhD Dissertation, University of Colorado at Boulder, 1994), pp. 1–4.
7. Virginia M. Duff, "Early English Women Novelists Testify to the Law's Manifest Cruelties against Women before the Marriage Act of 1753," *Women's Studies: An Interdisciplinary Journal* 29.5 (2000), 585.

8. John Stuart Mill, *On Liberty and Other Writings*, ed. Stefan Collini (Cambridge: Cambridge University Press, 1989), p. 147. As Carole Pateman has pointed out, contract theory involves not only property of material goods, land, and capital, but also the ownership of "property in the person," that is, the right to enter into contracts. Carole Pateman, *The Sexual Contract* (Stanford: Stanford University Press, 1988), p. 5.
9. Mill, *On Liberty and Other Writings*, p. 163.
10. Holcombe, *Wives and Property*, p. 5.
11. Many of the members of the Married Women's Property Committee were writers. Cheri Lin Larsen Hoeckley argues that they were seen as challenging the idea of separate spheres for men and women because they earned money from their writing: "Unlike family inheritances or gifts, which might give a woman property while still subsuming her under a familial economy, female literary earnings indicated an economic independence that belied the principles of domestic ideology." Cheri Lin Larsen Hoeckley, "Literary Ladies in Anomalous Positions: Victorian Women Writers and the Married Women's Property Act" (PhD Dissertation, University of California at Berkeley, 1997), p. 3. For a broader picture of the growing concern over working women, see Julie Hipp Schuetz, "Women, Property, and the Estate: Fiction and Legal Reform in Nineteenth-Century England, 1857–1882" (PhD Dissertation, Vanderbilt University, 2001).
12. Schuetz, "Women, Property, and the Estate," pp. 65–85, for a discussion of the work of the committee.
13. Schuetz, "Women, Property, and the Estate," p. 90. The Divorce Act, which transferred jurisdiction from the ecclesiastical courts to a new Court of Divorce and Matrimonial Causes, was, in Holcombe's analysis, essentially a conservative victory.
14. Schuetz, "Women, Property, and the Estate," p. 109.
15. Schuetz, "Women, Property, and the Estate," pp. 178–183.
16. Schuetz, "Women, Property, and the Estate," p. 195.
17. J. G. A. Pocock, *Virtue, Commerce, and History: Essays on Political Thought and History, Chiefly in the Eighteenth Century* (Cambridge: Cambridge University Press, 1985), pp. 103–104. It is interesting that "propriety," as used by Pocock, means "that which is proper for a person or situation." The word is also used to mean "conforming to the customs of polite society."
18. Pocock, *Virtue, Commerce, and History*, p. 113. Ann Louise Kibbie argues that these two kinds of property, the traditional estate in land and the circulating wealth of trade, are models for female character in eighteenth-century novels. In the first, the self is expressed as constant and removed from the instability of the marketplace, whereas in the second, female self-possession is expressed through alienation of the self. Ann Louise Kibbie, "The Woman in the Bargain: Property and Female Character in the Eighteenth Century Novel" (PhD Dissertation: University of California at Berkeley, 1990).

19. Catherine Ingrassia, *Authorship, Commerce, and Gender in Early Eighteenth-Century England: A Culture of Paper Credit* (Cambridge: Cambridge University Press, 1998), p. 5.
20. Ingrassia, *Authorship, Commerce, and Gender*, pp. 6–7.
21. Mona Scheuermann, "Women and Money in Eighteenth-Century Fiction," *Studies in the Novel* XIX (1987), 311–313. Edward Copeland agrees: "Whatever the political argument, whatever the social agenda, whatever the romantic entanglement in women's fiction, women can be heard talking about money, the lack of it, how to spend it, or how to get it." See his *Women Writing About Money: Women's Fiction in England, 1790–1820* (Cambridge: Cambridge University Press, 1995), p. 7.
22. April London, *Women and Property in the Eighteenth-century English Novel* (Cambridge: Cambridge University Press, 1999), p. 7.
23. Mary Poovey, *The Proper Lady and the Woman Writer: Ideology as Style in the Works of Mary Wollstonecraft, Mary Shelley, and Jane Austen* (Chicago: University of Chicago Press, 1984), p. 5.
24. Thomas Laqueur, *Making Sex: Body and Gender from the Greeks to Freud* (Cambridge: Harvard University Press, 1992), p. 150.
25. Laqueur, *Making Sex*, p. 156.
26. Nancy Armstrong, *Desire and Domestic Fiction: A Political History of the Novel* (Oxford: Oxford University Press, 1987), p. 8.
27. Armstrong, *Desire and Domestic Fiction*, p. 20.
28. Tim Dolin, *Mistress of the House: Women of Property in the Victorian Novel* (Aldershot: Ashgate, 1997), pp. 7–10.
29. Janet Todd, introduction to *Female Education in the Age of Enlightenment*, vol. I (London: William Pickering, 1996), p. vii.
30. Todd, introduction to *Female Education*, pp. viii–xv.
31. Mary Wollstonecraft, *A Vindication of the Rights of Woman* (New York: Dover Publications, Inc., 1966), p. 60.
32. Thomas Gisborne, *An Inquiry into the Duties of the Female Sex* in *Female Education in the Age of Enlightenment*, vol. 2 (London: William Pickering, 1996), pp. 215–216.
33. Gisborne, *An Inquiry into the Duties of the Female Sex*, p. 251.
34. James Fordyce, "On the Importance of the Female Sex," in *Female Education in the Age of Enlightenment*, vol. 1 (London: William Pickering, 1996), p. 24.
35. Fordyce, "On the Importance of the Female Sex," p. 449.
36. Jeff Nunokawa has suggested that in the Victorian novel there was a fear of portraying wives as property. "Trauma," he writes, "ensues there when wives are called commodities, not because they are thus cast as property, but rather because such property is thus cast among the uncertainties of the marketplace." See his *The Afterlife of Property: Domestic Security and the Victorian Novel* (Princeton: Princeton University Press, 1994), p. 7.
37. This view has been articulated by several critics, including Françoise Basch in her early analysis of Victorian fiction, *Relative Creatures: Victorian Women in Society and the Novel* (New York: Schocken Books, 1974); and

Joseph Allen Boone, *Tradition Counter Tradition: Love and the Form of Fiction* (Chicago: University of Chicago Press, 1987), among others.

38. Ruth Bernard Yeazell, *Fictions of Modesty: Women and Courtship in the English Novel* (Chicago: University of Chicago Press, 1991), p. 35.
39. Katherine Sobba Green, *The Courtship Novel 1740–1820: A Feminized Genre* (Lexington, KY: The University Press of Kentucky, 1991), pp. 2–3.
40. Green, *The Courtship Novel 1740–1820*, p. 13.
41. Julie Shaffer, "Not Subordinate: Empowering Women in the Marriage-Plot—The Novels of Frances Burney, Maria Edgeworth, and Jane Austen," *Criticism: A Quarterly for Literature and the Arts* 34.1 (1992), 53–57.
42. Judith Lowder Newton, *Women, Power, and Subversion: Social Strategies in British Fiction, 1778–1860* (Athens: The University of Georgia Press, 1981), p. 26.
43. Frances Burney, *Evelina*, ed. Kristina Straub (Boston: Bedford/St. Martin's, 1997), p. 55. All subsequent references will directly follow quotations in parentheses.
44. Shaffer, "Not Subordinate," 61.
45. Julia Epstein, *The Iron Pen: Frances Burney and the Politics of Women's Writing* (Bedminster: Bristol Classical Press, 1989), p. 96.
46. Epstein, *The Iron Pen*, p. 120.
47. Susan Fraiman, *Unbecoming Women: British Women and the Novel of Development* (New York: Columbia University Press, 1993), pp. 34–35.
48. Epstein, *The Iron Pen*, p. 96.
49. Fraiman, *Unbecoming Women*, p. 58.
50. Claudia L. Johnson, *Jane Austen: Women, Politics, and the Novel* (Chicago: University of Chicago Press, 1988), p. 6.
51. Johnson, *Jane Austen*, p. 14.
52. Johnson, *Jane Austen*, pp. xxiii–xxiv.
53. William H. Magee, "Instrument of Growth: The Courtship and Marriage Plot in Jane Austen's Novels," *Journal of Narrative Technique* 17.2 (1987), 198.
54. Magee, "Instrument of Growth," 205.
55. Charles H. Hinnant, "Jane Austen's 'Wild Imagination': Romance and the Courtship Plot in the Six Canonical Novels," *Narrative* 14.3 (2006), 294–295.
56. Hinnant, "Jane Austen's 'Wild Imagination,'" 295–298.
57. Hinnant, "Jane Austen's 'Wild Imagination,'" 305–306.
58. Jane Austen, *Sense and Sensibility* (New York: Dover Publications, 1996), p. 7; emphasis in the original. All subsequent references will directly follow quotations in parentheses.
59. Julie A. Shaffer, "The Ideological Intervention of Ambiguities in the Marriage Plot: Who Fails Marianne in Austen's *Sense and Sensibility*?" in *A Dialogue of Voices: Feminist Literary Theory and Bakhtin*, ed. Karen Hohne and Helen Wussow (Minneapolis: University of Minnesota Press, 1994), p. 145.
60. Laura Mooneyham White, "Jane Austen and the Marriage Plot: Questions of Persistence," in *Jane Austen and Discourses of Feminism*, ed. Devoney Looser (New York: St. Martin's Press, 1995), p. 78.

61. Jane Austen, *Pride and Prejudice* (Oxford: Oxford University Press, 2004), p. 1. All subsequent references will directly follow quotations in parentheses.
62. Karen Newman, "Can This Marriage Be Saved: Jane Austen Makes Sense of an Ending," *ELH* 50 (1983), 696.
63. Armstrong, *Desire and Domestic Fiction*, p. 50.
64. Poovey, *The Proper Lady*, p. 237.
65. Johnson, *Jane Austen*, p. 91.
66. Shaffer, "Not Subordinate," 66.
67. White, "Jane Austen and the Marriage Plot," pp. 81–82. White notes that it is not until the last fragment of the novel that a marital possibility enters.
68. George Eliot, *Middlemarch* (New York: The Modern Library, 2000), p. 1. Page citations will hereafter be in parentheses.
69. Sherry L. Mitchell, "Saint Teresa and Dorothea Brooke: The Absent Road to Perfection in *Middlemarch*," *The Victorian Newsletter* 92 (1997), 32–33. St. Theresa, she argues, directed the spiritual development of her nuns and engaged in prohibited theological discourse because of her privileged position in the convent. During her canonization, she was celebrated as a "virile woman" and a "manly soul."
70. There are, of course, others, such as Celia and Sir James, the Vincy parents, and Will Ladislaw's grandmother. Although all of these present other facets of the marriage issue in *Middlemarch*, I will only refer to them incidentally. In addition, both Dorothea and Rosamond have second marriages, which I will discuss later.
71. Here I differ from others who have investigated the Casaubon reference, who have not made the Hermetic link. For a synopsis of the argument, see Daniel Tyler, "Dorothea and the 'Key to All Mythologies,'" *The George Eliot Review: Journal of the George Eliot Fellowship* 33 (2002), 27–32; and Michelle Faubert, "A Possible Source for George Eliot's Edward Casaubon," *ANQ: A Quarterly Journal of Short Articles, Notes, & Reviews* 18.2 (2005), 46–54.
72. I am grateful to James Engell for this observation.
73. Margaret Homans, *Bearing the Word: Language and Female Experience in Nineteenth-century Women's Writing* (Chicago: University of Chicago Press, 1986), p. 144.
74. J. Hillis Miller, "A Conclusion in Which Almost Nothing is Concluded: *Middlemarch*'s 'Finale,'" in *Middlemarch in the Twenty-first Century*, ed. Karen Chase (Oxford: Oxford University Press, 2006), p. 142.
75. Jenni Calder, *Women and Marriage in Victorian Fiction* (New York: Oxford University Press, 1976), pp. 140–141.
76. Calder, *Women and Marriage*, p. 158.

6 Virginia Woolf's Women, Trapped and Freed

1. Virginia Woolf, *A Room of One's Own* (New York: Harcourt, Brace & World, Inc., 1929), p. 28.

2. David Dowling, *Mrs. Dalloway: Mapping Streams of Consciousness* (Boston: Twayne Publishers, 1991), pp. 21–23.
3. Naomi Black, *Virginia Woolf as Feminist* (Ithaca: Cornell University Press, 2004), p. 27.
4. Virginia Woolf, *Three Guineas* (New York: Harcourt, Inc., 1938), p. 3.
5. Black, *Virginia Woolf as Feminist*, p. 1.
6. Rachel Bowlby, *Feminist Destinations and Further Essays on Virginia Woolf* (Edinburgh: Edinburgh University Press, 1997), p. 18.
7. Black, *Virginia Woolf as Feminist*, p. 28.
8. Black, *Virginia Woolf as Feminist*, p. 13.
9. Christy L. Burns, "Re-dressing Feminist Identities: Tensions between Essential and Constructed Selves in Virginia Woolf's *Orlando*," *Twentieth Century Literature* 40.3 (1994), 342. Woolf, of course, uses biographical techniques throughout *Orlando*, as I will discuss later.
10. Virginia Woolf, *Mrs. Dalloway* (New York: Harcourt, Inc., 2005), pp. 7–8.
11. Denise Delory, "Parsing the Female Sentence: The Paradox of Containment in Virginia Woolf's Narratives," in *Ambiguous Discourse: Feminist Narratology and British Women Writers*, ed. Kathy Mezei (Chapel Hill: The University of North Carolina Press, 1996), p. 101.
12. Elizabeth Abel, "Narrative Structure(s) and Female Development: The Case of *Mrs.Dalloway*," *Virginia Woolf's Mrs Dalloway*, ed. Harold Bloom (New York: Chelsea House Publishers, 1985), 107.
13. Lisa Coughlin McGarry, *Orts, Scraps, and Fragments: The Elusive Search for Meaning in Virginia Woolf's Fiction* (Lanham, MD: University Press of American, 2007), p. 114.
14. Emily Blair, *Virginia Woolf and the Nineteenth-Century Domestic Novel* (Albany: State University of New York Press, 2007), pp. 173–179.
15. Dowling, *Mrs. Dalloway*, p. 33.
16. Dowling, *Mrs. Dalloway*, p. 107.
17. Jody R. Rosen, "Deviation and Acceleration: Time in the Story and Narrative of *Orlando*," *Virginia Woolf Miscellany* 70 (2006), 29.
18. Burns, "Re-dressing Feminist Identities," 342–345.
19. Nigel Nicolson, *Virginia Woolf* (New York: Viking, 2000), p. 107.
20. Virginia Woolf, *Orlando* (Harmondsworth, Middlesex: Penguin Books, 1975), p. 10.
21. Bowlby, *Feminist Destinations*, p. 49.
22. Burns, "Re-dressing Feminist Identities," 354.

7 Mid-nineteenth-century Russia: Women Writers Reject the Marriage Plot

1. Maria Tsebrikova, "Russia," in *The Woman Question in Europe: A Series of Original Essays*, ed. Theodore Stanton (New York: G.P. Putnam's Sons, 1884), p. 391.
2. Tsebrikova, "Russia," p. 392.

3. Eve Levin, "Women and Property in Medieval Novgorod: Dependence and Independence," *Russian History/Histoire Russe* 10.2 (1983), 156.
4. Levin, "Women and Property in Medieval Novgorod," 166.
5. Levin, "Women and Property in Medieval Novgorod," 156–158.
6. Levin, "Women and Property in Medieval Novgorod," 158–159. As Levin herself explains, Novgorod has a unique history as a semiautonomous city-state with widespread international economic activity. As a result, she does not generalize about its position on women's property to other East Slavic states, but rather compares it only to *Russkaia Pravda*.
7. Levin, "Women and Property in Medieval Novgorod," 169. In the *Sudebnik* of 1589, as Sandra Levy has noted, daughters could inherit if there were no sons, and if there were no daughters, then the property went to the nearest of kin of the father's *or* mother's side. "This suggested the validity of female inheritance as well as illustrates the strength of natal family ties preserved even after marriage." Sandra Levy, "Women and the Control of Property in Sixteenth-Century Muscovy," *Russian History/Histoire Russe* 10.2 (1983), 203.
8. William G. Wagner, *Marriage, Property, and Law in Late Imperial Russia* (Oxford: Clarendon Press, 1994), p. 228.
9. Michelle Lamarche Marresse, "From Maintenance to Entitlement: Defining the Dowry in 18th Century Russia," in *Women and Gender in 18th-Century Russia*, ed. Wendy Rosslyn (Aldershot: Ashgate, 2003), p. 210.
10. George G. Weickhardt, "Legal Rights of Women in Russia, 1100–1750," *Slavic Review* 55.1 (1996), 2.
11. Weickhardt, "Legal Rights of Women in Russia," 12–14. Weickhardt has shown elsewhere that the *pomest'e* evolved from land conditioned on state service to what was in essence a hereditary estate. Because of the tradition of private property in Russia, he argues, "the tsar was ultimately unable to suppress the desires of service landowners to acquire the incidents of private property." George G. Weickhardt, "The Pre-Petrine Law of Property," *Slavic Review* 52.4 (1993), 677.
12. Michelle Lamarche Marresse, *A Woman's Kingdom: Noblewomen and the Control of Property in Russia, 1700–1861* (Ithaca: Cornell University Press, 2002), p. 25.
13. Weichkhardt, "Legal Rights of Women in Russia," 17.
14. Marresse, *A Woman's Kingdom,* pp. 26–28.
15. Marresse, *A Woman's Kingdom,* p. 41.
16. Marresse, *A Woman's Kingdom,* pp. 30–31.
17. Marresse, "From Maintenance to Entitlement," p. 212.
18. Marresse, "From Maintenance to Entitlement," p. 211.
19. Marresse, *A Woman's Kingdom,* p. 39.
20. Marresse, "From Maintenance to Entitlement," p. 209.
21. Marresse, *A Woman's Kingdom,* p. 2.
22. Wagner, *Marriage, Property, and Law,* pp. 3–4.
23. Wagner, *Marriage, Property, and Law,* p. 62.

24. Richard Stites, *The Women's Liberation Movement in Russia: Feminism, Nihilism, and Bolshevism, 1860–1930* (Princeton: Princeton University Press, 1978), p. 7.
25. Carolyn Johnston Pouncy, ed. and trans., *The Domostroi: Rules for Russian Households in the Time of Ivan the Terrible* (Ithaca: Cornell University Press, 1994), pp. 20–21. There is no clearly identified author; Pouncy believes it was almost certainly written by a single person, most likely a man. See her discussion, pp. 37–41.
26. Pouncy, *The Domostroi*, pp. 27–28.
27. Pouncy, *The Domostroi*, p. 124.
28. Dorothy Atkinson, "Society and the Sexes in the Russian Past," in *Women in Russia*, ed. Dorothy Atkinson, Alexander Dalli, and Gail Warshofsky Lapidus (Stanford: Stanford University Press, 1977), p. 15.
29. Quoted in Atkinson, "Society and the Sexes."
30. Atkinson, "Society and the Sexes," p. 16.
31. As quoted in Barbara Alpern Engel, *Women in Russia, 1700–2000* (Cambridge: Cambridge University Press, 2004), pp. 8–9.
32. Engel, *Women in Russia*, p. 9.
33. Engel, *Women in Russia*, p. 12.
34. Stites, *Women's Liberation Movement,* p. 12.
35. Stites, *Women's Liberation Movement,* p. 14.
36. Engel, *Women in Russia*, p. 19. The idea of "obshchestvo" ("polite society") has been examined by William Mills Todd III, who shows how the ideal of a civilized society was a fragile one for Russia. The stresses and contradictions within Russian culture, he argues, challenged any normalizing of such uniformity. See his *Fiction and Society in the Age of Pushkin* (Cambridge: Harvard University Press, 1986).
37. Wagner, *Marriage, Property, and Law,* pp. 81–85.
38. Wagner, *Marriage, Property, and Law,* p. 5.
39. Wagner, *Marriage, Property, and Law,* pp. 9–10.
40. Robin Bisha, "Marriage, Church and Community in 18th-Century St. Petersburg," in *Women and Gender in 18th-Century Russia*, ed. Wendy Rosslyn (Aldershot: Palgrave, 2003), pp. 228–229.
41. Wagner, Wagner, *Marriage, Property, and Law,* p. 75.
42. Wagner, *Marriage, Property, and Law,* p. 259.
43. Wagner, *Marriage, Property, and Law,* p. 206–209.
44. Marresse, *A Woman's Kingdom*, p. 58.
45. Stites, *Women's Liberation Movement,* p. 8.
46. Barbara Alpern Engel, *Mothers and Daughters: Women of the Intelligentsia in Nineteenth-century Russia* (Cambridge: Cambridge University Press, 1983), p. 8.
47. Engel, *Mothers and Daughters,* pp. 9–11.
48. Joanna Hubbs, *Mother Russia: The Feminine Myth in Russian Culture* (Bloomington: Indiana University Press, 1993), pp. 95–96.
49. "Theotokos." *Encyclopedia Brittanica Online,* 2008. Encyclopedia Brittanica. July 12, 2008: http:brittanica.com/EpChecked/topic/591153 /Theotokos>Theotokos c/a.

50. "Theotokos," 100–101.
51. Engel, *Women in Russia*, p. 69.
52. For a complete discussion of the beginnings of the "Woman Question," see Stites, *Women's Liberation Movement,* pp. 30–45.
53. Stites, *Women's Liberation Movement,* pp. 4–6.
54. Tsebrikova, "Russia," p. 413.
55. Tsebrikova, "Russia," p. 412.
56. Engel, *Mothers and Daughters*, pp. 46–47. See also Linda Edmondson, "Equality and Difference in Women's History: Where Does Russia Fit In?," in *Women in Russia and Ukraine*, ed. and trans. Rosalind Marsh (Cambridge: Cambridge University Press, 1996), p. 103.
57. Engel, *Women in Russia*, pp. 75–77.
58. Engel, *Women in Russia*, pp. 70–71. This position has been challenged by Jane Costlow, who believes that women writers did not ignore the Woman Question, but rather approached it differently from men. See her article, "Love, Work, and the Woman Question in Mid Nineteenth-century Women's Writing," in *Women Writers in Russian Literature*, ed. Toby W. Clyman and Diana Greene (Westport, CT: Greenwood Press, 1994), p. 63.
59. Arja Rosenholm, *Gendering Awakening: Femininity and the Russian Woman Question of the 1860's* (Helsinski: Kikimora Publications, 1999), pp. 52–53.
60. Nikolai Chernyshevsky, *Chto delat'?* (Leningrad: Izdatelstvo Nauka, 1975), p. 630. English translation: *What Is To Be Done?* Michael R. Katz, trans., annotated by William G. Wagner (Ithaca: Cornell University Press, 1989), p. 344.
61. The popularity of George Sand, who wrote of women's right to love without regard to convention, spread to Russia beginning in 1836. This sparked a conservative backlash, led by the journalists Bulgarin and Grech, and a response by the intelligentsia. The intellectuals Belinsky and Herzen replied that marriage should be abolished and unions based on mutual love and respect. See Stites, *Women's Liberation Movement,* pp. 19–20.
62. Stites, *Women's Liberation Movement,* p. 53.
63. Barbara Heldt, *Terrible Perfection: Women and Russian Literature* (Bloomington: Indiana University Press, 1987), p. 5.
64. Heldt, *Terrible Perfection*, p. 2.
65. Heldt, *Terrible Perfection*, p. 13.
66. Ivan Turgenev, *Otsi e deti* (St. Petersburg: Akademicheski Proekt, 2000), p. 191. English translation: *Fathers and Sons*, trans. Constance Garnett (New York: Modern Library, 2001), pp. 178–179.
67. Jane T. Costlow, "'Oh-là-là' and 'No-no-no': Odintsova as Woman Alone in *Fathers and Children*," in *A Plot of Her Own: The Female Protagonist in Russian Literature*, ed. Sonia Stephan Hoisington (Evanston: Northwestern University Press, 1995), p. 23.
68. Rosalind Marsh, "Introduction: New Perspectives on Women and Gender in Russian Literature," in *Gender and Russian Literature: New Perspectives*, ed. Rosalind Marsh (Cambridge: Cambridge University Press, 1996), p. 3.

69. Marsh, "Introduction," pp. 12–13.
70. Vera Sandomirsky Dunham, "The Strong-Woman Motif," in *The Transformation of Russian Society*, ed. Cyril E. Black (Cambridge: Harvard University Press, 1960), p. 468.
71. Hubbs, *Mother Russia*, p. xv.
72. Hubbs, *Mother Russia*, pp. 230–231.
73. Engel, *Mothers and Daughters*, pp. 4–6.
74. S. K. Somerwil-Ayrton, *Poverty and Power in the Early Works of Dostoevsky* (Amsterdam: Rodopi, 1988), p. 1. See also Boris Christa, "Dostoevskii and Money," in *The Cambridge Companion to Dostoevskii*, ed. W. J. Leatherbarrow (Cambridge: Cambridge University Press, 2002), p. 109: "All of his characters," writes Christa, "are made to undergo trial by money... the elect few that rise above the temptations of money and remain uncontaminated are the true heroines and heroes of his novels." Similarly, Jacques Catteau has noted that money for Dostoevsky is the source of injustice, suffering, enslavement, and despiritualization. See his *La Creátion Littéraire Chez Dostoievski* (Paris: Institut D'Études Slaves, 1978), p. 209. As William Mills Todd III has shown, there was a turning point in Dostoevsky's own career when he lends his characters enough economic security to focus on ideological and psychological problems. See his "Dostoevskii as a Professional Writer" in Leatherbarrow, *The Cambridge Companion*, p. 66.
75. Fyodor Dostoevsky, *Sobranie sochinenii* (Leningrad: Akademia Nauk), v. 10 (1974). I use the English translation by Richard Pevear and Larissa Volokhonsky (New York: Vintage Books, 1995), occasionally modified. Page number citations to this translation will follow those for the Akademia Nauk edition (244,311).
76. Feodor Dostoevsky, *Sobranie sochinenii* (Leningrad: Akademia Nauk), v. 6 (1973). The English translation is taken from the Jessie Coulson edition, *Crime and Punishment* (New York: W.W. Norton & Company, 1989).
77. Nina Pelikan Straus, *Dostoevsky and the Woman Question: Rereadings at the End of a Century* (New York: St. Martin's Press, 1994), p. 125.
78. Marsh, "Introduction," p. 13.
79. Heldt, *Terrible Perfection*, p. 28.
80. Gary Rosenshield, "Afterword: The Problems of Gender Criticism; or, What Is To Be Done About Dostoevsky?" in Hoisington, *A Plot of Her Own*, pp. 126–127.
81. Hilde Maria Hoogenboom, *A Two-Part Invention: The Russian Woman Writer and Her Heroines from 1860 to 1917* (PhD Dissertation, Columbia University, 1996), p. 2.
82. Hoogenboom, *A Two-Part Invention*, p. 13.
83. Joe Andrew, *Narrative, Space and Gender in Russian Fiction: 1846–1903* (Amsterdam: Rodopi, 2007), p. 2.
84. Catriona Kelly, *A History of Russian Women's Writing, 1820–1992* (Oxford: Clarendon Press, 1994), p. 2.
85. Kelly, *A History of Russian Women's Writing*, pp. 1–2.

86. Kelly, *A History of Russian Women's Writing*, p. 33.
87. Kelly, *A History of Russian Women's Writing*, pp. 44–45.
88. Jehanne M. Gheith, *Finding the Middle Ground: Krestovskii, Tur, and the Power of Ambivalence in Nineteenth-Century Russian Women's Prose* (Evanston: Northwestern University Press, 2004), p. 16.
89. Gheith, *Finding the Middle Ground*, pp. 22–23. See also Rosenholm, *Gender Awakening*, p. 69, who believes that feminine heroines are not idealized and therefore do not reach the "high" standards of male writers.
90. Olga Demidova, "Russian Women Writers of the Nineteenth Century" in Marsh, *Gender and Russian Literature*, p. 103.
91. Mary F. Zirin, "Women's Prose Fiction in the Age of Realism," in Clyman and Greene, *Women Writers in Russian Literature*, p. 79.
92. Gheith, *Finding the Middle Ground*, p. 53.
93. Kelly, *A History of Russian Women's Writing*, pp. 57–61.
94. Kelly, *A History of Russian Women's Writing*, pp. 69–70.
95. Diana Greene, "Nineteenth-century Women Poets: Critical Reception vs. Self-Definition," in Clyman and Greene, *Women Writers in Russian Literature*, pp. 104–105.
96. Barbara Heldt, "Karolina Pavolva: The Woman Poet and the Double Life," prefatory essay to her translation of Karolina Pavlova, *A Double Life* (Oakland, CA: Barbary Coast Books, 1978), p. ii.
97. Donald Loewen, "Poetry, Perceptions and Personality: Finding Karolina Pavlova in Her Autobiographical Prose," *The Slavic and East European Journal* 47.4 (2003), 632.
98. Munir Sendich, *The Life and Works of Karolina Pavlova* (PhD Dissertation, New York University, 1968), p. 50.
99. Sendich, *The Life and Works of Karolina Pavlova*, p. i.
100. Alexander Lehrman, "The Poetics of Karolina Pavolva," in *Essays on Karolina Pavlova*, ed. Suzanne Fusso and Alexander Lehrman (Evanston: Northwestern University Press, 2001), p. 3.
101. Diana Greene, "Gender and Genre in Pavlova's *A Double Life*," *Slavic Review* 54.3 (1995), 563.
102. Loewen, "Poetry, Perceptions and Personality," 635–636.
103. Heldt, *Terrible Perfection*, pp. ii–vi.
104. Sendich, *The Life and Works of Karolina Pavlova*, pp. 63–64.
105. Sendich, *The Life and Works of Karolina Pavlova*, p. 243.
106. Ginger B. Lazarus, "Living Poetry: The Mute Poet and the Double Life," in Fusso and Lehrman, *Essays on Karolina Pavlova*, p. 97.
107. Stephanie Sandler and Judith Vowles, "Abandoned Meditation: Karolina Pavlova's Early Poetry," in Fusso and Lehrman, *Essays on Karolina Pavlova*, p. 46.
108. Sendich, *The Life and Works of Karolina Pavlova*, p. 229.
109. Sendich, *The Life and Works of Karolina Pavlova*, p. 232.
110. Greene, "Gender and Genre," 568–569.
111. Greene, "Gender and Genre," 572.

112. All English quotations come from Barbara Heldt's translation of Karolina Pavlova, *A Double Life* (Oakland: Barbary Coast Books, 1978), occasionally modified. The Russian edition is V. Briusov, ed., Karolina Pavlova, *Sobranie sochinenii* (Moscow: 1915). All page references will hereafter be in parentheses with Russian first, followed by English.
113. Anthony D. Briggs, "Twofold Life: A Mirror of Karolina Pavlova's Shortcomings and Achievements," *The Slavonic and East European Review* 49.114 (1971), 8.
114. Briggs, "Twofold Life," 6.
115. Marta Laura Wilkinson, *Antigone's Daughters: Gender, Family and Expression in the Modern Novel* (PhD Dissertation, University of California at Santa Barbara, 2000), p. 81.
116. Wilkinson, *Antigone's Daughters,* p. 108.
117. Rosenholm, *Gendering Awakening*, pp. 446–492.
118. See, e.g., Andrew, *Narrative, Space and Gender in Russian Fiction*, and the works of Jane Costlow, Hilde Maria Hoogenboom, Catriona Kelly, and Mary Zirin, cited earlier.
119. Kelly, *A History of Russian Women's Writing*, p. 59. *Pansionerka*, however, differs from other provincial tales in that it is not set on a country estate, but rather in a provincial town.
120. Kelly, *A History of Russian Women's Writing*, p. 63.
121. Gheith, *Finding the Middle Ground*, p. 55.
122. Gheith, *Finding the Middle Ground*, p. 57. This led to interesting consequences. In one case, a young woman named Catherine fell in love with her through her writings. Khvoshchinskaya played with the flirtation and put off telling her that she was a woman for a long time.
123. Gheith, *Finding the Middle Ground*, p. 62.
124. Gheith, *Finding the Middle Ground*, p. 70.
125. Gheith, *Finding the Middle Ground*, p. 104.
126. Gheith, *Finding the Middle Ground*, p. 18.
127. Nancy Folbre and Heidi Hartmann, "The Rhetoric of Self-Interest: Ideology and Gender in Economic Theory," in *The Consequences of Economic Rhetoric*, ed. Arjo Klamer, Donald N. McCloskey, and Robert M. Solow (Cambridge: Cambridge University Press, 1988), pp. 184–203.
128. Rosenholm, *Gendering Awakening*, p. 472.
129. Andrew, *Narrative, Space, and Gender in Russian Fiction*, p. 120.
130. N. D. Khvoshchinskaya, *Povesti i rasskazy* (Moscow: Khudozhestvennaya literatura, 1984). The English translations are from Karen Rosneck, ed. and trans., *The Boarding-School Girl* (Evanston: Northwestern University Press, 1999), occasionally modified.
131. Gheith, *Finding the Middle Ground*, pp. 174–176. Rosenholm agrees with this assessment. Andrew, on the other hand, believes Khvoshchinskaya intended the ending to be read as positive. See his *Narrative, Space, and Gender in Russian Fiction*, 122–126 for a discussion of both sides of the argument.

132. Catriona Kelly, "The First-Person 'Other': Sof'ia Soboleva's 1863 Story 'Pros and Cons' (I pro, I contra)," *Slavic and East European Review* 73.1 (1995), 67–69.
133. Kelly, "The First-Person 'Other,'" 65-66.
134. *Otechestvennye zapiski* 6 (1863), 295–337. English translation is from Catriona Kelly, *An Anthology of Russian Women's Writing, 1777–1992* (Oxford: Oxford University Press, 1994), modified occasionally.

BIBLIOGRAPHY

Medieval Bibliography

Abelard, Peter. *Opera theologica.* Turnholt: Brepols, 1987. *Corpus Christianorum Continuato Mediaevalis XIII.*

Aers, David. *Community, Gender, and Individual Identity: English Writing 1360–1430.* London: Routledge, 1988.

Alfonso, Pedro. *Disciplina Clericalis.* Zaragoza: Guara Editorial, S.A., 1980.

Allen, Peter L. "The Ambiguity of Silence: Gender, Writing, and *Le Roman De Silence.*" *Sign, Sentence, Discourse: Language in Medieval Thought and Literature.* Ed. Julian N. Wasserman and Lois Roney. Syracuse: Syracuse University Press, 1989. 98–112.

Allen, Prudence. *The Concept of Woman: The Aristotelian Revolution, 750 B.C.–A.D. 1250.* Montreal: Eden Press, 1985.

Ambrose, *De Virginibus.* Corpus Scriptorum Latinorum Paravianum. Ed. Egnatius Cazzaniga. Torino: G.B. Paravia, no date.

Angelos, Mark. "Urban Women, Investment, and the Commercial Revolution of the Middle Ages." *Women in Medieval Western European Culture.* Ed. Linda E. Mitchell. New York: Garland Publishing, Inc., 1999. 257–272.

Archibald, Elizabeth. "The Female Foundling and the Problem of Romance Genre." *The Spirit of Medieval Popular Romance.* Ed. Ad Putter and Jane Gilberg. Harlow, Essex: Longman, 2000. 39–55.

Arden, Heather. "The Lais of Marie De France and Carol Gilligan's Theory of the Psychology of Women." Marechal, 212–224.

Arjava, Antii. *Women and Law in Late Antiquity.* Oxford: Clarendon Press, 1998.

Armstrong-Partida, Michelle. "Mothers and Daughters as Lords: The Countesses of Blois and Chartres." *Medieval Prosopography* 26 (2005): 77–107.

Ashley, Kathleen. "Historicizing Margery: *The Book of Margery Kempe* as Social Text." *Journal of Medieval and Early Modern Studies* 28.2 (1998): 371–388.

Astell, Ann. *The Song of Songs in the Middle Ages.* Ithaca: Cornell University Press, 1990.

Augustine. *Confessiones.* Ed. Gillian Clark. Cambridge: Cambridge University Press, 1995.

______. *Confessions.* Trans. P. S. Pine-Coffin. London: Penguin Books, 1961.

______. *De Bono Coniugali, De Sancta Virginitate.* Trans. P. G. Walsh. Oxford: Clarendon Press, 1993.

______. *Marriage and Virginity: The Excellence of Marriage, Holy Virginity, the Excellence of Widowhood, Adulterous Marriage, Continence.* Trans. Ray Kearney. New York: New City Press, 1999.

Baldwin, John W. "Consent and the Marital Debt: Five Discourses in Northern France around 1200." Laiou, 257–270.

______. "Five Discourses of Desire: Sexuality and Gender in Northern France around 1200." *Speculum* 66 (1991): 797–819.

Barstow, Anne Llewellyn. *Married Priests and the Reforming Papacy: The Eleventh Century Debates.* New York: The Edwin Mellen Press, 1982.

Bennett, Judith. *History Matters: Patriarchy and the Challenge of Feminism.* Philadelphia: University of Pennsylvania Press, 2006.

Bernard of Clairvaux, St. *Sermones Super Cantica Canticorum.* Ed. H. Rochais, J. Leclerq, Ch. H. Talbot. Paris: Editions du Cerf, 1996–2007.

Berry, Craig. "What Silence Desires: Female Inheritance and the Romance of Property in the *Roman de Silence.*" *Translating Desire in Medieval and Early Modern Literature.* Ed. Craig R. Berry and Heather Richardson Hayton. Tempe, AZ: Arizona Center for Medieval and Renaissance Studies, 2005. 191–206.

Biddick, Kathleen. "Genders, Bodies, Borders: Technologies of the Visible." *Speculum* 66 (1993): 389–418.

Bingen, Hildegard of. *Hildegardis Bingensis Epistolarium.* Corpus Christianorum. Ed. Lieven Van Acker. Vol. 91. Turnholt, 1991.

Black, Nancy. *Medieval Narratives of Accused Queens.* Gainesville: University of Florida Press, 2003.

Blamires, Alcuin. *The Case for Women in Medieval Culture.* Oxford, 1998.

______. *Woman Defamed and Woman Defended: An Anthology of Medieval Texts.* Oxford: Clarendon Press, 1992.

Blanton, Virginia. "Chaste Marriage, Sexual Desire, and Christian Martyrdom in *La vie seinte Audrée.*" *Journal of the History of Sexuality* 19.1 (2010): 94–114.

______. *Signs of Devotion: The Cult of St. Aethelthryth in Meideval England, 695–1615.* University Park: Pennsylvania State University Press, 2007.

Bloch, R. Howard. *The Anonymous Marie De France.* Chicago: University of Chicago Press, 2003.

______. *Etymologies and Geneologies: A Literary Anthropology of the French Middle Ages.* Chicago: University of Chicago Press, 1983.

______. *Medieval Misogyny and the Invention of Western Romantic Love.* Chicago University of Chicago Press, 1991.

______. "The Medieval Text—Guigemar'—as a Provocation to the Discipline of Medieval Studies." *Romanic Review* 79 (1988): 63–73.

______. "Money, Metaphor, and Mediation of Social Differences in Old French Romance." *Symposium* 35 (1981):18–33.

Brahney, Kathleen J. "'When *Silence* Was Golden: Female Personae in the *Roman De Silence.*'" *The Spirit of the Court: Selected Proceedings of the Fourth Congress of the International Courtly Literature Society.* Ed. Glyn S. Burgess and Robert A. Taylor. Dover, NH: D.S. Brewer, 1985. 52–61.

Brooke, Christopher N. L. *The Medieval Idea of Marriage.* Oxford: Oxford University Press, 1991.

Brown, Catherine. "Muliebriter: Doing Gender in the Letters of Heloise." *Gender and Text in the Later Middle Ages.* Ed. Jane Chance. Gainesville: University of Florida Press, 1996. 25–51.

Brown, Peter. *The Body and Society: Men, Women, and Sexual Renunciation in Early Christianity.* New York: Columbia University Press, 1998.

Brundage, James A. "Implied Consent to Intercourse." Laiou, 245–256.

______. *Law, Sex, and Christian Society in Medieval Europe.* Chicago: University of Chicago Press, 1987.

"Sexual Equality in Medieval Canon Law." *Medieval Women and the Sources of Medieval History.* Ed. Joel T. Rosenthal. Athens, GA: University of Georgia Press, 1990. 66–79.

Burns, E. Jane. *Bodytalk: When Women Speak in Old French Literature.* Philadelphia: University of Pennsylvania Press, 1993.

Bynum, Caroline Walker. *Fragmentation and Redemption: Essays on Gender and the Human Body in Medieval Religion.* New York: Zone Books, 1992.

Cadden, Joan. *Meanings of Sex Difference in the Middle Ages: Medicine, Science, and Culture.* Cambridge: Cambridge University Press, 1993.

Callahan, Christopher. "Canon Law, Primogeniture, and the Marriage of Ebain and Silence." *Romance Quarterly* 49.1 (2002): 12–20.

Camille, Michael. *Image on the Edge: The Margins of Medieval Art.* London: Reaktion Books, 1988.

Carruthers, Mary. *The Book of Memory: A Study of Memory in Medieval Culture.* Cambridge: Cambridge University Press, 1992.

Cartlidge, Neil. *Medieval Marriage: Literary Approaches, 1100–1300.* Cambridge: D.S. Brewer, 1997.

Chance, Jane. "Classical Myth and Gender in the Letters of 'Abelard' and 'Heloise': Gloss, Glossed, Glossator." Wheeler, 161–185.

______. *The Literary Subversions of Medieval Women.* New York: Palgrave Macmillan, 2007.

Cherewatuk, Karen, and Ulrike Wiethaus, ed. *Dear Sister: Medieval Women and the Epistolary Genre.* Philadelphia: University of Pennsylvania Press, 1993.

Clanchy, M. T. *Abelard: A Medieval Life.* Oxford: Blackwell, 1997.

______. "The Letters of Abelard and Heloise in Today's Scholarship." Radice, lviii–lxxxvii.

Cooper, Helen. "When Romance Comes True." *Boundaries in Medieval Romance.* Ed. Neil Cartlidge. Rochester, NY: D.S. Brewer, 2008. 13–28.

Cooper, Kate. "Elle and *L*: Sexualized Textuality in *Le Roman de Silence.*" *Romance Notes* XXV.3 (1985): 341–360.

Cullum, P. H. "Gendering Charity in Medieval Hagiography." *Gender and Holiness.* Ed. Samantha Riches and Sarah Salih. London: Routledge, 2002. 135–151.

Davidson, Audrey, and Robert B. Ekelund, Jr., "The Medieval Church and Rents from Marriage Market Regulations." *Journal of Economic Behavior and Organization* 32 (1997): 215–245.

Delany, Sheila. "Sexual Economics, Chaucer's Wife of Bath and *The Book of Margery Kempe*." *Feminist Readings in Middle English Literature: The Wife of Bath and All Her Sect*. Ed. Ruth Evans and Lesley Johnson. London: Routledge, 1994. 72–87.

deTrafford, Claire. "Share and Share Alike? The Marriage Portion, Inheritance, and Family Politics." *Studies on Medieval and Early Modern Women: Pawns or Players?* Ed. Christine Meek and Catherine Lawless: Four Courts Press, 2000. 36–48.

Donahue, Charles, Jr. "The Canon Law on the Formation of Marriage and Social Practice in the Later Middle Ages." *Journal of Family History* 8 (1983): 144–158.

______. *Law, Marriage, and Society in the Later Middle Ages*. Cambridge: Cambridge University Press, 2008.

______. "What Causes Fundamental Legal Ideas?: Marital Property in England and France in the Thirteenth Century." *Michigan Law Review* 78 (1979): 59–88.

Dronke, Peter. *Abelard and Heloise in Medieval Testimonies*. Glasgow: University of Glasgow Press, 1976.

______. *Women Writers of the Middle Ages: A Critical Study of Texts from Perpetua (†203) to Marguerite Porete (†1310)*. Cambridge: Cambridge University Press, 1984.

Duby, Georges. *La Société aux XIe et XIIe Siècles Dans La Région Mâconnaise*. Paris: Librairie Armand Colin, 1953.

______. *Love and Marriage in the Middle Ages*. Chicago: University of Chicago Press, 1994.

______. *Medieval Marriage: Two Models from Twelfth-Century France*. Baltimore: Johns Hopkins University Press, 1978.

Earnshaw, Doris. *The Female Voice in Medieval Romance Lyric*. New York, 1998.

East, W. G. "This Body of Death: Abelard, Heloise and the Religious Life." *Medieval Theology and the Natural Body*. Ed. Peter Biller and A. J. Minnes. New York: Medieval Press, 1997. 43–59.

Edwards, Robert R. *The Flight from Desire: Augustine and Ovid to Chaucer*. New York: Palgrave Macmillian, 2006.

Eliott, Dyan. *Spiritual Marriage: Sexual Abstinence in Medieval Wedlock*. Princeton: Princeton University Press, 1993.

Evergates, Theodore, ed. *Aristocratic Women in Medieval France*. Philadelphia: University of Pennsylvania Press, 1999.

Faletra, Michael. "The Ends of Romance: Dreaming the Nation in the Middle English Havelok." *Exemplaria: A Journal of Theory in Medieval and Renaissance Studies* 17.2 (2005): 347–380.

Farmer, Sharon. "Persuasive Voices: Clerical Images of Medieval Wives." *Speculum* 61.3 (1986): 514–543.

Faust, Diana M. "Women Narrators in the Lais of Marie De France." *Stanford French and Italian Studies* 58 (1988): 17–28.

Feichtinger, Barbara. "Change and Continuity in Pagan and Christian (Invective) Thought on Women and Marriage from Antiquity to the Middle Ages." Smith, 182–209.

Fenster, Thelma S., and Clare A. Lees, ed. *Gender in Debate from the Early Middle Ages to the Renaissance.* New York: Palgrave, 2002.

Ferrante, Joan. *To the Glory of Her Sex: Women's Roles in the Composition of Medieval Texts.* Bloomington: Indiana University Press, 1997.

Fienberg, Nona. "Thematics of Value in *The Book of Margery Kempe.*" *Modern Philology* 87 (1989): 132–141.

Finke, Laurie A. *Feminist Theory, Women's Writing.* Ithaca: Cornell University Press, 1992.

______. *Women's Writing in English: Medieval England.* London: Longman, 1999.

Finke, Laurie A., and Martin B. Shichtman. "Magical Mistress Tour: Patronage, Intellectual Property, and the Dissemination of Wealth in the Lais of Marie De France." *SIGNS* 25 (2000): 479–503.

Fisher, Sheila, and Janet E. Halley, eds. *Seeking the Woman in Late Medieval and Renaissance Writings: Essays in Feminist Contextual Criticism.* Knoxville: University of Tennessee Press, 1988.

Fitz, Brewster. "The Prologue to the Lais of Marie De France and the Parable of the Talents: Gloss and Monetary Metaphor." *Modern Language Notes* 90 (1975): 558–596.

France, Marie de. *Lais de Marie De France.* Paris: GF Flammarion, 1994.

______. *The Lais of Marie De France.* Trans. Robert Hanning and Joan Ferrante. Grand Rapids: Baker Books, 1978.

Freeman, Michelle A. "Marie De France's Poetics of Silence: The Implications for a Feminine Translatio." PMLA 99 (1984): 860–883.

Friedrichs, Rhoda Lange. "Rich Old Ladies Mad Poor: The Vulnerability of Women's Property in Late Medieval England." *Medieval Prosopography: History and Collective Biography* 21 (2000): 211–219.

Fulton, Rachel. *From Judgment to Passion: Devotion to Christ and the Virgin Mary 800–1200.* New York: Columbia University Press, 2002.

Gaunt, Simon. *Gender and Genre in Medieval French Literature.* Cambridge: Cambridge University Press, 1995.

Gavigan, S. A. M. "Petit Treason in Eighteenth-Century England: Woman's Inequality Before the Law." *Canadian Journal of Women and the Law* 3.2 (1989–1990): 335–374.

Geary, Patrick. *Phantoms of Remembrance: Memory and Oblivion at the End of the First Milennium.* Princeton: Princeton University Press, 1996.

Georgianna, Linda. "Any Corner of Heaven: Heloise's Critique of Monasticism." *Mediaeval Studies* 49 (1987): 221–253.

Glasser, M. "Marriage and Medieval Hagiography." *Studies in Medieval and Renaissance History* 4 (1981): 3–34.

Gnarra, Irene, ed. and trans., *Philippe de Remy's "La Manekine": Text, Translation, Commentary.* New York: Garland Publishing, Inc., 1988.

Gold, Penny S. *The Lady and the Virgin: Image, Attitude and Experience in Twelfth-Century France.* Chicago: University of Chicago Press, 1985.

Goody, Jack. *The Development of the Family and Marriage in Europe.* Cambridge: Cambridge University Press, 1983.

______. "Inheritance, Property and Women: Some Comparative Considerations." *Family and Inheritance: Rural Society in Western Europe, 1200–1800.* Ed. Jack

Goody, Joan Thirsk, and E. P. Thompson. New York: Cambridge University Press, 1976. 10–36.

______. *Production and Reproduction: A Comparative Study of the Domestic Domain.* Cambridge: Cambridge University Press, 1976.

Griffin, Miranda. "Gender and Authority in the Medieval French Lai." *Forum for Modern Language Studies* 35 (1999): 42–56.

Hanawalt, Barbara. *The Wealth of Wives: Women, Law, and Economy in Late Medieval London.* Oxford: Oxford University Press, 2007.

______. "Women and the Household Economy: An Assessment of *Women, Work, and Family.*" *Journal of Women's History* 11.3 (1999): 10–16.

Hanning, Robert W. "The Talking Wounded: Desire, Truth Telling, and Pain in the Lais of Marie De France." *Desiring Discourse: The Literature of Love, Ovid through Chaucer.* Ed. James J. Paxson and Cynthia Gravlee. Selinsgrove: Susquehanna University Press, 1998. 140–161.

Harris, Barbara J. *English Aristocratic Women, 1450–1550: Marriage and Family, Property and Careers.* Oxford: Oxford University Press, 2002.

Harvey, Carol. "Incest, Identity and Uncourtly Conduct in *La Manekine.*" *The Court Reconvenes: Courtly Literature Across the Disciplines.* Ed. Barbara K. Altmann and Carleton W. Carroll. Rochester, NY: D.S. Brewer, 2002. 161–168.

Heldris de Cornuälle. *Silence: A Thirteenth-Century French Romance.* Ed. and trans. Sarah Roche-Mahdi. East Lansing: Michigan State University Press, 1999.

Heng, Geraldine. *Empire of Magic: Medieval Romance and the Politics of Cultural Fantasy.* New York: Columbia University Press, 2003.

Herlihy, David. "Land, Family, and Women in Continental Europe." *Traditio* XVIII (1962): 92–100.

______. "The Making of the Medieval Family: Symmetry, Structure, and Sentiment." *Journal of Family History* 8.2 (1983): 116–130.

______. *Medieval Households.* Cambridge: Cambridge University Press, 1985.

Hess, Erika E. "Inheritance Law and Gender Identity in the *Roman de Silence.*" *Law and Sovereignty in the Middle Ages.* Ed. Robert S. Sturges. Turnholt: Brepols, 2011. 215–235.

Hildegardis Bingensis Epistolarium. Ed. Lieven Van Acker. Turholt: Brepols, 1991. Corpus Christianorum 91.

Hirsch, John C. "Author and Scribe in *The Book of Margery Kempe.*" *Medium Aevum* 44 (1975): 145–150.

Hodgson, Frederick. "Alienation and the Otherworld in Lanval, Yonec, and Guigemar." *Comitatus: A Journal of Medieval and Renaissance Studies* 5 (1974): 19–31.

Holt, J. C. "Feudal Society and the Family in Early Medieval England: IV. The Heiress and the Alien." *Transactions of the Royal Historical Society.* Fifth Series, 35 (1985): 1–28.

Howell, Martha C. *The Marriage Exchange: Property, Social Place and Gender in the Cities of the Low Countries, 1300–1550.* Chicago: University of Chicago Press, 1998.

______. *Women, Production, and Patriarchy in Late Medieval Cities.* Chicago: University of Chicago Press, 1986.

Hughes, Diane Owen. "From Bridepiece to Dowry in Mediterranean Europe." *Journal of Family History* 3 (1978): 262–296.

Hurtig, Dolliann Margaret. "'I Do, I Do': Medieval Models of Marriage and Choice of Partners in Marie De France's Le Fraisne." *The Romantic Review* 94.2 (2001): 363–379.

Hutton, Shennan. *Women and Economic Activities in Late Medieval Ghent.* New York: Palgrave Macmillan, 2011.

Irvine, Martin. "Heloise and the Gendering of the Literate Subject." *Criticism and Dissent in the Middle Ages.* Ed. Rita Copeland. Cambridge: Cambridge University Press, 1996. 87–114.

Jambeck, Karen K. "'Femmes Et Tere': Marie De France and the Discourses of Lanval." *Discourses on Love, Marriage, and Transgression in Medieval and Early Modern Literature.* Ed. Albrecht Classen. Tempe: Arizona Center for Medieval and Renaissance Studies, 2004. 109–145.

Johnson, Cynthia. "Marriage Agreements from Twelfth-Century Southern France." Reynolds, *To Have and To Hold*, 215–259.

Jones, Nancy A. "By Woman's Tears Redeemed: Female Lament in St. Augustine's Confessions and the Correspondence of Abelard and Heloise " *Sex and Gender in Medieval and Renaissance Texts: The Latin Tradition.* Ed. Barbara K. Gold, Paul Allen Miller, and Charles Platter. Albany: State University of New York Press, 1997. 15–30.

Kamuf, Peggy. *Fictions of Feminine Desire: Disclosures of Heloise.* Lincoln: University of Nebraska Press, 1982.

Kaplan, Marion, ed. *The Marriage Bargain: Women and Dowries in European History.* New York: Harrington Park Press, 1983.

Karras, Ruth Mazzo. "Friendship and Love in the Lives of Two Twelfth-Century English Saints." *Journal of Medieval History* 14 (1998): 305–320.

______. *Sexuality in Medieval Europe: Doing Unto Others.* New York: Routledge, 2005.

Kauffman, Linda. *Discourses of Desire: Gender, Genre, and Epistolary Fictions.* Ithaca: Cornell University Press, 1986.

Kay, Sarah. *Courtly Contradictions: The Emergence of the Literary Object in the Twelfth Century.* Stanford: Stanford University Press, 2001.

Kellogg, Judith. *Medieval Artistry and Exchange: Economic Institutions, Society, and Literary Form in Old French Narrative.* New York: P. Lang, 1989.

Kempe, Margery. *The Book of Margery Kempe.* Ed. Lynn Staley. Kalamazoo: Western Michigan University, 1996.

______. Trans. B. A. Windeatt. Harmondsworth, Middlesex: Penguin Books, 1985.

Kettle, Ann J. "'My Wife Shall Have It': Marriage and Property in the Wills and Testaments of Later Mediaeval England." *Marriage and Property.* Ed. Elizabeth M. Craik. Aberdeen: Aberdeen University Press, 1984. 89–103.

Kinoshita, Sharon. "Cherchez La Femme: Feminist Criticism and Marie De France's Lai De Lanval." *Romance Notes* 34 (1994): 219–233.

______. "Male-Order Brides: Marriage, Patriarchy, and Monarchy in the Roman De Silence." *Arthuriana* 12.1 (2002): 64–75.

Krueger, Roberta L. "Beyond Debate: Gender in Play in Old French Courtly Fiction." Fenster and Lees, 79–95.

______. "'Transforming Maidens': Single Women's Stories in Marie De France's Lais and Later French Courtly Narratives." *Singlewomen in the European Past, 1250–1880.* Ed. Judith M. Bennett and Amy M. Froide. Philadelphia: University of Pennsylvania Press, 1999. 146–191.

______. *Women Readers and the Ideology of Gender in Old French Romance.* Cambridge: Cambridge University Press, 1993.

Labbie, Erin F. "The Specular Image of the Gender-Neutral Name: Naming Silence in *Le Roman De Silence.*" *Arthuriana* 7 2 (1997): 63–77.

Laiou, Angeliki E., ed. *Consent and Coercion to Sex and Marriage in Ancient and Medieval Societies.* Washington, D.C.: Dunbarton Oaks Research Library and Collection, 1993.

Leicester, H. Marshall, Jr. "The Voice of the Hind: The Emergence of Feminine Discontent in the Lais of Marie De France." *Reading Medieval Culture: Essays in Honor of Robert W. Hanning.* Ed. Robert M. Stein and Sandra Pierson Prior. Notre Dame: University of Notre Dame Press, 2005. 132–169.

Leongard, Janet Senderowicz. "Common Law for Margery: Separate But Not Equal." *Women in Medieval Western Culture.* Ed. Linda E. Mitchell. New York: Garland Publishing, 1999. 117–130.

______. "*Rationabilis Dos*: Magna Carta and the Widow's 'Fair Share' in the Earlier Thirteenth Century." *Wife and Widow in Medieval England.* Ed. Sue Sheridan Walker. Ann Arbor: University of Michigan Press, 1993. 81–108.

Lewis, Charleton T., and Charles Short. *A Latin Dictionary.* Oxford: Clarendon Press, 2002.

Livingstone, Amy. "Aristocratic Women in the Chartrain." Evergates, 44–73.

______. "Noblewomen's Control of Property in Early Twelfth-Century Blois-Chartres." *Medieval Prosopography: History and Collective Biography* 18 (1997): 55–71.

______. *Out of Love For My Kin: Aristocratic Family Life in the Lands of the Loire, 1000–1200.* Ithaca: Cornell University Press, 2010.

Makowski, Elizabeth. M. "The Conjugal Debt and Medieval Canon Law." *Journal of Medieval History* 3 (1977): 99–114.

Map, Walter. *De Nugis Curialium: Courtiers' Trifles.* Ed. M. R. James. Oxford: Clarendon Press, 1983.

Marbod of Rennes. *Liber decem capitulorum.* Roma: Herder Editrice e Libreria, 1984.

Marechal, Chantal A. *In Quest of Marie De France, a Twelfth-Century Poet.* Lewiston, NY: Edward Mellen Press, 1992.

Martindale, Janet. "Succession Politics in the Romance-Speaking World, c. 1000–1140." *England and Her Neighbours, 1066–1453: Essays in Honour of Pierre Chaplais.* Ed. Michael C. E. Jones and Malcolm Vale. London: The Hambleton Press, 1989. 19–41.

Matter, E. Ann. "The Undebated Debate: Gender and the Image of God in Medieval Theology." Fenster and Lees, 41–55.

______. *The Voice of My Beloved: The Song of Songs in Western Medieval Christendom.* Philadelphia: University of Pennsylvania Press, 1990.

McCash, June Hall. "Images of Women in the Lais of Marie De France." *Medieval Perspectives: Proceedings of the Twenty-First Annual Conference of the Southeastern Medieval Association* 11 (1996): 76–112.

McCash, June Hall, and Judith Clark Barban. *The Life of Saint Audrey: A Text by Marie de France.* Jefferson, NC: McFarland & Company, 2006.

McCracken, Peggy. "The Boy Who Was a Girl: Reading Gender in the *Roman de Silence*." *Romanic Review* 85 (1995): 517–536.

______. "The Curse of Eve: Female Bodies and Christian Bodies in Heloise's Third Letter." Wheeler, 217–230.

McLeod, Glenda. "'Wholly Guilty, Wholly Innocent': Self-Definition in Heloise's Letters to Abelard." Cherewatuk and Wiethaus, 64–86.

McNamara, Jo Ann. "The Herrenfrage: The Restructuring of the Gender System, 1050–1150." *Medieval Masculinities: Regarding Men in the Middle Ages.* Ed. Clare A. Lees. Minneapolis: University of Minnesota Press, 1994. 3–29.

______. "Women and Power Through the Family Revisted." *Gendering the Master Narrative: Women and Power in the Middle Ages.* Ed. Mary C. Erler and Maryanne Kowaleski. Ithaca: Cornell University Press, 2003. 17–30.

McNamara, Jo Ann, and Suzanne Wemple. "The Power of Women Through the Family in Medieval Europe: 500–1100." *Feminist Studies* 1.3/4 (1973): 126–141.

Mews, Constant J. *Abelard and Heloise.* Oxford: Oxford University Press, 2004.

______. *The Lost Love Letters of Heloise and Abelard: Perceptions of Dialogue in Twelfth-Century France.* New York: Palgrave, 1999.

Mikhaïlova, Miléna. "L'espace Dans Les Lais De Marie De France: Lieux, Structure, Rhétorique." *Cahiers de civilization medievale* 40 (1997): 145–157.

Mitchell, Linda. *Portraits of Medieval Women: Family, Marriage, and Politics in England 1225–1350.* New York: Palgrave Macmillan, 2003.

Moll, Richard J. "'Nest past autentik, mais apocrophum': Haveloks and Their Reception in Medieval England." *Studies in Philology* 105.2 (2008): 165–206.

Moore, Stephen D. "The Song of Songs in the History of Sexuality." *Church History* 69.2 (2000): 328–349.

Muckle, J. T. "The Letter of Heloise on Religious Life and Abelard's First Reply." *Mediaeval Studies* 17 (1955): 240–281.

______. "The Personal Letters between Abelard and Heloise." *Mediaeval Studies* 15 (1953): 47–94.

Murray, K. Sarah-Jane. "The Ring and the Sword: Marie De France's Yonec in Light of the Vie De Saint Alexis." *Romance Quarterly* 53.1 (2006): 25–42

Nelson, Janet L. "The Wary Widow." *Property and Power in the Early Middle Ages.* Ed. Wendy Davies and Paul Fouracre. Cambridge: Cambridge University Press, 1995. 82–113.

Newman, Barbara. *From Verile Woman to Womanchrist: Studies in Medieval Religion and Literature.* Philadelphia: University of Pennsylvania Press, 1995.

______. *God and the Goddesses: Vision, Poetry, and Belief in the Middle Ages.* Philadelphia: University of Pennsylvania Press, 2003.

______. "Hildegard and Her Hagiographers: The Remaking of Female Sainthood." *Gendered Voices: Medieval Saints and Their Interpreters*. Ed. Catherine M. Mooney. Philadelphia: University of Pennsylvania Press, 1999. 16–34.

______. "Sibyl of the Rhine: Hildegard's Life and Times." *Voice of the Living Light: Hildegard of Bingen and Her World*. Ed. Barbara Newman. Berkeley: University of California Press, 1998. 1–29.

______. *Sister of Wisdom: St. Hildegard's Theology of the Feminine*. Berkeley: University of California Press, 1987.

Nichols, Stephen G. "Medieval Women Writers: Aisthesis and the Powers of Marginality." *Yale French Studies* 75 (1988): 77–94.

______. "Rewriting Marriage in the Middle Ages." *Romanic Review* 79.1 (1988): 42–60.

Nouvet, Claire. "The Discourse of the 'Whore': An Economy of Sacrifice." *MLN* 105 (1990): 750–773.

Olson, Linda, and Kathryn Kerby-Fulton. *Voices in Dialogue: Reading Women in the Middle Ages*. Notre Dame: University of Notre Dame Press, 2005.

Partner, Nancy. "No Sex, No Gender." *Speculum* 68 (1993): 419–443.

Paterson, Linda. "Gender Negotiations in France During the Central Middle Ages: The Literary Evidence." *The Medieval World*. Ed. Peter Linehan and Janet L. Nelson. London: Routledge, 2001. 246–266.

______. "Women, Property, and the Rise of Courtly Love." *The Court Reconvenes: Courtly Literature across the Disciplines*. Ed. Barbara K. Altmann and Carleton W. Carroll. Cambridge: D.S. Brewer, 2003. 41–56.

Pederson, Frederik. "Marriage Contracts and the Church Courts of Fourteenth-Century England." *To Have and To Hold: Marrying and Its Documentation in Western Europe*. Ed. Phillip L. Reynolds and John Witte, Jr. Cambridge: Cambridge University Press, 2007. 287–331.

Pelikan, Jaroslav. *Mary through the Centuries: Her Place in the History of Culture*. New Haven: Yale University Press, 1996.

Radice, Betty. Revised by M. T. Clanchy. *The Letters of Abelard and Heloise*. London: Penguin Books, 2003.

Reid, Charles J. *Power over the Body, Equality in the Family: Rights and Domestic Relations in Medieval Canon Law*. Grand Rapids: William B. Eerdmans Publishing Company, 2004.

Rennes, Marbod of. *Liber Decem Capitulorum*. Roma: Herder Editrice e Libreria, 1984.

Resnick, Irven M. "Marriage in Medieval Culture: Consent Theory and the Case of Joseph and Mary." *Church History* 69.2 (2000): 350–371.

Reyerson, Kathryn, and Thomas Keuhn. "Women and Law in France and Italy." *Women in Medieval Western European Culture*. Ed. Linda E. Mitchell. New York: Garland Publishing, Inc., 1999. 130–141.

Reynolds, Philip L. *Marriage in the Western Church: The Christianization of Marriage During the Patristic and Early Medieval Periods*. Leiden: E.J. Brill, 1994.

______. *To Have and to Hold: Marrying and Its Documentation in Western Christendom, 400–1600*. Cambridge: Cambridge University Press, 2007.

Riddy, Felicity. "Text and Self in *The Book of Margery Kempe*." Olson and Kerby-Fulton, 435–453.

Ringer, Loren. "Exchange, Identity, and Transvestism in *Le Roman de Silence*." Dalhousie French Studies 28 (1994): 3–13.

Rollo-Koster, Joëlle. "The Boundaries of Affection: Women and Property in Late Medieval Avignon." *Across the Religious Divide: Women, Property, and Law in the Wider Mediterranean (ca. 1300–1800)*. Ed. Juta Gisela Sperling and Shona Kelly Wray. New York: Routledge, 2010. 38–50.

Rousseau, Constance M., and Joel T. Rosenthal. *Women, Marriage and Family in Medieval Christendom*. Kalamazoo, MI: Medieval Institute Publications, 1998.

Rubin, Miri. *Mother of God: A History of the Virgin Mary*. London: Penguin Books, 2009.

Sargent-Baur, Barbara N. "Dating the Romances of Philipe de Remi: Between an Improbable Source and a Dubious Adaptation." *Essays on the Poetic and Legal Writings of Philippe de Remy and His Son Philippe de Beaumanoir of Thirteenth-Century France*. Ed. Sarah-Grace Heller and Michelle Reichert. Lewiston, ME: The Edwin Mellen Press, 2001. 21–46.

Sawyer, Birgit. "Women as Landholders and Alienators of Property in Early Medieval Scandinavia." *Female Power in the Middle Ages: Proceedings of the 2. St. Gertrude Symposium*. Ed. Karen Glente and Lise Winther-Jenzen. Copenhagen: C.A. Reitzel, 1989. 156–171.

Schlauch, Margaret. *Chaucer's Constance and Accused Queens*. New York: New York University Press, 1027.

Shahar, Shulamith. *The Fourth Estate: A History of Women in the Middle Ages*. London: Routledge, 1983.

Sheehan, Michael. *Marriage, Family, and Law in Medieval Europe*. Toronto: University of Toronto Press, 1996.

Smith, Warren S., ed. *Satiric Advice on Women and Marriage: From Plautus to Chaucer*. Ann Arbor: University of Michigan Press, 2005.

Smithers, G., ed. *Havelok*. Oxford: Clarendon Press, 1987.

Solterer, Helen. *The Master and Minerva: Disputing Women in French Medieval Culture*. Berkeley: University of California Press, 1995.

Spiegel, Gabrielle M. *Romancing the Past: The Rise of Vernacular Prose Historiography in Thirteenth-Century France*. Berkeley: University of California Press, 1993.

Staley, Lynn. *Margery Kempe's Dissenting Fictions*. University Park: The Pennsylvania State University Press, 1984.

Staples, Kathryn. *Daughters of London: Inheritance Practice in Late Medieval London*. PhD Dissertation, University of Minnesota, 2006.

Stein, Robert M., and Sandra Pierson Prior. *Reality Fictions: Romance, History, and Governmental Authority, 1025–1180*. Notre Dame: University of Notre Dame Press, 2006.

Stock, Lorraine Kochanske. "The Importance of Being Gender 'Stable': Masculinity and Feminine Empowerment in *Le Roman De Silence*." *Arthuriana* 7.2 (1994): 7–34.

Stuard, Susan. "The Dominion of Gender: Women's Fortunes in the High Middle Ages." *Becoming Visible: Women in European History*. Ed. Renate

Bridenthal, Claudia Koonz, and Susan Stuard. Boston: Houghton Mifflin, 1987. 153–172.

Summit, Jennifer. "Women and Authorship." *The Cambridge Companion to Medieval Women's Writing.* Ed. Carolyn Dinshaw and David Wallace. Cambridge: Cambridge University Press, 2003. 91–108.

Szkilnik, Michelle. "The Grammar of the Sexes in Medieval French Romance." *Gender Transgressions: Crossing the Normative Barrier in Old French Literature.* Ed. Karen J. Taylor. New York: Garland Publishing, Inc., 1998. 61–88.

Toland, John. *Petrus Alfonsi and His Medieval Readers.* Gainesville: University Press of Florida, 1993.

Van Engen, John. "Letters and the Public Persona of Hildegard." *Hildegard Von Bingen in Ihrem Historischen Umfeld.* Ed. Alfred Haverkamp. Mainz: Verlag Philipp von Zabern, 2000. 375–418.

______. "Letters, Schools, and Written Culture in the Eleventh and Twelfth Centuries." *Dialektic Und Rhetorik Im Fruheren Und Holen Mittelatler.* Ed. Johannes Fried. Munchen: R. Oldenbourg Verlag, 1997. 97–132.

Van Houts, Elizabeth. *Memory and Gender in Medieval Europe, 900–1200.* Toronto: University of Toronto Press, 1999.

Wack, Mary Frances. *Lovesickness in the Middle Ages: The Viaticum and its Commentaries.* Philadelphia: University of Pennsylvania Press, 1990.

Walsh, P.G. "Antifeminism in the High Middle Ages." Smith, 222–242.

Watson, Nicholas. "The Making of *The Book of Margery Kempe.*" Olson and Kerby-Fulton, 395–434.

Weinburger, Stephen. "Women, Property, and Poetry in Eleventh Century Provence." *Proceedings of the Annual Meeting of the Western Society for French History* 8 (1981): 24–32.

Weiss, Judith. "The Power and Weakness of Women in Anglo-Norman Romance." *Women and Literature in Britain, 1150–1500.* Ed. Carol M. Neale. Cambridge: Cambridge University Press, 1996. 7–23.

______. "Structure and Characterization in Havelok the Dane." *Speculum* 44.2 (1969): 247–257.

Wemple, Suzanne Fonay. *Women in Frankish Society: Marriage and the Cloister 500 to 900.* Philadelphia: University of Pennsylvania Press, 1981.

Wheeler, Bonnie. *Listening to Heloise: The Voice of a Twelfth-Century Woman.* New York: St. Martin's Press, 2000.

Whetter, K. S. "*Gest* and *Vita*, Folktale and Romance in *Havelok.*" *Parergon* 20.2 (2003): 21–46.

Williams, Bernadette. "'Cursed Be My Parents': A View of Marriage from the Lais of Marie De France." *The Fragility of Her Sex?: Medieval Irishwomen in Their European Context.* Ed. Christine Meek and Katherine Simms. Dublin: Four Courts Press, 1996. 73–86.

Wilson, Katharine, and Glenda McLeod. "Textual Strategies in the Abelard/Heloise Correspondence." Wheeler, 121–142.

Wilson, Katharine, and Elizabeth M. Makowski. *Wykked Wives and the Woes of Marriage: Misogamous Literature from Juvenal to Chaucer.* Albany: State University of New York Press, 1990.

Winer, Rebecca Lynn. *Women, Wealth, and Community in Peripignan, c. 1250–1300: Christians, Jews, and Enslaved Muslims.* Aldershot: Ashgate, 2006.

Wogan-Browne, Jocelyn. "Rerouting the Dower: The Anglo-Norman Life of St. Audrey by Marie (of Chatteris?)." *Power of the Weak: Studies on Medieval Women.* Ed. Jennifer Carpenter and Sally-Beth MacLean. Urbana: University of Chicago Press, 1995. 27–56.

______. "Saints' Lives and the Female Reader." *Forum for Modern Language Studies* 27 (1981): 314–332.

Ziolkowski, Jan M. *Letters of Peter Abelard, Beyond the Personal.* Washington, D.C.: The Catholic University of America Press, 2006.

______. "Lost and Not yet Found" Heloise, Abelard, and the Epistolae Duorum Amantium." *Journal of Medieval Latin* 14 (2004): 171–202.

Russian Bibliography

Andrew, Joe. *Narrative and Desire in Russian Literature, 1822–1849.* New York: St. Martin's Press, 1993.

______. *Narrative, Space, and Gender in Russian Fiction: 1846–1903.* Amsterdam: Rodopi, 2007.

Atkinson, Dorothy. "Society and the Sexes in the Russian Past." *Women in Russia.* Ed. Dorothy Atkinson, Alexander Dallin, and Gail Warshofsky Lapidus. Stanford: Stanford University Press, 1977. 3–38.

Bisha, Robin. "Marriage, Church and Community in 18th Century St. Petersburg." *Women and Gender in 18th-Century Russia.* Ed. Wendy Rosslyn. Aldershot: Ashgate, 2003. 227–242.

Briggs, Anthony D. "Twofold Life: A Mirror of Karolina Pavlova's Shortcomings and Achievements." *The Slavonic and East European Review* 49.114 (1971): 1–17.

Catteau, Jacques. *La Création Littéraire Chez Dostoievski.* Paris: Institut D'Études Slaves, 1978.

Chernyshevsky, Nikolai. *Chto Delat'?* Leningrad: Izdatelstvo Nauka, 1975.

______. *What Is To Be Done?* Trans. Michael R. Katz. Ithaca: Cornell University Press, 1989.

Christa, Boris. "Dostoevskii and Money." Leatherbarrow, 93–110.

Clyman, Toby W., and Diana Greene, ed. *Women Writers in Russian Literature.* Westport, CT: Praeger, 1994.

Costlow, Jane T. "Love, Work, and the Woman Question in Mid-Nineteenth-Century Women's Writing." Clyman and Greene 61–75.

______. "Oh-là-là and No-no-no: Odintsova as Woman Alone in *Fathers and Children.*" Hoisington, 21–32.

Demidova, Olga. "Russian Women Writers of the Nineteenth Century." Marsh, 92–111.

Dostoevsky, Feodor. *Crime and Punishment.* Trans. Jessie Coulson. New York: W.W. Norton & Company, 1989.

______. *Demons.* Trans. Richard Pevear and Larissa Volokhonsky. New York: Vintage Books, 1995.

______. *Sobranie Sochinenii.* Leningrad: Aademia Nauk, 1973–1974.

Dunham, Vera Sandomirsky. "The Strong-Woman Motif." *The Transformation of Russian Society: Aspects of Social Change Since 1861.* Ed. Cyril E. Black. Cambridge: Harvard University Press, 1960. 459–483.

Edmondson, Linda. "Equality and Difference in Women's History: Where Does Russia Fit In?" *Women in Russia and Ukraine.* Ed. Rosalind Marsh. Cambridge: Cambridge University Press, 1996. 94–108.

Engel, Barbara Alpern. *Mothers and Daughters: Women of the Intelligentsia in Nineteenth-Century Russia.* Cambridge: Cambridge University Press, 1983.

______. *Women in Russia, 1700–2000.* Cambridge: Cambridge University Press, 2004.

______. "Women's Rights à La Russe." *Russian Review* 58.3 (1999): 355–360.

Freeze, Gregory L. "The Soslovie (Estate) Paradigm and Russian Social History." *American Historical Review* 91.1 (1986): 11–36.

Fusso, Suzanne, and Alexander Lehrman, ed. *Essays on Karolina Pavlova.* Evanston: Northwestern University Press, 2001.

Gheith, Jehanne. *Finding the Middle Ground: Krestovskii, Tur, and the Power of Ambivalence in Nineteenth-Century Russian Women's Writing.* Evanston: Northwestern University Press, 2004.

______. "A Slanted Perspective: Russian Literary Criticism and Women's Prose in the Nineteenth Century." *Teksty drugie* 4 (1993): 213–224.

Greene, Diana. "Gender and Genre in Pavlova's a Double Life." *Slavic Review* 53.3 (1995): 563–577.

______. "Nineteenth-Century Women Poets: Critical Reception Vs. Self-Definition." Clyman and Greene, 95–109.

Grenier, Svetlana. *Representing the Marginal Woman in Nineteenth-Century Russian Literature: Personalism, Feminism, and Polyphony.* Westport, CT: Greenwood, 2001.

Heldt, Barbara. *Terrible Perfection: Women and Russian Literature.* Bloomington: Indiana University Press, 1987.

Hoisington, Sonia Stephan, ed. *A Plot of Her Own: The Female Protagonist in Russian Literature.* Evanston: Northwestern University Press, 1995.

Hoogenboom, Hilde Maria. "A Two-Part Invention: The Russian Woman Writer and Her Heroines from 1860 to 1917." PhD Dissertation, Columbia University, 1996.

Hubbs, Joanna. *Mother Russia: The Feminine Myth in Russian Culture.* Bloomington: Indiana University Press, 1998.

Kelly, Catriona. *An Anthology of Russian Women's Writing, 1777–1992.* Oxford: Oxford University Press, 1994.

______. "The First-Person 'Other': Sof'ia Soboleva's 1863 Story 'Pros and Cons.'" *Slavonic and East European Review* 73.1 (1995): 61–81.

______. *A History of Russian Women's Writing, 1820–1992.* New York: Oxford University Press, 1994.

Khvoshchinskaya, Nadezda. *The Boarding-School Girl.* Trans. Karen Rosneck. Evanston: Northwestern University Press, 1999.

______. *Povesti I Rasskazy*. Moscow: Khudozhestvennaya literatura, 1984.

Lazarus, Ginger. "Living Poetry: The Mute Poet and the Double Life." Fusso and Lehrman, 86–98.

Leatherbarrow, W. J. *The Cambridge Companion to Dostoevskii*. Cambridge: Cambridge University Press, 2002.

Lehrman, Alexander. "The Poetics of Karolina Pavlova." Fusso and Lehrman, 3–20.

Levin, Eve. "Women and Property in Medieval Novgorod: Dependence and Independence." *Russian History/Histoire Russe* 10.2 (1983): 154–169.

Levy, Sandra. "Women and the Control of Property in Sixteenth-Century Muscovy." *Russian History* 10 (1983): 201–212.

Loewen, Donald. "Poetry, Perceptions and Personality: Finding Karolina Pavlova in Her Autobiographical Prose." *The Slavic and East European Journal* 47.4 (2003): 631–647.

Marresse, Michelle Lamarche. "From Maintenance to Entitlement: Defining the Dowry in 18th-Century Russia." Rosslyn, 209–226.

______. *A Woman's Kingdom: Noblewomen and the Control of Property in Russia, 1799–1861*. Ithaca: Cornell University Press, 2002.

Marsh, Rosalind, ed. *Gender and Russian Literature: New Perspectives*. Cambridge: Cambridge University Press, 1996.

______. *Women and Russian Culture: Projections and Self-Perceptions*. New York: Berghahn Books, 1998.

Murav, Harriet. "Reading Woman in Dostoevsky." Hoisington, 44–57.

Norton, Barbara, and Jehanne Gheith. *An Improper Profession: Women, Gender, and Journalism in Imperial Russia*. Durham, NC: Duke University Press, 2001.

Pavlova, Karolina. *A Double Life*. Trans. Barbara Heldt. Oakland, CA: Barbary Coast Books, 1978.

______. ed. *Sobranie Sochinenii*. Moscow: K.F. Nekrasova, 1915.

Pouncy, Carolyn Johnston, ed. *The Domostroi: Rules for Russian Households in the Time of Ivan the Terrible*. Ithaca: Cornell University Press, 1994.

Ransel, David. *The Family in Imperial Russia: New Lines of Historical Research*. Urbana: University of Illinois Press, 1978.

Riff, Victor. "Turgenev as Social Novelist: The Problem of the Part and the Whole." *Literature and Society in Imperial Russia 1800–1914*. Ed. William Mills Todd III. Stanford: Stanford University Press, 1978. 237–257.

Rosenholm, Arja. *Gender Awakening: Femininity and the Russian Woman Question of the 1860's*. Helsinki: Kikimora Publications, 1999.

______. "The 'Woman Question' Of the 1860's and the Ambiguity of The 'Learned Woman.'" Marsh, 112–128.

______. "Writing the Self: Creativity and the Female Author: Nadezhda Dmitrievna Khvoshchinskaia (1824–1889)." *Gender Restructuring in Russian Studies*. Tampere: University of Tampere Press, 1993. 193–208.

Rosenshield, Gary. "Afterword: The Problems of Gender Criticism; or, What is to Be Done About Dostoevsky?" Hoisington, 114–127.

Rosenthal, Charlotte. "The Silver Age: Highpoint for Women?" Edmondson, 32–47.

Rosslyn, Wendy, ed. *Women and Gender in 18th-Century Russia.* Aldershot: Ashgate, 2003.

Sandler, Stephanie, and Judith Vowles. "Abandoned Meditation: Karolina Pavlova's Early Poetry." Fusso and Lehrman, 32–52.

Sendich, Munir. "The Life and Work of Karolina Pavlova." PhD Dissertation, New York University, 1968.

Soboleva, Sofia. "I pro i contra: Mechty i dumy nadvornoi sovetnitsy Lisitsynoi" *Otechestvennye zapiski* 6 (1863): 295–337.

______. "Pros and Cons: The Thoughts and Dreams of Madame Court Counsellor Lisitsyna." *An Anthology of Russian Women's Writing, 1777–1992.* Ed. and trans. Catriona Kelly. Oxford: Oxford University Press, 1994. 71–113.

Solomon, Karla Thomas. "Nadezhda Khvoshchinskaia." *Russian Women Writers,* vol. I. Ed. Christine D. Tomei. New York: Garland, 1999. 261–267.

Somerwil-Ayrton, S. K. *Poverty and Power in the Early Works of Dostoevsky.* Amsterdam: Rodopi, 1988.

Stites, Richard. *The Women's Liberation Movement in Russia: Feminism, Nihilism and Bolshevism, 1860–1930.* Princeton: Princeton University Press, 1990.

Straus, Nina Pelikan. *Dostoevsky and the Woman Question: Rereadings at the End of a Century.* New York: St. Martin's Press, 1994.

Todd, William Mills III. "Dostoevskii as a Professional Writer." Leatherbarrow, 66–92.

______. *Fiction and Society in the Age of Pushkin.* Cambridge: Cambridge University Press, 1986.

______. ed. *Literature and Society in Imperial Russia 1800–1914.* Stanford: Stanford University Press, 1978.

Tomei, Christine D., ed. *Russian Women Writers.* New York: Garland, 1999.

Tsebrikova, Maria. "Russia." *The Woman Question in Europe: A Series of Original Essays.* Ed. Theodore Stanton. New York: G.P. Putnam's Sons, 1884. 391–423.

Turgenev, Ivan. *Fathers and Sons.* Trans. Constance Garnett. New York: Modern Library, 2001.

______. *Otsi E Deti.* St. Petersburg: Akademischeski Proekt, 2000.

Wagner, William G. *Marriage, Property, and Law in Late Imperial Russia.* Oxford: Clarendon Press, 1994.

Weickhardt, George. "Legal Rights of Women in Russia, 1100–1750." *Slavic Review* 55.1 (1996): 1–23.

______. "The Pre-Petrine Law of Property." *Slavic Review* 52.4 (1993): 663–679.

Wilkinson, Marta Laura. "Antigone's Daughters: Gender, Family, and Expression in the Modern Novel." PhD Dissertation, University of California at Santa Barbara, 2000.

Zirin, Mary F. "Women's Prose Fiction in the Age of Realism." Clyman and Greene, 77–794.

British Bibliography

Abel, Elizabeth. "Narrative Structure(s) and Female Development: The Case of Mrs. Dalloway." *Virginia Woolf's Mrs. Dalloway*. Ed. Harold Bloom. New York: Chelsea House Publishers, 1985. 103–126.

Armstrong, Nancy. *Desire and Domestic Fiction: A Political History of the Novel*. Oxford: Oxford University Press, 1987.

Austen, Jane. *Pride and Prejudice*. Oxford: Oxford University Press, 2004.

______. *Sense and Sensibility*. New York: Dover Publications, 1996.

Backscheider, Paula R. "The Novel's Gendered Space." *Revising Women: Eighteenth-Century 'Women's Fiction' and Social Engagement*. Ed. Paula R. Backscheider. Baltimore: Johns Hopkins University Press, 2000. 1–30.

Basch, Francoise. *Relative Creatures: Victorian Women in Society and the Novel*. New York: Schocken Books, 1974.

Black, Naomi. *Virginia Woolf as Feminist*. Ithaca: Cornell University Press, 2004.

Blair, Emily. *Virginia Woolf and the Nineteenth-Century Domestic Novel*. Lanham, MD: University Press of American, 2007.

Boone, Joseph Allen. *Tradition Counter Tradition: Love and the Form of Fiction*. Chicago: University of Chicago Press, 1987.

Bowlby, Rachel. *Feminist Destinations and Further Essays on Virginia Woolf*. Edinburgh: Edinburgh University Press, 1997.

Burney, Frances. *Evelina*. Ed. Kristina Straub. Boston: Bedford/St. Martin's, 1997.

Burns, Christy L. "'Re-Dressing Feminist Identities: Tensions between Essential and Constructed Selves in Virginia Woolf's Orlando.'" *Twentieth-Century Literature* 40.3 (1994): 342–364.

Calder, Jenni. *Women and Marriage in Victorian Fiction*. New York: Oxford University Press, 1976.

Copeland, Edward. *Women Writing About Money: Women's Fiction in England, 1790–1820*. Cambridge: Cambridge University Press, 1995.

Delory, Denise. "Parsing the Female Sentence: The Paradox of Containment in Virginia Woolf's Narratives." *Ambiguous Discourse: Feminist Narratology and British Women Writers*. Ed. Kathy Mezei. Chapel Hill: University of North Carolina Press, 1996. 93–108.

Dolin, Tim. *Mistress of the House: Women of Property in the Victorian Novel*. Aldershot: Ashgate, 1997.

Dowling, David. *Mrs. Dalloway: Mapping Streams of Consciousness*. Boston: Twayne Publishers, 1991.

Duff, Virginia M. "Early English Women Novelists Testify to the Law's Manifest Cruelties against Women before the Marriage Act of 1753." *Women's Studies: An Interdisciplinary Journal* 29.5 (2000): 583–618.

______. "Woman and Property, Woman as Property: Woman, Property, and Law as Imagined by British Female Novelists 1680–1740." PhD Dissertation, University of Colorado at Boulder, 1994.

Eliot, George. *Middlemarch*. New York: Modern Library, 2000.

Epstein, Julia. *The Iron Pen: Frances Burney and the Politics of Women's Writing.* Bedminster: Bristol Classical Press, 1989.

Faubert, Michelle. "A Possible Source for George Eliot's Edward Casaubon." *ANQ: A Quarterly Journal of Short Articles, Notes, & Reviews* 18.2 (2005): 46–54.

Fordyce, James. "On the Importance of the Female Sex." *Female Education in the Age of Enlightenment.* Vol. I. London: William Pickering, 1996.

Fraiman, Susan. *Unbecoming Women: British Women and the Novel of Development.* New York: Columbia University Press, 1993.

Gisborne, Thomas. "An Inquiry into the Duties of the Female Sex." *Female Education in the Age of Enlightenment.* Vol. II. London: William Pickering, 1996.

Green, Katherine Sobba. *The Courtship Novel 1740–1820: A Feminized Genre.* Lexington, KY: The University Press of Kentucky, 1991.

Hinnant, Charles H. "Jane Austen's 'Wild Imagination': Romance and the Courtship Plot in the Six Canonical Novels." *Narrative* 14.3 (2006): 284–310.

Hinz, Evelyn J. "Hierogamy Versus Wedlock: Types of Marriage Plots and Their Relationship to Genres of Prose Fiction." PMLA 91.5 (1976): 490–493.

Hoad, T. F. *The Concise Oxford Dictionary of English Entymology.* Oxford: Oxford University Press, 1993.

Hoeckley, Cheri Lin Larsen. "Literary Ladies in Anomalous Positions: Victorian Women Writers and the Married Women's Property Act." PhD Dissertation, University of California at Berkeley, 1997.

Holcombe, Lee. *Wives and Property: Reform of the Married Women's Property Law in Nineteenth-Century England.* Toronto: University of Toronto Press, 1983.

Homans, Margaret. *Bearing the Word: Language and Female Experience in Nineteenth-Century Women's Writing.* Chicago: University of Chicago Press, 1986.

Hunt, Margaret R. *The Midling Sort: Commerce, Gender, and the Family in England, 1680–1780.* Berkeley: University of California Press, 1996.

Ingrassia, Catherine. *Authorship, Commerce, and Gender in Early Eighteenth-Century England: A Culture of Paper Credit.* Cambridge: Cambridge University Press, 1998.

Johnson, Claudia L. *Jane Austen: Women, Politics, and the Novel.* Chicago: University of Chicago Press, 1988.

Kibbie, Ann Louise. "The Woman in the Bargain: Property and Female Character in the Eighteenth-Century Novel." PhD Dissertation, University of California at Berkeley, 1990.

Laqueur, Thomas. *Making Sex: Body and Gender from the Greeks to Freud.* Cambridge: Harvard University Press, 1992.

London, April. *Women and Property in the Eighteenth-Century English Novel.* Cambridge: Cambridge University Press, 1999.

Magee, William H. "Instrument of Growth: The Courtship and Marriage Plot in Jane Austen's Novels." *Journal of Narrative Technique* 17.2 (1987): 198–208.

McGarry, Lisa Coughlin. *Orts, Scraps, and Fragments: The Elusive Search for Meaning in Virginia Woolf's Fiction.* Lanham, MD: University Press of America, 2007.

Mill, John Stuart. *On Liberty and Other Writings*. Ed. Stefan Collini. Cambridge: Cambridge University Press, 1989.

Miller, J. Hillis. "A Conclusion in Which Almost Nothing Is Concluded: Middlemarch's 'Finale'." *Women and Marriage in Victorian Fiction*. Ed. Karen Chase. New York: Oxford University Press, 2006. 133–156.

Mitchell, Sherry L. "Saint Teresa and Dorothea Brooke: The Absent Road to Perfection in *Middlemarch*." *The Victorian Newsletter* 92 (1997): 32–37.

Newman, Karen. "Can This Marriage Be Saved: Jane Austen Makes Sense of an Ending." *ELH* 50 (1983): 693–710.

Newton, Judith Lowder. *Women, Power, and Subversion: Social Strategies in British Fiction, 1778–1860*. Athens: The University of Georgia Press, 1981.

Nicolson, Nigel. *Virginia Woolf*. New York: Viking, 2000.

Nunokawa, Jeff. *The Afterlife of Property: Domestic Security and the Victorian Novel*. Princeton: Princeton University Press, 1994.

Okin, Susan Moller. "Patriarchy and Married Women's Property in England: Questions on Some Current Views." *Eighteenth-Century Studies* 17.2 (1983–1984): 121–138.

Pocock, J. G. A. *Virtue, Commerce, and History: Essays on Political Thought and History, Chiefly in the Eighteenth Century*. Cambridge: Cambridge University Press, 1985.

Poovey, Mary. *The Proper Lady and the Woman Writer: Ideology as Style in the Works of Mary Wollstonecraft, Mary Shelley, and Jane Austen*. Chicago: University of Chicago Press, 1984.

Rosen, Jody R. "Deviation and Acceleration: Time in the Story and Narrative of Orlando." *Virginia Woolf Miscellany* 70 (2006): 29–30.

Scheuermann, Mona. "Women and Money in Eighteenth-Century Fiction." *Studies in the Novel* XIX (1987): 311–322.

Schuetz, Julie Hipp. "Women, Property, and the Estate: Fiction and Legal Reform in Nineteenth-Century England." PhD Dissertation, Vanderbilt University, 2001.

Shaffer, Julie. "The Ideological Intervention of Ambiguities in the Marriage Plot: Who Fails Marianne in Austen's *Sense and Sensibility*." *A Dialogue of Voices: Feminist Literary Theory and Bakhtin*. Ed. Karen Ann Hohne and Helen Wussow. Minneapolis: University of Minnesota Press, 1994. 128–151.

______. "Not Subordinate: Empowering Women in the Marriage-Plot—the Novels of Frances Burney, Maria Edgeworth, and Jane Austen." *Criticism: A Quarterly for Literature and the Arts* 34.1 (1992): 51–73.

Spring, Eileen. *Land, Law, and Family: Aristocratic Inheritance in England, 1300–1800*. Chapel Hill: University of North Carolina Press, 1993.

Staves, Susan. *Married Women's Separate Property in England, 1660–1833*. Cambridge: Harvard University Press, 1990.

Stone, Lawrence. *The Family, Sex, and Marriage in England, 1500–1800*. New York: Harper & Row, 1977.

Todd, Janet. "Introduction." *Female Education in the Age of the Enlightenment*. Vol. I. London: William Pickering, 1996.

Tyler, Daniel. "Dorothea and the 'Key to All Mythologies'." *The George Eliot Review: Journal of the George Eliot Fellowship* 33 (2002): 27–32.

White, Laura Mooneyham. "Jane Austen and the Marriage Plot: Questions of Persistence." *Jane Austen and Discourses of Feminism*. Ed. Devoney Looser. New York: St. Martin's Press, 1995. 71–86.

Wollstonecraft, Mary. *A Vindication of the Rights of Woman*. New York: Dover Publications, 1966.

Woolf, Virginia. *Mrs. Dalloway*. New York: Harcourt, Inc., 2005.

______. *Orlando*. Harmondsworth, Middlesex: Penguin Books, 1975.

______. *A Room of One's Own*. New York: Harcourt, Brace & World, Inc., 1929.

______. *Three Guineas*. New York: Harcourt, Inc., 1938.

Yeazell, Ruth Bernard. *Fictions of Modesty: Women and Courtship in the English Novel*. Chicago: University of Chicago Press, 1991.

General Bibliography

Cixous, Hélène. "The Laugh of the Medusa." Trans. Keith Cohen and Paula Cohen. *Signs: Journal of Women in Culture and Society* 1.4 (1976): 815–893.

Dickinson, Emily. "I am afraid to own a body." *The Poems of Emily Dickinson: Variorum Edition*. Ed. Ralph W. Franklin. Cambridge: The Belknap Press of Harvard University Press, 1998.

Engels, Frederich. *The Origin of the Family, Private Property, and the State*. New York: Pathfinder Press, 1972.

Folbre, Nancy, and Heidi Hartmann. "The Rhetoric of Self-Interest: Ideology and Gender in Economic Theory." *The Consequences of Economic Rhetoric*. Ed. Arjo Klamer, Donald M. McCloskey, and Robert M. Solow. Cambridge: Cambridge University Press, 1988. 184–203.

Lanser, Susan Sniader. *Fictions of Authority: Women Writers and Narrative Voice*. Ithaca: Cornell University Press, 1992.

Pateman, Carole. *The Sexual Contract*. Stanford: Stanford University Press, 1988.

Rose, Carol M. *Property and Persuasion: Essays on the History, Theory, and Rhetoric of Ownership*. Boulder: Westview Press, 1994.

Rubin, Gayle. "The Traffic in Women: Notes on the 'Political Economy' of Sex." *Toward an Anthropology of Women*. Ed. Rayna R. Reiter. New York: Monthly Reviw Press, 1975. 157–210.

Spivak, Gayatri Chakravorty. *A Critique of Postcolonial Reason: Toward a History of the Vanishing Present*. Cambridge: Harvard University Press, 1999.

INDEX

9780230115064